A LUTHERAN *looks at...* CATHOLICS

Curtis A. Jahn

NORTHWESTERN PUBLISHING HOUSE
Milwaukee, Wisconsin

Art Director: Karen Knutson
Designer: Pamela Dunn

Northwestern Publishing House
1250 N. 113th St., Milwaukee, WI 53226-3284
www.nph.net

Published 2014
Printed in the United States of America
ISBN 978-0-8100-2502-8
ISBN 978-0-8100-2613-1 (e-book)

23 24 25 26 27 28 11 10 9 8 7 6 5 4 3

CONTENTS

INTRODUCTION

Whenever I teach a course on modern Catholicism to a group of Lutherans, I begin the course by asking the members of the class, "How many of you have a friend, neighbor, or coworker who is a Catholic? Raise your hand." All the class members always raise their hands. To the question, "How many of you have a spouse or relatives who are Catholic?" quite a few raise their hands. To the question, "How many of you are former Catholics?" there are always a few who raise their hands.

Because there are so many Catholics, it is natural that Lutherans and Catholics interconnect in many ways. Because those connections give us opportunities to compare notes on our churches and to share what we believe with Catholics, it is helpful to know something about the Catholic Church and its teachings. We will want to know what Lutherans and Catholics have in common and also where our churches' teachings differ. That's the reason for this book, which is part of the series A Lutheran Looks At.

This book looks at the Roman Catholic Church today from a confessional Lutheran perspective, that is, with the conviction that the teachings of the Lutheran church as confessed in *The Book of Concord* of 1580 are true and correct because they are based on the written Word of God—Holy Scripture. Where we find Catholic teaching in agreement with Scripture and our Lutheran Confessions, we rejoice; and where we find that Catholic teaching conflicts with Scripture, love and honesty demand that we frankly say so. In presenting the teachings of the Catholic Church in this book, I strove to do so by quoting from its own official documents, such as the *Catechism of the*

Catholic Church, and the decrees of popes and church councils. Occasionally, I also referenced the writings of modern Catholic theologians as they present Catholic teaching, including some of the more liberal theologians who take issue with official Catholic teaching on some points.

A word may be necessary about how I use the words *Catholic* and *Roman Catholic*. In this book, I use the words interchangeably. While the official name is simply the Catholic Church and seems to be preferred by most Catholics, Roman Catholic is also in fairly common usage.

Within the Catholic Church, there are what are called *Latin-* or *Western-rite* Catholics. And there are *Eastern-rite* Catholics, who adhere to various rites traditional in countries to the east of Europe. Eastern rites include the Armenian, Coptic, Syriac, Maronite, Chaldean, and Ukrainian rites. The Eastern-rite Catholic churches are very similar to their Eastern Orthodox church counterparts, the major difference being that the Eastern-rite Catholics accept the primacy and authority of the pope, while still keeping their distinctly Eastern forms of worship and church laws.

Probably the most noticeable differences between Eastern- and Western-rite Catholics are the rules regarding the marriage of priests. Eastern-rite Catholics allow married men to be priests. With only a very few special exceptions, the Western or Latin rite, which is set by the pope, does not. This book will limit itself to the Western- or Latin-rite Catholic Church, which makes up the vast majority of Catholics in the world.[1]

MODERN CATHOLICISM
An Overview

This first chapter will offer an overview of the Roman Catholic Church today. We will look at some of the general characteristics of the Catholic Church: how it is organized, various statistics, and some general religious trends within contemporary Catholicism. To facilitate this overview, we will look at the Catholic Church using eight categories. We can say the Catholic Church is each of the following:

- a huge church
- a diverse church
- a changing church
- an unchanging church
- a troubled church
- a sacramental church
- a hierarchical church
- a creedal (Christian) church[2]

A huge church

The size of the Catholic Church is perhaps its most obvious characteristic. Of the approximately 2 billion Christians in the world, 1.1 billion are Roman Catholics. Of the other billion Christians, somewhere between two hundred and three hundred million are Eastern Orthodox. Most of the other seven hundred million are Protestants (Anglicans, Baptists, Episcopalians, Lutherans, Methodists, Presbyterians, various holiness and Pentecostal groups, and others). Half of the world's Catholics live in the Western Hemisphere; about

68 million live in the United States, with most of the rest living in Central and South America. About one-third of all US Catholics are Hispanic. About one million US Catholics are African-American. The 68 million US Catholics represent about 23 percent of the US population. By comparison, there are about 74 million Lutherans worldwide and about 7.4 million Lutherans in the United States.[3]

Comparison of worldwide Catholic and Lutheran populations

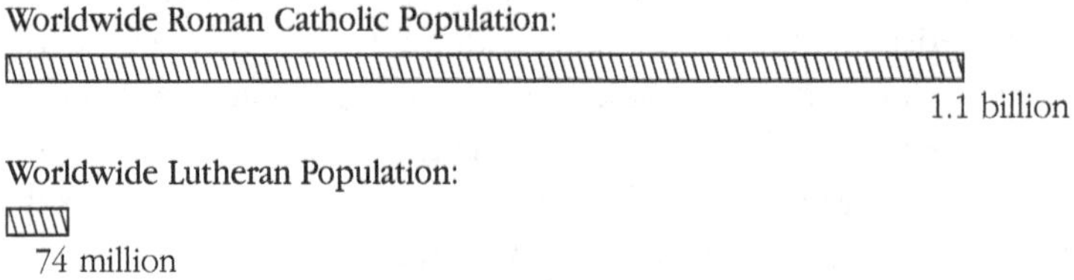

Comparison of US Catholic and Lutheran populations

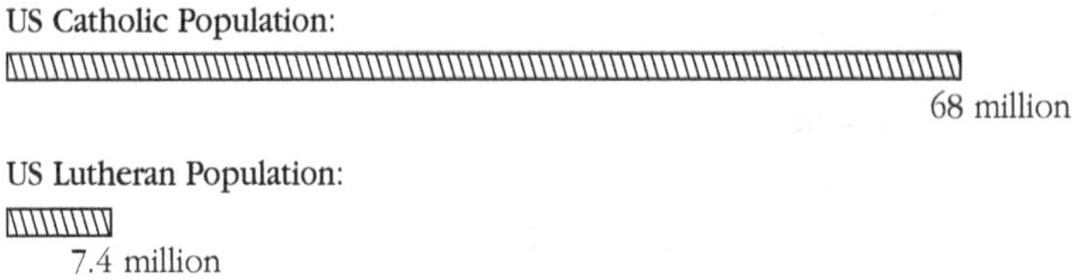

To further compare the number of Catholics and the number of Lutherans in the United States, we could note the following:

- There are more Catholics in the state of California (11 million) than there are Lutherans in the entire United States.
- There are almost as many Catholics in the archdiocese of Chicago (2.3 million) as there are Lutherans in the entire Lutheran Church—Missouri Synod.

- The number of Catholics in the archdiocese of Milwaukee (630,000) is almost double the total number of Lutherans in the entire Wisconsin Evangelical Lutheran Synod (390,000).

What are Lutherans to make of such large numbers? We might question whether Catholic membership figures are accurate and if they are an apples-to-apples comparison with membership figures of other denominations. Aren't many people who are counted as members of the Catholic Church "Catholic in name only"? Perhaps they were baptized Catholic, but for whatever reason, they are nonpracticing or seldom-practicing Catholics. In answer, Catholics themselves, when talking about their numbers in the United States, often say it this way: "The Catholic Church is the largest denomination in the United States. And fallen-away Catholics make up the second largest denomination!" Catholics suggest that there are about 25 million lapsed or nominal Catholics in the United States. The large percentage of nominal Catholics compared to practicing Catholics reflects the fact that Catholic parishes usually will not remove the names of baptized members from their membership rolls unless a person specifically asks to have his or her name removed—in other words, unless the person publicly renounces the Catholic faith. By contrast, Lutheran parishes tend to remove the names of inactive members from their church rosters if attempts to reinstate them appear to be futile.

Because the number of Catholics—active, inactive, and fallen away—is so large, Lutherans have many opportunities to talk to Catholics about religion—about what Lutherans and Catholics have in common and where they differ. Many Lutheran pastors can relate stories of former Catholics who have stated that they never had heard a clear presentation of the gospel until they came to a Lutheran church. They appreciate having the burden of their sin and guilt removed from them by the message of God's unconditional forgiveness, which Jesus won for all people on the cross and gives to them for free in the gospel only through believing in him.

Because of its size, the Catholic Church often will have a noticeable presence and influence in a community. Often their churches and parochial schools are among the largest in a local community. Catholic bishops often have more of a presence in the local, state, and national news media than the clergy from other denominations.

Media attention, of course, can be both an advantage and a disadvantage. On the one hand, such exposure helps remind people in the community of your church's presence. Catholics effectively use the media for making known their church's position on such moral issues as abortion.

On the other hand, it can also be a disadvantage, especially when church scandals become public, such as the current sexual abuse scandal. This crime began to receive enormous national media attention in the United States in 2002. Even though it has been pointed out that the percentage of Catholic priests who have sexually abused children over the years is probably about the same as the percentage of clergy from other denominations involved in such crimes, news coverage of the Catholic scandals has been much more intense and extensive, no doubt because of the sheer numbers of priests and victims involved.

When Lutherans compare their denomination's size with that of the Catholic Church, they must always remember that the size of a church building or the size of a church's membership list never determines which church's teachings are true. Jesus says, "Your [God's] word is truth" (John 17:17). Religious error, whether taught by many or by few, is always error. On the other hand, when a church faithfully preaches and teaches God's Word, God promises to bless that church's ministry, whether the outward number of members is large or small. The only way to know for sure whether a church's teachings are true or not is by comparing them to Scripture.

A diverse church

Non-Catholics sometimes assume that the Catholic Church is the most monolithic organization on earth and that it enjoys a high degree of doctrinal unity among both clergy and lay members. The fact that the Catholic Church has a universal leader, the pope in Rome, who claims to be the supreme teaching authority for all Catholics, contributes to that impression. What's more, all Catholic bishops pledge loyalty and obedience to the pope, and all Catholic priests pledge loyalty and obedience to their bishops.

Yet in spite of this outward organizational unity, there is considerable doctrinal diversity within the Catholic Church. This diversity ranges from what we might call ultra-traditionalism on the one extreme to ultraliberalism on the other, with varying degrees of conservatism and liberal progressivism in between. We can place these general categories on a spectrum, as follows:

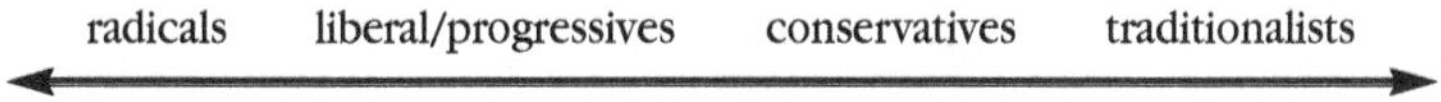

Catholics themselves refer to these general categories when they describe their church. Catholic liberal/progressives for the most part promote the following agenda:

- married priests
- female priests
- the laity involved to a certain extent in the election of bishops
- democratization of church authority
- relative autonomy of national churches (that is, decisions arrived at by national bishops not subject to the pope's approval)
- downgrading of papal authority
- greater tolerance of theological diversity

- total repeal of the ban on the use of contraceptives
- a more flexible moral code with regard to divorce, abortion, homosexuality, and premarital sex

The agenda of the conservative camp is the opposite:

- male priests only
- celibate priesthood
- papal control over the election of bishops
- papal approval for national church decisions
- affirmation of papal authority over the whole Catholic Church
- no tolerance for theological dissent
- staunchly pro-life; opposed to abortion, euthanasia, artificial contraception, divorce, and homosexuality

In general, theologically conservative Catholics believe that there is such a thing as absolute, objective truth, which has been revealed by God through the Catholic Church. Conservative Catholics are also confident of the truth of their historical Catholic faith. They endeavor to measure contemporary culture against the standards suggested by that faith.

Liberal Catholics, on the other hand, hold that the historical Christian faith and Catholic doctrine came about entirely by processes of human development and this also applies to the Bible. The liberal dogma is "all truth is relative" and "we have no right answers." Liberals express confidence in the normative value of contemporary culture in determining what the church's agenda should be.

On the extreme ends of the liberal-conservative spectrum are the radicals and the traditionalists. The radicals include such fringe groups as Call to Action, Dignity, and We Are Church. The radicals call for what amounts to a renunciation of the Catholicism of the past and bringing about a "new church" of perpetual change. Some radical Catholics are experimenting with various New Age beliefs, including goddess worship.

By contrast, on the far right are what we might call the ultratraditionalists. Many of them belong to a group called the Society of St. Pius X, founded by Archbishop Marcel Lefebré, often referred to as Lefebrists. This group holds that many of the changes initiated by the Second Vatican Council in the 1960s—the changes made to the Mass, ecumenism, views toward non-Christian religions, and religious liberty—are heretical and that no pope since Pope Pius XII (d. 1958) has been legitimate. After all attempts by the Vatican to get Archbishop Lefebré to reconcile with the Catholic Church failed, Pope John Paul II excommunicated Lefebré in 1988. All members of the Society of St. Pius X are considered by the Catholic Church to be in schism—a very grave sin. In recent years the leadership of the society and high-level Vatican officials have been meeting to try to resolve their differences. Discussions remain ongoing.

Besides these theological/ideological categories of Catholics, we can point out a few other categories: nominal Catholics, cultural Catholics, cafeteria Catholics, charismatic Catholics, and syncretistic Catholics.

Nominal Catholics probably make up the largest single group of Catholics worldwide. They are Catholic largely in name only. They were likely baptized in a Catholic church but do not participate in a local Catholic parish or avail themselves of the ministry of the Catholic Church. They remain members only because the church does not remove them, and they have not taken steps to remove themselves. Perhaps the only times they enter a Catholic church is to attend a funeral or wedding. Their worldview is usually shaped more by the culture in which they live than by the church and its official teachings.

Cultural Catholics are similar to nominal Catholics in that the only time they avail themselves of the church's ministry is when they want to get married, have their children baptized, or have a Catholic relative buried. Occasionally they may attend a Christmas Eve or Easter Mass.

Cafeteria Catholics tend to be more active in their local parish. They may attend church more than cultural Catholics do, but they pick and choose what aspects of Catholic teaching they wish to believe and practice. The teaching of angels may appeal to them, so they believe what the church teaches about angels. But if they don't like the Catholic teachings about purgatory and hell, they ignore those teachings. Many Catholics today have chosen to ignore their church's teachings on sexual morality, birth control, divorce, and remarriage. According to many religious surveys, the majority of American Catholics do not accept the Catholic Church's teaching that the pope is infallible in his official teachings. They choose instead to think of him merely as an important "symbol of unity" in the church, whatever that means.

The charismatic movement entered the Catholic Church in the late 1960s and early 1970s, as it did in most of the mainline Protestant denominations. At first, most bishops and Vatican officials were suspicious of the movement. It seemed to have a highly Protestant flavor to it. Catholic charismatics had little problem fellowshiping with Protestant charismatics, and many of them seemed to have little time or need for the ministries of the ordained priests and bishops. Since the Catholic Church holds that the Holy Spirit truly comes only through the sacramental ministries of the ordained priests and bishops, this was obviously a source of contention.

The bishops seem to have worked out these problems. Catholic charismatics have affirmed the validity of the Sacrament of Baptism and the necessity of the ministries of their priests and bishops. The Catholic charismatic movement no longer seems to be growing as fast in North America as it was in the 1970s and 1980s. Evidence suggests, however, that the movement is still growing among Catholics in Africa and Latin America.

Syncretism refers to the practice of mixing the teachings and practices of different religions or belief systems. This form of Catholicism is seen especially in developing countries, such as Haiti and Papua New Guinea, and among Brazilian Indians, where many baptized Catholics also practice voodoo and other forms of pagan superstition. For centuries, it has been a Catholic mission practice to "convert" heathen people by "baptizing" their heathen gods and festivals by identifying them with Catholic saints and saints' days, which blurs the distinction and makes it easier for people to retain heathen practices.

The image the Catholic Church tries to promote of itself, namely, that it is a unified church with a single faith, is clearly a myth. Lutherans need to keep this in mind when they talk to their Catholic friends and relatives. Just because people say that they are Catholic doesn't mean that they necessarily accept all the teachings of Catholicism. Many do; many do not. It is always important to ask the individual Catholic what he or she believes. Some will confess genuine Christian faith in Christ as their Savior. Others will mostly reveal their doubts, confusion, and spiritual ignorance. As God gives us opportunities to share our faith and hope in Christ with Catholics, what the apostle Peter wrote applies to us today: "Always be prepared to give an answer to everyone who asks you to give the reason for the hope that you have. But do this with gentleness and respect" (1 Peter 3:15).

A changing yet unchanging church

Anyone who has been a part of the Catholic Church or closely observed it is aware that it went through a great deal of change in the second half of the 20th century, particularly since the Second Vatican Council (1962–1966). (The next chapter will look at the Second Vatican Council in detail.) Here is a partial list of those changes:

- replacing the old Latin Mass with a new Mass in the vernacular
- allowing laypeople to touch the Sacred Host and sacred Communion vessels
- in certain circumstances, receiving Communion under both kinds (bread and wine) is accepted

- receiving Communion while standing instead of kneeling
- receiving Communion with the hand instead of only on the tongue
- removing the Communion rail in church
- allowing altar girls and women to be Communion servers
- practically eliminating the Lenten fast
- eliminating the meatless Friday law
- downgrading traditional devotions to Mary, including praying the Rosary
- major revising of the church calendar and eliminating many saints' days
- allowing Catholics to get married in Protestant churches
- no longer insisting on children's attendance at Catholic schools
- encouraging Catholic laypeople to read the Bible
- removing many traditional religious statues from churches
- no longer referring to non-Catholic Christians as heretics (which includes all Protestants, even Lutherans) or schismatics (in reference to the Eastern Orthodox) but as "separated brethren"

In many cases, it seems that the bishops and local parish priests implemented many of these changes without spending much time instructing the people as to why the changes were being made. As a result, many Catholics living at the time of the changes were left feeling confused and hurt, believing that their religion was being taken away from them. Still others, probably a majority in the United States, eagerly welcomed most of the changes.

Lutherans will recognize that the list of changes is comprised mostly of external and peripheral things, not of doctrinal and theological matters as such. Since the changes appear to be made in external, nontheological matters, Lutherans will sometimes say, "The Catholic Church has not really changed its doctrines." This is more or less true. Yet careful observers of Catholicism can also point to changes in emphasis in areas of theology as well.

For example, as we will see later in this book, the teaching of purgatory isn't gone, but it certainly isn't emphasized in Catholic instruction the way it once was. When Lutherans attend the funeral of a Catholic acquaintance, they will sometimes notice that the priest speaks of the soul of the deceased Catholic as being not in purgatory but in heaven. Another example: Many Catholics no longer hear their priests speak of the Mass as a *sacrifice* for the sins of the living and the dead in as emphatic a way as they once did. There is more emphasis on the Mass as a *meal that celebrates* the presence of the community of God's people gathered together. Speaking of sin, many older Catholics have noted that the "s-word" is seldom mentioned anymore in many priests' homilies. Two more examples: The teaching of evolution is generally accepted throughout the Catholic Church today as being in harmony with Catholic teaching. And the negative "critical" view of the Bible—that it is a book that reflects the human weaknesses of its authors—is the view held by most Catholic theologians today. All of these examples reflect a general liberalizing trend in theology, similar to what has taken place in many mainline Protestant denominations, that is different from what Catholics were taught a century ago.

When Lutherans say that nothing of doctrinal substance has changed in Catholic teaching, they are likely referring to the basic doctrinal issues that have divided Lutherans and Catholics since the time of the Reformation in the 16th century. We will examine several of those issues in later chapters of this book.

A troubled church

When we speak of the Catholic Church as a troubled church, the first thing that comes to mind is the huge sexual abuse scandal that became public in 2002. Scores of priests have been accused and convicted of sexually abusing children, especially adolescent boys. (This represents more than 80 percent of all sexual abuse victims in the United States.) The scandal has resulted in payouts to victims and legal fees totaling more than a billion dollars. Some of the monetary damages that juries awarded to sexual abuse victims were so huge that some dioceses filed for bankruptcy. The emotional damage to the victims and their families is beyond calculation.

While the priest sex-abuse scandal certainly is the most sensational trouble facing the Catholic Church, it is not the only example of the Catholic Church's troubles. Consider the following statistics of the Catholic Church in the United States:[4]

	1965	2002
Number of priests in USA	59,000	46,000
Number of parishes without a priest	3%	15%
Number of priests for every 10,000 Catholics	7.87	4.6
Number of seminarians	49,000	4,700
Number of religious sisters	180,000	75,500 (half age 70+)
Number of parochial grade school students	4.5 million	1.9 million

It would seem difficult to deny that such statistics describe a church facing considerable challenges. But there is more.

During that same period (1965–2002) and continuing to the present, the Catholic Church has been plagued by a problem unlike any it faced in previous centuries: doctrinal dissent among its priests and theologians. The match that lit the fuse on the powder keg of dissent was the 1968 encyclical of Pope Paul VI, *Humanae Vitae,* which affirmed the Catholic ban on the use of all artificial means of birth control. The encyclical touched off a firestorm of public protest among Catholic theologians and educators all over the world.

The next logical step for the dissenters was to publicly question and deny the pope's claims to be the infallible teaching authority in the Catholic Church. Many theologians began questioning every Catholic and Christian doctrine imaginable. The bishops, who are supposed to exercise doctrinal oversight and discipline in their respective dioceses, often seemed nearly helpless to do anything to confront this onslaught of doctrinal rebellion. Other bishops even seemed sympathetic to it.

To this day, doctrinal dissent seems to be fashionable among many professional Catholic theologians in Catholic colleges and universities. The strategy of Pope John Paul II and the Vatican to counter doctrinal dissent seemed to be twofold: discipline only relatively few of the most outspoken dissenting theologians in order to make an example of them; and as older, theologically liberal bishops retire, replace them with younger, more theologically conservative bishops.

It has been observed that, in general, the younger priests—those who have received their seminary training since about the late 1980s—appear to be more doctrinally conservative and more zealous for promoting historical, orthodox Catholic teaching than many older priests who received their training from the 1950s through the early 1980s. Nevertheless, doctrinal dissent remains imbedded throughout the Catholic educational system. Consider, for instance, the following list, which gives the percentage of lay religion teachers in US Catholic elementary schools in the year 2000 who *agreed* with official Catholic teaching on various topics:[5]

contraception	10%
abortion	26%
infallibility of the pope	27%
male-only priesthood	33%
the Real Presence	63%
life after death	74%
the resurrection	87%
the divinity of Christ	91%
the existence of God	98%

A hierarchical church

The Catholic Church can be characterized as *hierarchical* in its organization. All authority in the church resides with the ordained clergy. Within the clergy are three ranks: *bishops, priests,* and *deacons.* The Catholic Church has divided up the entire world into geographical areas called *dioceses* and *archdioceses* (an archdiocese is simply a large diocese). Currently there are 2,023 dioceses and 578 archdioceses in the world. The United States is divided into 152 dioceses with an additional 34 archdioceses. Each diocese is governed by a bishop, and each archdiocese by an archbishop. Archbishops will often have one or more auxiliary bishops to assist them. All of the bishops (and archbishops) together form the *college of bishops,* which is headed by the *pope,* who is the bishop of Rome.

Catholics view the pope as the supreme pastor (or shepherd) of the entire Catholic Church. Each bishop is the pastor of all the Catholics in his respective diocese. Each diocese is made up of a number of local *parishes* over which ordained priests preside, perhaps with ordained deacons to assist the priests. Catholics teach that this hierarchy was instituted by Christ and that it is absolutely necessary in order for the true Christian church to exist. (We will examine this teaching in the light of Scripture in the next chapter.)

So where do laypeople fit in? They are on the bottom. Sometimes more progressive Catholics will object to that description and say, "The hierarchical model may have been true in the past, but the Second Vatican Council (1962–1965) changed all that. If the Catholic Church was once a pyramid with the pope on the top and the laypeople at the bottom, Vatican II turned that pyramid on its side. Laypeople now have a much greater role in the church." In response we point out: It is still the case that no one can be a bishop without the pope's appointment and approval. And within each diocese, no one can serve as a priest except by the bishop's appointment and approval. Laypeople have no say or vote whatsoever in who will be the bishop of their diocese or who will be the priest of their local parish. When it comes to who decides whether a parish will open, or close, or be merged with another parish, laypeople and even priests have no deciding vote. The bishop makes the decision, and his decision is final.

The hierarchical nature of the Catholic Church is shown by the fact that when a man is ordained to be a priest, he has to solemnly pledge his loyalty and obedience to his bishop. When a priest is ordained as a bishop, he must solemnly pledge his loyalty and obedience to the bishop of Rome. While it is true that lay Catholics have been given many of the responsibilities in local parishes and in diocesan offices that once were handled exclusively by priests (or perhaps with the help of religious brothers and sisters), the fact remains that all official church authority resides in the bishops, with the pope as the head of the college of bishops. The documents of the Second Vatican Council quite emphatically reaffirmed that Catholic teaching.

Who chooses the pope? The pope is elected by a group of men called *cardinals,* who together are called the *college of cardinals.* Cardinals are the highest officials in the Catholic Church, second only to the pope. Cardinals are appointed by the pope. Almost all cardinals are either archbishops or top church officials who work directly under the pope in the Vatican. The college of cardinals has almost always elected a new pope from within its own ranks.

The pope resides in the *Vatican,* which is short for the State of Vatican City. Vatican City is the smallest sovereign state in the world, covering an area of only 108.7 acres. St. Peter's Basilica is the focal point of Vatican City and is the largest church building in the world. Somewhere between five hundred and one thousand people live in Vatican City, and another three to four thousand people work there on a daily basis.

The Vatican once comprised several states within central Italy, formerly known as the Papal States. The size of the Vatican was reduced in the 1800s by various European political powers, but it still maintains some characteristics of a sovereign state. It has its own post office and bank. The vestige of the papal army is the famed Swiss Guard. Most notably, as a sovereign nation, it maintains an international diplomatic core. In fact, the Vatican maintains full diplomatic relations and exchanges ambassadors with more countries around the world than does the United States.

Two other terms are used to refer to the central administration of the Catholic Church in Rome: the *Holy See* and the *Apostolic See.* The word *see* is derived from the Latin word for seat, referring to a seat of authority. The Holy See (or Apostolic See) refers to the supreme authority, sovereignty, and jurisdiction exercised by the pope over the entire Catholic Church. While technically the term *the Vatican* refers to the geographical city-state, it is often used as a synonym for the Holy or Apostolic See.

The central government of the Catholic Church within the Vatican, which assists the pope in the day-to-day governing of the church, is known as the Roman curia. The word *curia* is from the Latin word for circle, here in reference to the circle of Vatican officials. The curia is comprised of several departments, which are called sacred congregations, councils, tribunals, and commissions. Members of the curia serve solely at the pleasure of the pope.

The pope serves for life. Very rarely has a pope ever resigned. Catholic Church historians count only about 11 papal resignations in the history of the papacy. (Pope Benedict XVI resigned in 2013.) One unresolved question is what should happen if a pope becomes senile and refuses to resign or is unable to resign by his own volition. While the Vatican has in place very clear rules and protocols to follow when a pope dies and a specific procedure to follow in electing a new pope, there are no clear guidelines for how to remove a pope if he becomes incapacitated so that he can no longer rule and is unable to resign or refuses to do so. The Catholic priest-scholar Thomas Reese remarks:

> There are currently no canonically acceptable procedures for removing a mentally ill or senile pope. In the good old days his staff might lock him in his rooms and run the church until he died. In the bad old days someone would poison him. Either strategy would be difficult to carry out in the full blaze of today's media attention. How many crazy popes the church has suffered through in the past is uncertain. Some who today might be classified as sociopaths governed through terror and violence. Others became senile or paranoid but continued to reign.
>
> There are no easy solutions to the problem. How crazy does a pope have to be to be incompetent to govern? Who makes that decision? Any process for removing a pope for psychological reasons would be open to corruption, abuse, bad judgment, or misinterpretation.[6]

A creedal (Christian) church

The question may be asked, "With all the theological diversity and doctrinal dissent within the Catholic Church, is it possible to state with any certainty what the official position of the Catholic Church is on any given doctrine and to compare that teaching with Scripture?" The answer is yes. It is possible because the Catholic Church is a creedal church. Like the Lutheran church, the Catholic Church has adopted certain creeds and confessions as its official statements of faith. In fact, Catholics and Lutherans have three of those creeds in common. They are the three ecumenical (universal) creeds that all Christians share: the Apostles' Creed, the Nicene Creed, and the Athanasian Creed. In confessing these creeds, Catholics, along with Lutherans, confess the basic articles of the Christian faith: that God is triune—Father, Son, and Holy Spirit; that Jesus Christ is true God and true man; that Jesus suffered and died for the eternal salvation of mankind; and that Jesus bodily rose from the dead, ascended into heaven, and will return on the Last Day to judge the living and the dead. With Lutherans, Catholics confess the Sacrament of Baptism instituted by Christ.

Because of these common Christian confessions as articulated in the three historic Christian creeds, Lutherans have always held that the Catholic Church is a Christian church—and Lutherans rejoice in that fact. We give thanks to God whenever biblical truth is taught and Christian faith is confessed, and that includes in the Catholic Church.

At the same time, we Lutherans are also compelled to testify that when other teachings of the Catholic Church are compared with Scripture, it is evident that grave, faith-destroying errors pervade the Catholic Church. This was true at the time of the Reformation in the 16th century. It is just as true today. Lutherans find no joy in making this accusation of false teaching, but it is our conviction that honesty and love require us to do so.

As we examine the main teachings of the Catholic Church in this book, we will attempt to let the Catholic Church speak for itself. That is, I have quoted from its own official doctrinal sources, such as the official statements of Catholic Church councils and the official *Catechism of the Catholic Church*. At times I also have quoted from the private writings of Catholic theologians when those writings state Catholic teaching in a way that's easy to understand or to give examples of more liberal theological views that are popular among many present-day Catholics.

Following the example of the first Christians in the New Testament, we will compare those teachings with the written Word of God to determine whether they are true or false (Acts 17:11; 1 Thessalonians 5:21,22).

Before we examine specific Catholic teachings, it will be helpful to look at the Second Vatican Council, or simply Vatican II, which took place during the 1960s. That event was probably the most significant event in the history of the Catholic Church since the time of the Reformation.

2 VATICAN II

The concept of councils

An official meeting of bishops is called a *council*. Councils can be either *regional* or *ecumenical* (or *general*). A regional council would be the meeting of the bishops from a particular region or country. Decisions of a regional council are binding only on the bishops of that particular region or country.

Vatican II was what the Catholic Church calls an *ecumenical* or *general* council. An ecumenical or general council is a meeting that all the Catholic bishops in the world are invited to attend. When Catholics speak of general councils as *ecumenical*, they are using the word in its meaning of "universal," or "worldwide," not in the sense that representatives of non-Catholic churches are invited to participate on equal footing with the Catholic bishops.

Only the pope can convene an ecumenical council, and such a council's decisions and actions, once the pope has ratified them, are regarded as binding on all Catholics throughout the world. The Catholic Church teaches that ecumenical councils are guided in a special way by the Holy Spirit and that when such councils make official pronouncements of doctrine, those pronouncements—again, when ratified by the pope—are considered to be infallible and binding on all Catholics for all time.

Since the year 1545, the Catholic Church has held only three general councils: the Council of Trent (1545–1563), the First Vatican Council (Vatican I, 1869–1870), and the Second Vatican Council (Vatican II, 1962–1965). Before we look more closely at Vatican II, we'll provide a little background about the Council of Trent and Vatican I because we will be referring to both of those councils, along with Vatican II, in subsequent chapters of this book.

The Council of Trent

A general council was called by Pope Paul III in 1537 and began its meeting in the northern Italian city of Trent in 1545. The council held a number of sessions during the years 1545–1547, 1551–1552, and 1562–1563. The Council of Trent was the Catholic Church's answer to the Reformation. It reaffirmed all the traditional teachings of the medieval church, including justification by faith *and* good works, Scripture and sacred tradition as the sources of doctrine, the seven sacraments, the sacrifice of the Mass, transubstantiation, masses for the dead, the veneration of Mary and the saints, and purgatory. Trent officially rejected the Lutheran Reformation teachings of salvation by grace alone, salvation through faith alone, salvation in Christ alone, as revealed in Scripture alone. It also pronounced dozens of solemn curses on Lutherans and Reformed Protestants who believed anything different from what the Catholic Church teaches. The Catholic Church adopted an adversarial approach in its dealings with all non-Catholics that lasted for four centuries, up until the time of Vatican II in the 1960s.

Besides reaffirming traditional Catholic doctrine and rejecting the teachings of the Reformation, Trent also mandated that the bishops carry out a number of church reforms. Bishops were called on to take better care of their churches than they had generally been doing and to establish seminaries for training priests. Worship was reformed. The council insisted on worship uniformity, worshiping exactly as it was done in Rome and using Latin exclusively. Interestingly, Trent also instituted some reforms in respect to the buying and selling of indulgences. While Trent reaffirmed the work-righteousness theology of indulgences, it sought to curtail some of the crass merchandizing practices of the past. Indulgences were pieces of paper, approved by the pope, which gave time off from purgatory for sins committed against church laws. Lutherans will recall that the selling of indulgences was the spark that ignited the Reformation, prompting Luther to post his famous Ninety-five Theses against indulgences.

The Council of Trent provided the Catholic Church with its theological agenda for the next four centuries. In general, we could describe that agenda like this: Whatever the Lutheran Reformation emphasized, Catholics emphasized the opposite. While Lutherans taught that Christ is the only Savior and mediator between sinners and God, Catholics emphasized the role of Mary and the saints as co-mediators. While Lutherans emphasized the Bible as the sole source of all Christian doctrine, preaching, and teaching; Catholics downplayed the Bible and instead emphasized church tradition, decrees of popes and church councils, and stories about the saints. Where Lutherans worshiped in the language of the people, Roman Catholic worship was conducted only in Latin. While Lutherans emphasized that Holy Communion is Christ's gift of his body and blood to all communicants to be eaten and drunk for the forgiveness of sins, Catholics emphasized the priest's work of sacrificing the Mass over and over, with the priest alone drinking the wine. And so on. Actually, it was the Council of Trent that set the stage for Vatican II in the 1900s. By the middle of the 20th century, some reformed-minded Catholics were thinking it was time to make some adjustments in some of those emphases.

But first we need to look at a few things about Vatican I.

The First Vatican Council

Pope Pius IX convened the First Vatican Council in 1869, and it lasted until the following year when the council fathers (the bishops) were forced to leave Rome because of political upheaval going on throughout Italy. In that relatively short time, however, Pope Pius IX got the bishops to make a very important statement of faith. They issued a document that solemnly defined the infallibility of the pope and asserted that the pope was the absolute ruler over the Catholic Church.

Papal infallibility was not a new teaching in the Catholic Church. It had been confessed for a long time. So why call a council at this time to define and officially decree that Catholics must accept this teaching?

In part, the teaching of papal infallibility was the Catholic Church's response to the many ideas and movements that had risen since the start of the Enlightenment in the mid 1600s. These movements included rationalism, secularism, nationalism, and individualism.

Basically, the Enlightenment was man's declaration of independence from God. According to rationalist thinkers, man no longer needed God, his Word, or his church. Man could arrive at truth on his own simply by using his reason. The Enlightenment and rationalistic thinking wreaked theological havoc on the protestant Church of England and the Lutheran churches in Germany and Scandinavia. Many pastors and teachers of theology fell under the sway of rationalism with the result that they rejected the miracles in the Bible and any doctrine that wasn't "reasonable" or couldn't be proven by "science." They held that the Bible is not the inspired Word of God and not literally true in everything it teaches. Rather, they held that Scripture was only the words of men, full of conflicting man-made stories and myths. They theorized how all these stories gradually developed over time into what made up the individual books of the Bible. These theories came to be known as the "historical-critical method" of Bible interpretation.

As a result, many people had become very antireligious and specifically anti-Christian and anti-Catholic. While some faithful Lutherans and other conservative Protestants reacted to rationalism by reaffirming the infallibility of the Bible, the Catholic Church responded by reaffirming the infallibility of the pope. Like the Council of Trent, Vatican I condemned and solemnly cursed all non-Roman Catholic Christians, with the addition of condemning all who did not accept the pope's claims to be the infallible teacher and absolute ruler of Christ's church on earth.

Pope John XXIII convenes the next general council

Vatican I set the tone for how the Catholic Church dealt with Enlightenment modernism and liberalism up through the papacy of Pius XII, who reigned from 1939 to 1958. After Pius XII died, a new pope was elected, Angelo Roncalli, who took the name John XXIII.

Most Catholics thought that John XXIII would be merely a "caretaker pope." He was almost 77 years old when he was elected and not in good health. It was assumed that he would have a short reign with little more impact than providing the transition from the 19-year-long reign of Pius XII to whoever would succeed him. It therefore came as a huge surprise to the entire Catholic world when he announced on January 25, 1959, just three months into his reign, that he was calling an ecumenical council. It came as a surprise also because it seems that Roncalli had discussed the idea with almost no one. In fact, Roncalli himself said that the idea of calling a council came to him in a sudden moment of "inspiration."

The news of a council came as a surprise to most Catholic bishops for another reason. Historically, church councils were called when there was some heresy threatening the church or because some other major problem needed attention. In 1959 there were no new heresies to contend with and no huge problems to address. In fact, in many countries, such as the United States, the Catholic Church seemed to be doing better than ever. Attendance at Sunday Mass was high. Seminaries were full of young men training for the priesthood. Religious orders of sisters and brothers (traditionally called nuns and monks) provided ample teachers for the vast Catholic parochial school system. And except for the oppression that the church continually faced in communist countries, the 1950s was a period of relative peace and calm for the Catholic Church. So why call a council?

In the months following his announcement, Pope John explained his reasons. The purpose of this council was not to make any new definitions of church doctrine or to condemn heresies. Rather, it would address pastoral concerns. It would modernize and update the church so it could better relate to the modern world and have a more positive impact on it. Pope John's vision was that by being open to the ideas of the modern world and learning from those ideas, the modern world in turn would become more open to the teachings of the Catholic Church and be influenced by them. Pope John didn't seem to want to impose any more of a specific agenda on the council beyond that.

Pope John's vision for the council soon caught on with many Catholics, including many bishops. Some church leaders, however, especially some of the more conservative cardinals who worked in the Vatican, feared that calling a council with such a vague and naïve agenda would only spell trouble for the church.

In the following months, Pope John invited all the bishops to relate to the Vatican their ideas and suggestions for what should be placed on the council's agenda. The pope appointed committees, called commissions, within the Vatican to review the bishops' suggestions and to forge them into working documents for the council to consider. Most of the commissions were chaired by the more conservative cardinals in the Vatican, who were not enthusiastic about the council. So, many of the documents these commissions presented for discussion at the upcoming council did little more than present traditional Catholic teaching in very traditional ways, including condemnations of those who disagreed with Catholic teaching.

The Second Vatican Council begins

The Second Vatican Council officially began on October 11, 1962. The opening ceremonies included a lengthy procession through Saint Peter's Square of all 2,500 bishops, archbishops, and cardinals present, all wearing their liturgical robes. As was still customary at the time, the pope was carried through the square and into Saint Peter's Basilica on his gestatorial throne, wearing his triple-crown golden tiara. Near the end of the long processional line was one of the youngest bishops, the auxiliary bishop of Krakow, Poland, Karol Wojtyla (voy-TEE-wah), who later would become Pope John Paul II.

One of the more dramatic and significant events of the council occurred on the first full day of council business. The council used "commissions" similar to a church convention's floor committees. The commissions were responsible for framing documents and proposals and steering them through the discussion and debate sessions of the full body of bishops. The cardinals in the Roman curia chose the bishops for these commissions, and they tended to choose the more conservative, change-resistant bishops. Their proposed lists of bishops had to be ratified by the council, and when the cardinals presented their lists, one of the more progressive cardinals suggested that the council postpone accepting the nominees until the bishops could get to know one another better in formal and informal gatherings, at which point the bishops themselves would come up with their own lists of commission members. The proposal was adopted. Pope John seemed pleased. From that moment on, it was clear that the bishops themselves would be in charge of the council and not the Roman curia. What's more, it became clear that the more reform-minded bishops were in the majority and those who resisted change were in the minority.

The entire council took place over a period of four years in four sessions:

First session:	October 11–December 8, 1962
Second session:	September 29–December 4, 1963
Third session:	September 14–November 21, 1964
Fourth session:	September 14–December 8, 1965

In between the formal sessions, the bishops worked at framing and revising the many documents to be discussed by the full council.

Another significant event took place in June 1963, between the first and second sessions. Pope John died. According to Catholic Church law, the council was suspended until a new pope was elected who would decide whether to reconvene the council or not. Cardinal Montini of Milan, viewed as a moderate progressive, was elected as the new pope and took the name Paul VI. He said the council would continue, promising to carry forward Pope John's vision for church reform.

Vatican II's accomplishments

Even though Vatican II took place more than 40 years ago, it set a broad agenda for the Catholic Church for years to come, which the church's leaders use as an authoritative guide in how they govern the church today. At the same time, Catholic bishops, theologians, and historians continue to debate what the documents of Vatican II exactly meant and taught. The discussion reflects the current Catholic theological diversity of theologians, bishops, and the laity.

The council produced 16 concrete documents officially endorsed by the pope, which gives them the highest authority in the church. The documents are as follow:

Constitutions

Constitution on the Sacred Liturgy
Dogmatic Constitution on the Church
Dogmatic Constitution on Divine Revelation
Pastoral Constitution on the Church in the Modern World

Decrees

Decree on the Means of Social Communications
Decree on the Catholic Churches of the Eastern Rite
Decree on Ecumenism
Decree Concerning the Pastoral Office of Bishops in the Church
Decree on the Ministry and Life of Priests
Decree on Priestly Training
Decree on Renewal of Religious Life
Decree on the Apostolate of the Laity
Decree on the Mission Activity of the Church

Declarations

Declaration on Religious Freedom
Declaration on Christian Education
Declaration on the Relation of the Church to Non-Christian Religions[7]

The documents of Vatican II produced a book of roughly 650 pages, about the size of the Lutheran *Book of Concord.* Catholics do not regard the documents to be divinely inspired like the Bible, but they do hold that the Holy Spirit guided the council in writing the documents. As such, Catholics view these documents as providing the authoritative, broad-based agenda for their church well into the future, at least until the next general council.

Some key teachings of Vatican II

What are the basic teachings of Vatican II? It did not formally change any historic doctrines of the Catholic Church. In fact, it reaffirmed many of them. However, in a number of areas, it called for changes in emphases. Catholic theologians still vigorously debate just what those changes were and how they should be implemented, no doubt because many sections of the documents are written in the language of compromise, reflecting the theological pluralism of the bishops.

The main question under debate among Catholics, regarding the meaning and intent of the renewal forged by the council, seems to be this: Are the changes that Vatican II called for to be understood as making a decisive break with the church's past, or are they to be understood as maintaining continuity with the past? The more liberal, progressive theologians argue for the break-with-the-past approach. The more conservative theologians maintain the continuity-with-the-past approach. In general, it seems the liberal view held sway for the first dozen years or so after the council. But Pope John Paul II and then Pope Benedict XVI clearly imposed a more conservative view.

One of the most prominent American Catholic theologians, Avery Dulles, who was made a cardinal by Pope John Paul II, identifies ten basic principles of Vatican II.[8]

Aggiornamento

Aggiornamento is the Italian word for the updating, modernization, and adaptation to current thought and practice popularized by Pope John XXIII. Instead of being suspicious and critical of modern ideas, philosophy, and science, as the Catholic Church often had been in past centuries, Vatican II called for an openness to modern ideas. This is a very broad principle and subject to much interpretation.

Reformability of the church

This idea took many Catholics by surprise. Before Vatican II, Catholics tended to think of church reform as a Protestant idea and tended to avoid it. Instead, they emphasized that the Catholic Church never changes and is always the same. Vatican II said that some things can change. Again, this is a very broad principle, which Catholics are still debating.

Renewed attention to the Word of God

The council called for Catholics to read the Bible more, for more translations of the Bible to be made in modern languages, and for Catholic scholars to study the Bible in the original languages. It also called for an expanded lectionary (a book containing Scripture readings to be used in worship services) so that more of the Bible would be read in church. The council also opened the door for wide acceptance of historical-critical methods of Bible interpretation, which liberal protestant churches had been using for a century or more.

Collegiality

This term defines how the bishops and pope should work together in governing the Catholic Church. The bishops make up what the council called a *college of bishops,* with the pope as the head. The bishops must pledge loyalty and obedience to the pope as the absolute ruler and infallible teacher of the whole Catholic Church.

Active role of the laity

Prior to Vatican II, the Catholic laity had a mostly passive role in the church. The work of the church was carried out by the clergy, along with the men and women in religious orders. The laity's job, it was sometimes said, was simply to "pray, pay, and obey." Vatican II called for the laity to take a more active role in the church. It was to be their church too, not just the clergy's.

Regional and local variety

In the past, uniformity was the emphasis in church organization and worship. Vatican II made the provision for a certain amount of diversity in worship language and allowed parishes to incorporate elements of the local culture into their worship. Again, this is a broad principle that continues to spark debate among Catholics.

Ecumenism

Before Vatican II, the Catholic Church studiously avoided any formal involvement in the ecumenical movement (the movement whose goal is to merge all Christian churches into one). It held that the Roman Catholic Church alone was the one true church. Catholics regarded the Eastern Orthodox as schismatics and Protestants as heretics who should repent of their schisms and heresies and "come home to Rome." The council maintained that the Roman Catholic Church is still the one, true church instituted by Christ, but it called for dialogue with other Christians to replace confrontation. Non-Catholics should now be referred to with the less pejorative term "separated brothers and sisters," and in a certain sense to be members of the Catholic Church even though they don't realize it.

Dialogue with non-Christian religions

The changing attitude of Catholics toward other Christian churches was marked by a corresponding shift in their attitude toward non-Christian religions. While the Catholic Church has always allowed for the possibility of people being saved without faith in Christ, Vatican II spoke more positively of other religions than the church had ever officially done in the past. This is true especially in regard to Judaism.

Religious freedom

In the past, Catholic theologians and popes had advocated the principle that "error has no rights." In other words, non-Catholic Churches or religions should have no legal rights. It was the duty of the civil government to promote the Catholic Church and to suppress any other church or religion. Vatican II backed off from this position and taught that while the Catholic Church alone has the full truth of God, this truth should not be imposed on others by force, that is, by trying to make them Catholics against their will.

The social mission of the church

In the past the Catholic Church tended to emphasize its mission mostly as a religious one—saving souls through membership in the Catholic Church, receiving the Catholic sacraments, and striving to live according to Catholic teaching. Vatican II endorsed the trend established by several of the popes who reigned in the years leading up to the council who spoke out on social issues and saw the mission of the church to include helping to create a just and moral society (making this world a better place in which to live).

Much more, of course, could be said about the teachings of Vatican II. We will expand on some of them in other chapters of this book. Suffice it again to say that while Vatican II changed some of the outward ways that Catholicism expresses and organizes itself and while it put a different emphasis on some aspects of Catholic teaching, it did not officially change any of the basic teachings of the Catholic Church.

Aftermath of Vatican II

In general, we can say that Vatican II opened the door for the liberalization of much of Catholic teaching, similar in many respects to what we see happening in modern liberal Protestantism. Higher critical views of the Bible, which allow for errors and conflicting teachings in Scripture, are now taught in the Catholic Church. Modern theories of evolution are assumed to be true, even though they contradict the literal teachings of the Bible. The teaching of sin and God's judgment on sin tends to be downplayed. Likewise, the corresponding need for Jesus Christ as the Savior from sin by his atoning sacrifice is downplayed, perhaps even more so than in the past.

To many Catholics, both clergy and laity, the changes that were implemented in the years following the council seemed like a revolution. For centuries the emphasis had been on uniform obedience to Rome and that nothing ever changes in the Catholic Church. But now the Mass has changed—the priest faces the people and speaks in their language. And centuries-old customs, such as meat-less Friday fasts and various traditional devotions to Mary, have been abandoned. Many Catholics became confused and disillusioned. While some felt that not enough had changed, others thought that too much was changing too fast.

Many Catholics assumed that if it was okay to make these kinds of changes, it was also okay to make other changes, like dropping the ban on the use of artificial contraception, allowing priests to marry, and ordaining women as priests. Many Catholics assumed that Vatican II's teaching on religious freedom meant that individual Catholics now had the right to make up their own rules of right and wrong.

In recent years, however, the pendulum seems to be swinging back in a more conservative direction, due in a large measure to the influence of Pope John Paul II (reigned 1978–2005) and then Pope Benedict XVI. These popes sought to rein in some of the more outspoken radical theologians who publicly dissented with papal statements and official Catholic teachings. During his long reign, Pope John Paul II replaced the older more liberal bishops with younger, often more conservative, bishops. The general "agenda" in the Catholic Church in recent years seems to put less emphasis on what the church can learn from the rest of the world and from other religions. There is more emphasis on shoring up "Catholic identity" and reaffirming ties with the Catholic Church's heritage.

Students of Catholicism notice this trend toward a somewhat more conservative, traditional Catholicism among many of the younger priests and laypeople. Many in the new generation don't seem to be as liberal as the older priests or their own Catholic parents who lived through the 1960s and early 1970s. Nevertheless, as huge and diverse as the Catholic Church is, the debate continues among Catholics over what Vatican II really means and how its documents should be implemented.

3 THE PAPACY

Beginning in this chapter, we will examine several doctrinal teachings over which Lutherans and Catholics have always disagreed. The two main or central teachings of Christian doctrine have to do with *teaching authority* and *salvation*. Specifically, this chapter looks at the papacy; and the next, at Scripture and tradition. Chapter 5 looks at the teaching of justification.

Who or what decides whether a teaching is from God? Who or what determines how God defines a holy life? Lutherans find their answers to these questions in the Scriptures. The Bible is the divinely inspired, revealed Word of God (1 Thessalonians 2:13; 2 Thessalonians 2:15; 2 Peter 1:20,21). In the Bible, God reveals everything Christians need to know about his plan of salvation (2 Timothy 3:15-17). God's Word, revealed in the Scriptures, is a "lamp to [our] feet and a light for [our] path" (Psalm 119:105). When answering questions about what is true doctrine, what is false doctrine, what is God's holy will for our lives, and what is sinful, Lutherans respond, "Here is what God's Word teaches." God's Word of truth alone binds our consciences. The Bible alone is our supreme authority.

"Supreme church authority"

The Catholic Church has an entirely different way of defining authority in the church. In Canon 331 of the official *Code of Canon Law,* the Catholic Church addresses the question of "supreme church authority" like this:

> The bishop of the Church of Rome, in whom resides the office given in a special way by the Lord to Peter, first of the Apostles and to be transmitted to his successors, is

> the head of the college of bishops, the Vicar of Christ and Pastor of the universal Church; therefore, in virtue of his office he enjoys supreme, full, immediate and universal ordinary power in the Church, which he can always freely exercise.[9]

In other words, the supreme and final authority in the Catholic Church is not the Word of God but the pope, the bishop of Rome. Some of the pope's official titles include:

- Bishop of Rome
- Vicar of Jesus Christ
- Successor of the Prince of the Apostles
- Supreme Pontiff of the Universal Church
- Primate of Italy
- Archbishop and Metropolitan of the Roman Province
- Sovereign of the Vatican City State
- Servant of the Servants of God[10]

The pope claims that by divine right, he is the head of the whole Christian church on earth and that only the church over which he is the head is the one true church of Jesus Christ. He claims to receive this authority directly from Christ himself and not from any other source, not even from a church council consisting of all the Catholic bishops in the world. He claims the divine right to define doctrines that people are conscience bound to believe as true, even if they are not found in the Bible or even directly contradict the Bible. Such doctrines include purgatory, the immaculate conception of Mary, and Mary's bodily assumption into heaven. When he makes such official pronouncements of doctrine, he claims that he is infallible and that his doctrines cannot be changed. He also claims the right to issue laws and decrees that people are conscience bound to obey, such as the laws regarding worship and fasting, the law that forbids priests to marry, and the law that absolutely prohibits all use of artificial contraceptives, even by married couples.

Papal primacy

Two key concepts involved in the Catholic definition of papal authority are *primacy* and *infallibility*. The concept of primacy refers to everything the pope does as the supreme leader and ruler of the Catholic Church. He claims to have a divine right to appoint and depose bishops and the right to confirm or overrule the decisions of bishops or even the entire college of bishops meeting in a church council such as Vatican II. The pope claims the right to establish rules for worship and what orders of worship can be used throughout the entire world.

When a group of bishops—for example, all the Catholic bishops in the English-speaking world—wants to make a new English translation of the various liturgical rites and worship books, it has to get official approval from the pope. If the pope disapproves of their English translation, the bishops are not allowed to use it until they have corrected it according to the pope's wishes. In practice, much of the pope's oversight is carried on by the various departments within the Roman curia, but they must run their decisions by the pope for his official approval.

Papal infallibility

Papal primacy refers to the pope's day-to-day governance of the church. His claim of infallibility, on the other hand, is invoked on a more limited basis, such as when he officially defined the doctrines of the immaculate conception of the virgin Mary in 1854 and Mary's bodily assumption into heaven in 1950. Also, when a pope officially approves of the pronouncements and decrees of a church council, such as the Council of Trent or Vatican II, all of those pronouncements and decrees are considered infallible. But even in his day-to-day teaching in sermons, encyclicals (formal teaching letters), and other official documents, the pope is always to be obeyed because he is functioning as the Vicar of Christ, the visible head of the whole Christian church on earth.

Vatican I on papal authority

The two most recent ecumenical church councils of the Catholic Church have taught and reaffirmed the teachings of papal primacy and infallibility. Here is how Vatican Council I (1869–1870) defined the dogma of papal infallibility:

> We teach and define that it is a dogma divinely revealed that the Roman Pontiff, when he speaks *ex cathedra,* that is, when in discharge of the office of pastor and doctor of all Christians, by virtue of his supreme Apostolic authority, he defines a doctrine regarding faith and morals to be held by the universal Church, by the divine assistance promised to him in blessed Peter, is possessed of that infallibility with which the divine Redeemer willed that his Church should be endowed for defining doctrine regarding faith or morals and that therefore such definitions of the Roman Pontiff are irreformable of themselves, and not from the consent of the Church.[11]

Regarding papal primacy, Vatican I teaches:

> We renew the definition of the ecumenical Council of Florence, in virtue of which all the faithful of Christ must believe that the holy Apostolic See and the Roman Pontiff possesses the primacy over the whole world, and that the Roman Pontiff is the successor of blessed Peter, Prince of the Apostles, and is the true vicar of Christ, and head of the whole Church, and father and teacher of all Christians, and that full power was given to him in blessed Peter to rule, feed, and govern the universal Church by Jesus Christ our Lord, . . . Hence we teach and declare that by the appointment of our Lord the Roman Church possesses a superiority of ordinary power over all other churches, and that this power of jurisdiction of the Roman Pontiff, which is truly episcopal, is immediate; to which all, of whatever right and dignity, both pastors and faithful, both individually and collectively, are bound, by their duty of hierarchial subordination and true

> obedience, to submit not only in matters which belong to faith and morals, but also in those which appertain to the discipline and government of the Church throughout the world, so that the Church of Christ may be one flock under one supreme pastor. . . . This is the teaching of Catholic truth, from which no one can deviate without loss of faith and salvation.[12]

So where does that leave Lutherans and all other Christians who reject the papal claims of divine authority? Here is the answer of Vatican I:

> If anyone, therefore, shall say that blessed Peter the apostle was not appointed the Prince of all the apostles and the visible Head of the whole Church militant; or that the same directly and immediately received from the same our Lord Jesus Christ a primacy of honor only, and not of true and proper jurisdiction: let him be anathema.
>
> If, then, any should deny that it is by institution of Christ the Lord or by divine right, that blessed Peter should have a perpetual line of successors in the Primacy over the universal Church, or that the Roman Pontiff is the successor of blessed Peter in this primacy: let him be anathema.
>
> If, then, any shall say that the Roman Pontiff has the office merely of inspection or direction, and not full and supreme power of jurisdiction over the universal Church, not only in things which belong to faith and morals, but also in those which relate to the discipline and government of the Church spread throughout the world; or assert that he possesses merely the principal part, and not all the fullness of this supreme power; or that power which he enjoys is not ordinary and immediate, both over each and all the churches, and over each and all the pastors and the faithful: let him be anathema.
>
> This is the teaching of Catholic truth, from which no one can deviate without loss of faith and salvation.[13]

Note the *anathemas* issued against those who refuse to acknowledge the authority of the pope. An anathema is a solemn curse: "Let him be damned to hell!"

Vatican II on papal authority

The First Vatican Council took place in 1869–1870. Ninety years later, Pope John XXIII recognized that times had changed and felt it was time for the Catholic Church to change also. In his opening speech to the Second Vatican Council, he stated that while the substance of Catholic doctrine does not change, perhaps it would be wise to adopt a milder, more winsome manner of speaking, especially to non-Catholics. Pope John saw the opportunity for the Catholic Church to become a key player in the modern (then mainly Protestant) ecumenical movement. To attract non-Catholic Christians to Catholic teaching, Catholics would have to "tone down the rhetoric" a little without losing the Catholic substance. So Vatican II established the model of refraining from anathema statements while still affirming full papal authority over the church.

At the same time, Vatican II clearly defined and reaffirmed the role of the bishops, individually and collectively in church councils, in relation to the pope's authority:

> The college or body of bishops has for all that no authority unless united with the Roman Pontiff, Peter's successor, as its head, whose primatial authority, let it be added, over all, whether pastors or faithful, remains in its integrity. For the Roman Pontiff, by reason of his office as Vicar of Christ, namely, and as pastor of the entire Church, has full, supreme and universal power over the whole Church, a power which he can always exercise unhindered. . . . Together with their head, the Supreme Pontiff, and never apart from him, they have supreme and full authority over the universal Church; but this power cannot be exercised without the agreement of the Roman Pontiff. The Lord made Peter alone the rock-

> foundation and the holder of the keys of the Church (cf. Mt. 16:18-19), and constituted him shepherd of his whole flock (cf. Jn. 21:15ff.). It is clear, however, that the office of binding and loosing which was given to Peter (Mt. 16:19), was also assigned to the college of the apostles united to its head (Mt. 18:18; 28:16-20).[14]

The hellfire and brimstone anathemas of Vatican I were not repeated at Vatican II. Actually, they didn't have to be; they were still in effect. And papal primacy and authority were affirmed as much as ever.

Catholic bishops and papal authority

Where do the bishops fit in? Vatican I had clearly settled the question debated within the Catholic Church for centuries, namely, whether the pope or a church council has the highest authority. Vatican I made it clear that the pope does; he has the last word. But there were still some unanswered questions about the bishops. What is the nature of their authority? Is it merely derived from the pope? How obligated are Catholics to obey the teachings and decisions of their individual bishops? Here is part of Vatican II's answer:

> Bishops who teach in communion with the Roman Pontiff are to be revered by all as witnesses of divine and Catholic truth; the faithful, for their part, are obliged to submit to their bishops' decision, made in the name of Christ, in matters of faith and morals, and to adhere to it with a ready and respectful allegiance of mind. This loyal submission of the will and intellect must be given, in a special way, to the authentic teaching authority of the Roman Pontiff, even when he does not speak *ex cathedra* in such wise, indeed, that his supreme teaching authority be acknowledged with respect, and that one sincerely adhere to decisions made by him, conformably with his manifest mind and intention, which is made known principally either by the character of the documents in question, or by the frequency with which

a certain doctrine is proposed, or by the manner in which the doctrine is formulated.

Although the bishops, taken individually, do not enjoy the privilege of infallibility, they do, however, proclaim infallibly the doctrine of Christ on the following conditions: namely, when, even though dispersed throughout the world but preserving for all that amongst themselves and with Peter's successor the bond of communion, in their authoritative teaching concerning matters of faith and morals, they are in agreement that a particular teaching is to be held definitively and absolutely. This is still more clearly the case when, assembled in an ecumenical council, they are, for the universal Church, teachers of and judges in matters of faith and morals, whose decisions must be adhered to with the loyal and obedient assent of faith.

This infallibility, however, with which the divine redeemer wished to endow his Church in defining doctrine pertaining to faith and morals, is co-extensive with the deposit of revelation, which must be religiously guarded and loyally and courageously expounded. The Roman Pontiff, head of the college of bishops, enjoys this infallibility in virtue of his office, when, as supreme pastor and teacher of all the faithful—who confirms his brethren in the faith (cf. Lk. 22:32)—he proclaims in an absolute decision a doctrine pertaining to faith or morals. For that reason his definitions are rightly said to be irreformable by their very nature and not by reason of the assent of the Church, in as much as they were made with the assistance of the Holy Spirit promised to him in the person of blessed Peter himself; and as a consequence they are in no way in need of the approval of others, and do not admit of appeal to any other tribunal. For in such a case the Roman Pontiff does not utter a pronouncement as a private person, but rather does he expound and defend

> the teaching of the Catholic faith as the supreme teacher of the universal Church, in whom the Church's charism of infallibility is present in a singular way. The infallibility promised to the Church is also present in the body of bishops when, together with Peter's successor, they exercise the supreme teaching office. Now, the assent of the Church can never be lacking to such definitions on account of the same Holy Spirit's influence, through which Christ's whole flock is maintained in the unity of the faith and makes progress in it.[15]

So, while the bishops are not equal to the pope in authority, they also exercise infallible teaching authority when they make doctrinal pronouncements in church councils in agreement with (and only when they are in agreement with) the pope.

Is obedience to the pope necessary for salvation?

The pope's claims to primacy over the Christian church is not just the matter of authority. It spills over into how sinners receive salvation. The Bible clearly teaches that all who believe in Jesus Christ as their Savior receive full and complete forgiveness for their sins, eternal life, and salvation (John 3:16; Romans 3:21-24). Contrary to this, the pope claims that salvation comes only to those who obey him. Consider the pope's own words from an official decree made by Pope Boniface VIII (*Unam Sanctam,* 1302):

> We are compelled with a firm faith to believe [in] the Holy Catholic and Apostolic Church itself and to hold that . . . outside of it there is no salvation or remission of sins. . . . Furthermore we declare, say, define and pronounce that it is absolutely necessary for salvation that every human being should be subject to the Roman pope.

What did Vatican II say about this claim, namely, that submitting to the pope's supreme authority is necessary for salvation? Here the Catholic Church made one significant shift in its doctrine (Catholics prefer to call it a development). It now refers to non-Catholic Christians as "separated brethren." Protestants, including Lutherans, are recognized as Christians and having some kind of "connection" with the Catholic Church through Baptism. It is also acknowledged that they have the Bible and Christian prayer. But they still are not members of the one and only true saving church, which is the Catholic Church ruled by the pope. Vatican II stated:

> It is through Christ's Catholic Church alone, which is the all-embracing means of salvation, that the fullness of the means of salvation can be obtained. It was to the apostolic college alone, of which Peter is the head, that we believe our Lord entrusted all the blessings of the New Covenant.[16]

Prior to Vatican II, Catholic teaching more commonly emphasized that salvation comes only through the Catholic Church. Since Vatican II, however, Catholic teaching is that the *fullness of the means of salvation* comes only through the Catholic Church. This leaves the door open for the possibility of salvation for non-Catholics.

At the same time, as recently as the year 2000, in an official document titled *Dominus Iesus* (Jesus Is Lord), the Vatican reaffirmed Vatican II's teaching on this point. The Vatican also made it clear that Lutherans and all other Protestant churches aren't real churches. According to Catholic teaching, Lutherans have neither a true absolution nor a true sacrament of the Lord's Supper. According to the pope, when a Lutheran pastor pronounces the words of absolution, "I forgive you all your sins in the name of the Father, and of the Son, and of the Holy Spirit," he is speaking only empty words that convey no real forgiveness from God. When a Lutheran pastor speaks Christ's words of institution ("This is my body"; "This is my blood") over the bread and wine in the Lord's Supper and distributes them, there is only bread and wine and no forgiveness of sins. Therefore, to receive the "fullness of the means of salvation," it is still necessary to submit to the authority of the pope and become a member of the Catholic Church.

Where is the papacy taught in the Bible?

Lutherans (and other non-Catholic Christians) may wonder: Do Catholics try to prove their teachings about the papacy from the Bible? Yes, they do, kind of. We say, "kind of," because nowhere does the Bible say that Christ instituted the Roman papacy. So how do they arrive at the teachings that the papacy is a divine institution and has primacy over all other church authorities? The Catholic Church points to Jesus' words to the apostle Peter in Matthew chapter 16. Peter had just made his great confession of faith in answer to Jesus' question to his disciples, "Who do you say I am?" (verse 15). Responding for all of the disciples, Peter confessed, "You are the Christ, the Son of the living God" (verse 16). Then, speaking directly to Peter, Jesus replied:

> Blessed are you, Simon son of Jonah, for this was not revealed to you by man, but by my Father in heaven. And I tell you that you are Peter, and on this rock I will build my church, and the gates of Hades will not overcome it. I will give you the keys of the kingdom of heaven; whatever you bind on earth will be bound in heaven, and whatever you loose on earth will be loosed in heaven. (verses 17-19)

Catholics are quick to point out that in Greek Peter (*petros*) means "rock." They hold that Peter is the rock on which Christ established his church. They hold that in these verses, Christ was making Peter the first pope and bishop of Rome, with primacy and authority over the other apostles and over the whole Christian church.

In response to this view, it should be pointed out that the original Greek word used in Matthew's gospel for "rock," on which Jesus says he will build his church, is not *petros* (Peter); it is *petra*. The words are related but do not refer to the same thing. *Petros* means rock, in the sense of a stone, like a building block. *Petra* refers to a massive rock, like bedrock.

What is the bedrock foundation on which Jesus builds his church? It is the same foundation on which Peter's faith rested. It is the confession that Peter had just made, that Jesus is the Christ, the promised Savior, the Son of God. That confession, Jesus told Peter, is no mere human opinion but a divinely revealed truth of God. God had revealed it to Peter and the other disciples through Jesus' preaching and teaching.

That Christ himself is the foundation and Rock on which the Christian church is built is taught in many other places in Scripture. Already in the Old Testament, the psalm writers referred to the Lord, their Savior-God, as their Rock, the foundation of their faith:

> The LORD is my rock, my fortress and my deliverer; my God is my rock, in whom I take refuge. . . . For who is God besides the LORD? And who is the Rock except our God? The LORD lives! Praise be to my Rock! Exalted be God my Savior! (Psalm 18:2,31,46)

> May the words of my mouth and the meditation of my heart be pleasing in your sight, O LORD, my Rock and my Redeemer. (Psalm 19:14)

> To you I call, O LORD my Rock; do not turn a deaf ear to me. (Psalm 28:1)

In the New Testament, Peter himself refers to Jesus as the rock foundation of the Christian church:

> As you come to him, the living Stone—rejected by men but chosen by God and precious to him—you also, like living stones, are being built into a spiritual house to be a holy priesthood, offering spiritual sacrifices acceptable to God through Jesus Christ. For in Scripture it says: "See, I lay a stone in Zion, a chosen and precious cornerstone, and the one who trusts in him will never be put to shame." (1 Peter 2:4-6)

And Paul says that the church is built on the foundation of God's Word with Jesus as the chief cornerstone:

> Consequently, you are no longer foreigners and aliens, but fellow citizens with God's people and members of God's household, built on the foundation of the apostles and prophets, with Christ Jesus himself as the chief cornerstone. In him the whole building is joined together and rises to become a holy temple in the Lord. And in him you too are being built together to become a dwelling in which God lives by his Spirit. (Ephesians 2:19-22)

To claim that Jesus in Matthew chapter 16 set Peter above the other apostles in rank, power, and authority, completely contradicts what Jesus says about such things in other places. For example:

> You are not to be called "Rabbi," for you have only one Master and you are all brothers. And do not call anyone on earth "father," for you have one Father, and he is in heaven. Nor are you to be called "teacher," for you have one Teacher, the Christ. The greatest among you will be your servant. For whoever exalts himself will be humbled, and whoever humbles himself will be exalted. (Matthew 23:8-12)

> They came to Capernaum. When he was in the house, he asked them, "What were you arguing about on the road?" But they kept quiet because on the way they had argued about who was the greatest. Sitting down, Jesus called the Twelve and said, "If anyone wants to be first, he must be the very last, and the servant of all." (Mark 9:33-35)

> Jesus called them together and said, "You know that those who are regarded as rulers of the Gentiles lord it over them, and their high officials exercise authority over them. Not so with you. Instead, whoever wants to become great among you must be your servant, and whoever wants to be first must be slave of all. For even the Son of Man did not come to be served, but to serve, and to give his life as a ransom for many." (Mark 10:42-45)

Jesus emphatically taught the kinship of all Christians. The only divine authority in Christ's church is God's Word, which he moved prophets in the Old Testament and the apostles in the New Testament to write down. The "keys" are Scripture's message of forgiveness for all, which opens heaven to those who believe, and the message of judgment on all who refuse to believe that Christ died for them. The keys that Christ gave to Peter in Matthew 16:19 were clearly not given only to Peter but to all the apostles and to the entire church (Matthew 18:15-20).

Besides all that has been said so far in response to the Catholic claims about Peter in Matthew chapter 16, it should be pointed out that nowhere does the New Testament ever say that Jesus appointed Peter to be the first bishop of Rome. The New Testament is silent about Peter ever being in Rome. Likewise, the New Testament says nothing about Jesus commanding a line of successors to Peter, who were to receive primacy over the whole church. That Peter died a martyr's death in Rome is Christian historical tradition, which is probably true; but it is only historical tradition, not something taught in the Bible.

The institution of the Roman papacy developed only very gradually over several centuries until it became fully developed in the Middle Ages. (To trace that history is beyond the scope of this book. See the "For Further Reading" list at the end of this chapter for sources that trace the historical development of the papacy.)

The papacy is the Antichrist

How do confessional Lutherans view the papacy and its claims? Lutherans reject the papacy and its claims to be a divine institution along with its claims of primacy and infallibility as the vicar of Christ. In fact Lutherans recognize the papacy as the fulfillment of the scriptural prophecies regarding the Antichrist, a great false teacher who would arise in the church.

Scripture speaks of all false teachers in the church as "antichrists." The prefix *anti* in the original Greek language, from which the English prefix *anti* comes, means not only "against" but also "instead of." By his false teaching, the Antichrist claims to be the highest authority in people's hearts *instead of* Christ and his Word, and in that way he stands *against* Christ. It is no coincidence that the pope has added to his official titles the phrase "vicar of Christ." *Vicar* is a Latin word that means "substitute." The pope claims to be Christ's substitute in this world until Christ returns.

The apostle John writes in his first epistle: "Dear children, this is the last hour; and as you have heard that the antichrist is coming, even now many antichrists have come. . . . They went out from us, but they did not really belong to us" (1 John 2:18,19). John speaks of many false prophets and antichrists troubling the church already in his day, and he also speaks of one great antichrist, "the antichrist," who is distinguished from other false teachers and in John's day was still to come.

In 2 Thessalonians chapter 2, the apostle Paul also speaks of this great false teacher, referring to him there as the man of lawlessness (sin). After warning his readers not to let false teachers upset their faith with false prophecies about the end of the world, Paul writes:

> Don't let anyone deceive you in any way, for that day will not come until the rebellion occurs and the man of lawlessness is revealed, the man doomed to destruction. He will oppose and will exalt himself over everything that is called God or is worshiped, so that he sets himself up in God's temple, proclaiming himself to be God. (verses 3,4)

Here Paul says that the Antichrist would lead a great spiritual rebellion against God and his Word, resulting in a great falling away from the Christian faith. In view of this, we know that the Antichrist is clearly a religious teacher within the Christian church ("God's temple"), not a secular ruler who would attack the church from the outside. In his rebellion, this false teacher would act like God, claiming authority in the church that belongs only to God.

Paul continues in 2 Thessalonians chapter 2:

> Don't you remember that when I was with you I used to tell you these things? And now you know what is holding him back, so that he may be revealed at the proper time. For the secret power of lawlessness is already at work; but the one who now holds it back will continue to do so till he is taken out of the way. (verses 5-7)

The opposition to Christ was already at work in Paul's day, but God was holding it back. As long as Christians loved the truth of God's Word, the Antichrist would be prevented from working too openly. But eventually as love for the truth of God's Word would grow cold in the church, God would let him work openly. (For more information on this passage, see the pages of The People's Bible commentary, *1,2 Thessalonians,* referenced in the section "For Further Reading" at the end of this chapter.)

Paul writes: "Then the lawless one will be revealed, whom the Lord Jesus will overthrow with the breath of his mouth and destroy by the splendor of his coming" (verse 8). Later, the Antichrist will be exposed ("revealed") for what he really is, and finally he will be destroyed by Christ himself at his second coming at the end of the world.

But how can the Antichrist have such spiritual influence over so many people's hearts? Paul says that Satan and his demonic power are behind the power of the Antichrist:

> The coming of the lawless one will be in accordance with the work of Satan displayed in all kinds of counterfeit miracles, signs and wonders, and in every sort of evil that deceives those who are perishing. They perish because they refused to love the truth and so be saved. (verses 9,10)

The devil gives this man of sin the power to do counterfeit miracles, signs, and wonders—"counterfeit" not in the sense that they are not miraculous but because they seem to be miracles performed by God's power but are not. Because outwardly they seem to be signs that only Christ can perform, they lead people away from Christ and his teachings and into the camp of the Antichrist and his false teachings.

Why does God allow such a terrible false teacher to plague people right within the visible Christian church? Paul's answer is sobering for us all. He says that it is God's judgment on those who do not believe and love his Word:

> They perish because they refused to love the truth and so be saved. For this reason God sends them a powerful delusion so that they will believe the lie and so that all will be condemned who have not believed the truth but have delighted in wickedness. (verses 10-12)

When we observe the development and claims of the institution of the papacy and compare it with the marks of the great false teacher to come, as Paul describes him, we see all the details of Paul's prophecy fulfilled in the Roman papacy.

- He operates from within the Christian church.
- He usurps Christ's authority in the church by claiming to be the visible head of the church on earth.
- He opposes God by claiming the right to develop and teach doctrines that are not found in the Bible and are contrary to the Bible, such as salvation through submission to his authority, purgatory, various doctrines about Mary, the veneration of Mary and the saints, the sacrifice of the Mass, and forbidding priests to marry.
- He is a man but also a succession of men—an institution that continues throughout history until finally destroyed by Christ at his second coming on the Last Day.
- He claims miracles—for example, the many miraculous healings performed in the name of Mary at Lourdes and other places—to confirm his false teachings and bolster his hold on people's hearts.

We must conclude that only one institution in history fits all of the scriptural marks of the Antichrist: the Roman papacy.

Martin Luther and the other Lutheran confessors at the time of the Reformation identified the papacy with the Antichrist prophesied in Scripture. In the Smalcald Articles, one of the official confessions of the Lutheran church written by Martin Luther, Lutherans confess:

> This teaching shows forcefully that the pope is the true Endchrist or Antichrist [1 John 2:18]. He has exalted himself above and opposed himself against Christ. For he will not permit Christians to be saved without his power, which, nevertheless, is nothing, and is neither ordained nor commanded by God. This is, properly speaking, how he "exalts himself against every so-called god" as Paul says (2 Thessalonians 2:4). Even the Turks or the Tartars, great enemies of Christians as they are, do not do this. They take bodily tribute and obedience from Christians, but they allow whoever wishes to believe in Christ.
>
> The pope, however, bans this faith. He says that to be saved a person must obey him. This we are unwilling to do, even though we must die in God's name because of this. This all proceeds from the pope wishing to be called the supreme head of the Christian Church by divine right. So he had to make himself equal and superior to Christ. He had to have himself proclaimed the head and then the lord of the Church, and finally of the whole world. This makes him simply God on earth, to the point that he has dared to issue commands even to the angels in heaven. When we distinguish the pope's teaching from, or compare it to, Holy Scripture, it is clear that the pope's teaching at its best has been taken from the imperial and heathen law. It deals with political matters and decisions or rights, as the decretals show. His law also teaches ceremonies about churches, garments, food, persons, and childish, theatrical, and comical things without measure. But in all of this, nothing at all is taught about Christ,

> faith, and God's commandments. Finally, the papacy is nothing else than the devil himself, because above and against God the pope pushes his falsehoods about Masses, purgatory, the monastic life, one's own works, and false worship. (This, in fact, is the papacy.) He also condemns, murders, and tortures all Christians who do not exalt and honor [his] abominations above all things. Therefore, just as we cannot worship the devil himself as Lord and God, so we cannot endure his apostle—the pope or Antichrist—in his rule as head or lord. For what his papal government really consists of (as I have very clearly shown in many books) is to lie and kill and destroy body and soul eternally.[17]

Another official Lutheran confession, the Treatise on the Power and Primacy of the Pope (written by Luther's coreformer Philip Melanchthon), also clearly identifies the Roman papacy as the fulfillment of all the scriptural marks of the Antichrist:

> It is clear that the Roman pontiffs, with their followers, defend godless doctrines and godless services. And the marks of Antichrist plainly agree with the kingdom of the pope and his followers. For Paul, in describing Antichrist to the Thessalonians, calls him an enemy of Christ, "Who opposes and exalts himself against every so-called god or object of worship, so that he takes his seat in the temple of God" (2 Thessalonians 2:4). He is not speaking about heathen kings, but about someone ruling in the Church. He calls him the enemy of Christ, because he will invent doctrine conflicting with the Gospel and will claim for himself divine authority.
>
> Furthermore, it is clear, in the first place, that the pope rules in the Church and has established this kingdom for himself by the claim of churchly authority and of the ministry. He gives these words as a basis, "I will give you the keys" [Matthew 16:19]. Second, the doctrine of the

pope conflicts in many ways with the Gospel. [Third,] the pope claims for himself divine authority in a threefold manner: (a) He takes for himself the right to change Christ's doctrine and services instituted by God, and wants his own doctrine and his own services to be observed as divine. (b) He takes to himself the power not only of binding and loosing in this life, but also jurisdiction over souls after this life. (c) He does not want to be judged by the Church or by anyone and puts his own authority ahead of the decision of councils and the entire Church. To be unwilling to be judged by the Church or by anyone else is to make oneself God. Finally, he defends these horrible errors and this impiety with the greatest cruelty and puts to death those who disagree.

This being the case, all Christians should beware of participating in the godless doctrine, blasphemies, and unjust cruelty of the pope. They should desert and condemn the pope with his followers as the kingdom of Antichrist, just as Christ has commanded, "Beware of false prophets" [Matthew 7:15]. Paul commands that godless teachers should be avoided and condemned as cursed [Galatians 1:8; Titus 3:10]. And he says, "Do not be unequally yoked with unbelievers. . . . What fellowship has light with darkness?" (2 Corinthians 6:14)[18]

These quotations make it clear that identifying the papacy as the Antichrist was not just a private, personal opinion of Martin Luther. It is the official teaching of the Lutheran church, clearly set forth in its official public confessions in the *Book of Concord* of 1580. It might also be mentioned that all the Protestant reformers of the 16th century, including non-Lutherans, identified the papacy as the Antichrist.

But what about today? Hasn't the papacy changed a lot since the 16th century? Haven't recent popes spoken a lot about Christ and encouraged peace and good will among people in the world? Haven't recent popes been prominent spokesmen for the defense of human life in the face of secular institutions that promote abortion and euthanasia? Confessional Lutherans answer that the papacy has not renounced any of its historic claims, as we have seen in our examination of the doctrine of the papacy in the proceedings of Vatican II. The more recent official *Catechism of the Catholic Church* also reaffirms the historic Catholic teaching about the papacy.[19] The teaching of the Lutheran Confessions remains as valid today as it was in the 16th century. The papacy fulfills all the scriptural marks of the Antichrist.

When Catholics hear the Lutheran confession about the papacy, they sometimes assume that Lutherans are declaring that all Roman Catholics are not Christians and condemned to hell. That is not the case at all. The Lutheran Confessions, in identifying the *papacy* as the great false teacher prophesied in Scripture, are not discussing the eternal fate of individual Roman Catholics. Lutherans believe and teach that sinners, whether Lutherans or Catholics, are saved from their sins through believing and trusting in Jesus Christ as their Savior and in no other way. Lutherans are convinced that the claims the papacy makes for itself undermine the authority of God's Word and Christ's place as Savior in people's hearts.

One thing confessional Lutherans and Romans Catholics can agree on, though, is that a person cannot remain neutral regarding the papacy. You cannot just say the pope is a nice man and an important religious teacher, a symbol of religious unity who talks a lot about peace in the world. That bland assessment would be calling the pope a liar because he himself claims to be a whole lot more than that. There are really only two choices. One must either believe the pope's own claims about his authority and submit to him as the vicar of Christ on earth or one must regard him for what the Scriptures expose him to be: the great Antichrist who tries to take Christ's place in the church and in every Christian's heart. Either the pope is the vicar of Christ on earth, the head of the whole Christian church by God's command, and our salvation is dependent on obeying what he teaches, even when he teaches contrary to Scripture; or he is, as Scripture teaches, the very Antichrist.

The Lutheran confession regarding the papacy is not a popular position to take today. But it is one that confessional Lutherans, in obedience to Scripture, hold very soberly and seriously.

For Further Reading

John F. Brug, *The Ministry of the Word* (Milwaukee: Northwestern Publishing House, 2009), pp. 253-276.

Theodore Hoyer, "The Papacy," in *The Abiding Word,* Vol. 2, edited by Theodore Laetsch (St. Louis: Concordia Publishing House, 1947).

David P. Kuske, *1,2 Thessalonians,* in The People's Bible series (Milwaukee: Northwestern Publishing House, 2000), pp. 87-100.

W. F. Schink, "The Scriptural Doctrine of the Antichrist," in *Our Great Heritage,* Vol. 3, edited by Lyle W. Lange (Milwaukee: Northwestern Publishing House, 1991).

"Statement on the Antichrist," in *Doctrinal Statements of the WELS,* prepared by the Commission on Inter-Church Relations of the Wisconsin Evangelical Lutheran Synod (Milwaukee: Northwestern Publishing House, 1997).

4 SCRIPTURE *and Tradition*

In chapter 3 we began our study of authority in the Catholic Church. We discussed the papacy and the pope's claim that his word binds people's consciences as to what they should believe and how they should act. In this chapter we will continue our look at how Lutherans and Catholics differ on the question of authority in the church. We will discuss Scripture and tradition. We will see again that significant differences continue to divide the two churches. Lutherans confess that the Bible alone (*sola Scriptura* in Latin) is the only source and norm of Christian doctrine. By contrast, the Catholic Church adds to Scripture other documents that it considers sources of truth and binding on the Christian church.

The two positions compared

Two classic statements that express the Lutheran church's conviction about the church's source of truth are found in the Lutheran Confessions. The first statement was penned by Martin Luther in the Smalcald Articles: "It will not do to frame articles of faith from the words and the works of the holy Fathers. . . . The true rule is this: God's Word shall establish articles of faith, and no one else, not even an angel can do so [Galatians 1:8]."[20] In this statement, when Luther speaks of "God's Word," he is clearly referring to the Bible.

The second confessional statement comes from the Formula of Concord:

> We believe, teach, and confess that the only rule and norm according to which all teachings, together with all

> teachers, should be evaluated and judged [2 Timothy 3:15-17] are the prophetic and apostolic Scriptures of the Old and New Testaments alone. . . .
>
> However, other writings by ancient or modern teachers—no matter whose name they bear—must not be regarded as equal to the Holy Scriptures. All of them are subject to the Scriptures [1 Corinthians 14:32]. Other writings should not be received in any other way or as anything more than witnesses that show how this pure doctrine of the prophets and apostles was preserved after the time of the apostles, and at what places.[21]

The Formula of Concord also specifies that "the prophetic and apostolic Scriptures of the Old and New Testaments [are] the pure, clear fountain of Israel. They are the only true standard or norm by which all teachers and doctrines are to be judged."[22]

Lutherans hold that the Scriptures are both the source of Christian doctrine (the "pure, clear fountain of Israel"), as well as the "only rule and norm," "the only true standard or norm," by which all teachers and teachings in the church are to be judged.

At the Council of Trent in 1546, the Roman Catholic Church officially rejected the Lutheran Reformation teaching of Scripture alone. Instead, Trent held that both Scripture and Sacred Tradition are the sources of Christian doctrine.

> [The Catholic Church] receives and venerates with an equal piety and reverence all the books of the Old Testament as well as of the New, since one God is the author of both, and no less the traditions themselves, both those pertaining to faith and those pertaining to morals, as having been spoken orally by Christ himself or dictated by the Holy Spirit, and preserved in the Catholic Church by the succession of bishops.[23]

Exactly what Trent meant by Sacred Tradition, the relationship between Scripture and Tradition, and how

Tradition is determined, etc., were all debated by the bishops at Trent but they could not agree. So they left these issues open and unanswered.

Four centuries later, at the Second Vatican Council (1965), the Catholic Church reiterated its rejection of the Bible alone as the only source of God's Word and Christian doctrine and likewise reaffirmed Sacred Tradition as being on the same level as the Bible.

> Sacred Tradition and sacred Scripture, then, are bound closely together, and communicate one with the other. For both of them, flowing out from the same divine well-spring, come together in some fashion to form one thing, and move towards the same goal. Sacred Scripture is the speech of God as it is put down in writing under the breath of the Holy Spirit. And Tradition transmits in its entirety the Word of God which has been entrusted to the apostles by Christ the Lord and the Holy Spirit. It transmits it to the successors of the apostles so that, enlightened by the Spirit of truth, they may faithfully preserve, expound and spread it abroad by their preaching. Thus it comes about that the Church does not draw her certainty about all revealed truths from the holy Scriptures alone. Hence, both Scripture and Tradition must be accepted and honored with equal feelings of devotion and reverence.
>
> Sacred Tradition and sacred Scripture make up a single sacred deposit of the Word of God, which is entrusted to the Church.[24]

Clearly, there is a clear and longstanding difference between Lutherans and Catholics over what should be the source and norm of doctrine in the Christian church.

A closer look at Lutheran *sola Scriptura*

We will now take a close look at the Lutheran teaching of *sola Scriptura* (Scripture alone) and then the Catholic teaching of Scripture and Tradition.

The Lutheran teaching of *sola Scriptura* does not mean that the Bible contains all knowledge on all subjects, like an exhaustive encyclopedia. It does not answer every question that scientists, mathematicians, and historians might ask.

Sola Scriptura also does not mean that the Bible is a record of every word God ever spoke to the prophets or Jesus spoke to his disciples. At the end of his gospel, the apostle John states: "Jesus did many other things as well. If every one of them were written down, I suppose that even the whole world would not have room for the books that would be written" (John 21:25).

Sola Scriptura does not mean that the Christian church does not have authority to publicly preach and teach God's Word. God himself has established the preaching and teaching ministry of the gospel (Matthew 28:18-20; John 20:21-23; Acts 6:2). God himself provides his church with public ministers of the gospel (Ephesians 4:11). God wants his people to "remember" and "obey" the spiritual leaders he has given them in the church as those leaders preach and teach God's Word (Hebrews 13:7,17). At the same time, God wants his people to hold their ministers accountable and insist that their preaching and teaching conform to the truth of the Bible (Acts 17:11).

Sola Scriptura does not deny that the Word of God was often presented orally in the past. God spoke directly to Abraham, Moses, and other prophets. They, in turn, preached God's Word to others. Jesus, during his earthly ministry, taught and preached orally, as did his apostles. *Sola Scriptura* acknowledges that in the past, God's Word was both spoken and written. At the same time, confessional Lutherans confidently hold that the Bible is God's complete revelation to the human race today. The Bible is the only divinely inspired and revealed Word that the Christian church possesses today. The Bible does not need to be supplemented by new revelations or by human sources.

By *sola Scriptura,* Lutherans do not reject every kind of "tradition" or forbid its use. In his book, *Examination of the*

Council of Trent, Martin Chemnitz, a second-generation Lutheran theologian, compiled a list of how the word *tradition* is used in the Bible and in the church.[25] The following is a summary of Chemnitz' list:

1. The Greek word for tradition in the New Testament is used as a verb and a noun. As a verb it means "to pass on, to hand on," synonymous with *teach*. As a noun it is used for the teachings that were passed on. The apostle Paul received his teachings from Christ. Paul, in turn, passed on (taught) those teachings (traditions) to others. He did this both orally and in writing. This is how Paul used the word in 1 Corinthians 15:1-4:

> Now, brothers, I want to remind you of the gospel I preached to you, which you received and on which you have taken your stand. By this gospel you are saved, if you hold firmly to the word I preached to you. Otherwise, you have believed in vain. For *what I received I passed on to you* as of first importance: that Christ died for our sins *according to the Scriptures,* that he was buried, that he was raised on the third day *according to the Scriptures*. (Italic added.)

Notice how Paul closely tied together the teachings that he orally passed on to the Corinthians with what was taught (written) in Scripture. They are the same teachings.

Similarly, Paul writes in 2 Thessalonians 2:15: "So then, brothers, stand firm and hold to the teachings [Greek: traditions] we passed on to you, whether by word of mouth or by letter." Paul never implied or even hinted that what he taught orally and in person was anything different from what he taught in his inspired writings, which are in the New Testament.

2. A second use of the word *tradition* in the early church referred to the careful transmission of the Scriptures from one generation to the next. Martin Chemnitz observed: "By this tradition the church confesses that it is bound to that voice of doctrine which sounds forth in the Scripture,

and when it passes on this tradition, it teaches that posterity also is bound to the Scripture."[26]

3. Some of the early church fathers used the word *tradition* for what they also labeled the "rule of faith." This referred to a brief creedal summary of the Christian faith, as taught in Scripture. What we call the Apostles' Creed, one example of an early Christian creed, along with others were titled the "rule of faith." Lutherans accept the orthodox Christian creedal tradition because it is based on Scripture. The "rule of faith" does not contain any teachings that are contrary to or not found in Scripture.
4. Closely related to the third kind of tradition is a fourth: the true exposition and understanding of Scripture received from the apostles and handed down to future generations.
5. Christian doctrines not explicitly stated in Scripture but drawn from clear Scripture on the basis of sound reason are also referred to as "traditions" in the early church. An example would be infant Baptism. Jesus did not explicitly command, "Baptize infants." But since he did command to baptize "all nations" (Matthew 28:19), without adding any restrictions, sound reason recognizes that in his command to baptize "all nations," children and infants are included.
6. Lutherans also accept the teachings of the early church fathers as they taught Scripture. As Chemnitz said, "We love and praise the testimonies of the fathers which agree with the Scripture."[27]
7. Many ancient rites and ceremonies were designated as apostolic, though there was not always direct proof from Scripture that they actually originated with the apostles. Examples that Chemnitz cites include making the sign of the cross, turning to the east in prayer, the renunciation of Satan in Baptism, and others. Other ancient customs and practices clearly do have their origins already in the New Testament, such as replacing the Jewish Sabbath

with Sunday as the regular weekly day for worship, also the laying on of hands when ordaining, installing, and commissioning a minister of the gospel for public service in the church (1 Timothy 4:14; 2 Timothy 1:6). In Christian freedom, we may observe such ceremonies as they serve the preaching of the gospel.

8. The only traditions Lutherans object to are those that pertain to doctrine and Christian life, have no foundation in Scripture, and are used as sources of doctrines—placed on the same level as the doctrines clearly taught in Scripture. Many such doctrines based on such traditions are found in the Catholic Church. Examples of doctrines derived from "Sacred Tradition" include the primacy and infallibility of the papacy, the sacrifice of the Mass, prayers for the dead, purgatory, indulgences, the invocation of Mary and the saints, the immaculate conception and bodily assumption of Mary into heaven, and the sacraments of confirmation, marriage, ordination, and last rites, etc. Chemnitz sums up this objectionable kind of tradition as "whatever the Roman church believes, holds, and observes, which cannot be proved by any testimony of the Scripture, must be believed to have been handed down by the apostles."[28] In summary: *sola Scriptura* does not mean that Lutherans reject all tradition, only that kind of tradition that claims to be a source of doctrines that are not found in Scripture.

We have looked at what *sola Scriptura,* according to Lutherans, is not. Now we will briefly state what it is.

The doctrine of *sola Scriptura* is that the Bible alone is the source of God's special revelation to the human race. The Bible is in a category by itself as the verbally inspired and infallible Word of God. All the words of the Bible are the actual words of God.

Sola Scriptura means that everything a Christian needs to believe is found in Scripture. In Scripture, God reveals everything necessary for salvation and for Christians to lead God-pleasing lives.

Sola Scriptura means that what is not revealed in Scripture is not binding on Christians. This includes many human traditions, rites, and ceremonies, which Christians are free to use or not to use, depending, in their judgment, as to whether they serve the preaching of the gospel today.

Finally, *sola Scriptura* means that all teachers in the church, their teachings and writings, and all human traditions are subject to the higher authority of Scripture.

The biblical teaching of *sola Scriptura*

The Lutheran doctrine of *sola Scriptura* reflects how Scripture describes itself. It is the unique, divinely inspired Word of God. The Old Testament prophets claimed of their writings, "This is what the LORD says" ("Thus saith the Lord" is the familiar translation of the King James Version). And the prophets' words are my words "declares the LORD." The Old Testament also records many instances where God specifically commanded the prophets to *write* down his Word (Exodus 17:14; 34:27; Deuteronomy 27:3,8; Jeremiah 30:2).

New Testament writers, when quoting from the Old Testament, used formulas like "all this took place to fulfill *what the Lord had said* through the prophet" (Matthew 1:22, italic added) to underline the divine source of the quotation. New Testament writers also claimed that they preached and wrote by the inspiration of God, which means that their words were also the words of God (1 Corinthians 2:13; 1 Thessalonians 2:13). Paul referred to his preaching and writings as the basis for the Christian faith (2 Thessalonians 2:15). The apostle Peter spoke of Paul's writings as "Scripture" (2 Peter 3:15), and put them on the same level as the Old Testament Scriptures. The apostle John ended the book of Revelation with the warning that no one should presume to add any man-made words or doctrines to the book of Revelation (Revelation 22:18,19), similar to the solemn warnings and threats of divine curses Moses described in the first five books of the Bible.

The doctrine of the inspiration of Scripture is summed up by Paul in 2 Timothy 3:15-17:

> From infancy you have known the holy Scriptures, which are able to make you wise for salvation through faith in Christ Jesus. All Scripture is God-breathed ["given by inspiration of God," as the King James Version translates it] and is useful for teaching, rebuking, correcting and training in righteousness, so that the man of God may be thoroughly equipped for every good work.

Because Scripture is God-breathed, that is, because it has its origin in God, it is "able to make you wise for salvation," not just in part but completely. Scripture is also "useful for teaching, rebuking, correcting and training in righteousness." What is more, Paul assured his coworker, Pastor Timothy, that armed with the Scriptures, he and the members of his congregation would be "*thoroughly* equipped for *every* good work" (italic added). The Scriptures would not just partially equip Timothy for *some* good works but for everything God wanted him to believe and do. There is not a hint in what Paul says that Scripture is insufficient, needing to be supplemented by some unwritten tradition that would only gradually come to light and develop over many centuries, as Roman Catholics claim. This passage (2 Timothy 3:15-17) clearly teaches what is called the *sufficiency* of Scripture. All that Timothy needed for his salvation, to live as a Christian, and to serve as a pastor in Christ's church, he already possessed in the inspired written Word of God, the Holy Scriptures.

Roman Catholics vehemently deny the *sufficiency* of Scripture and defend tradition as a source of doctrine equal to Scripture. This is especially true in their apologetic writings.[29] Because their distinctively Catholic teachings—papal infallibility, dogmas about Mary, purgatory, etc.—are not found in Scripture, they are forced to deny that Scripture is the sole source of divine doctrine and knowledge of salvation in Christ. Tradition, therefore, becomes necessary as a source of Catholic doctrine.

Another attribute of Scripture that is affirmed by Lutherans is the *clarity* of Scripture. The Bible itself says that its message is clear. Speaking to the Israelites as God's inspired writer, Moses said this about the Word that God had revealed to him:

> Now what I am commanding you today is not too difficult for you or beyond your reach. It is not up in heaven, so that you have to ask, "Who will ascend into heaven to get it and proclaim it to us so we may obey it?" Nor is it beyond the sea, so that you have to ask, "Who will cross the sea to get it and proclaim it to us so we may obey it?" No, the word is very near you; it is in your mouth and in your heart so you may obey it. (Deuteronomy 30:11-14)

The Israelites could not claim that they couldn't follow God's Word because it was too hard to understand. In the future, if their memory of what Moses personally had told them failed, they always had recourse to Moses' inspired written record, the first five books of the Bible, written in clear human language that they could know and understand.

Similarly, the psalm writer called God's Word "a lamp to my feet and a light for my path" (Psalm 119:105). And David wrote in Psalm 19:8: "The commands of the LORD are radiant, giving light to the eyes." David could not have written those things if the Bible was a dark book, unclear in its message. It is clear that to David, Scripture was not a book that led people spiritually astray from the truth and that required some outside, human source to shed light on it before people could understand its meaning. Rather, the clear message of Scripture illuminates our minds, hearts, and understanding.

Lutherans make an important distinction about the clarity of Scripture itself and our frequent lack of ability to grasp what it is saying. Lutheran theologian Lyle Lange describes the distinction this way:

> The Bible is *outwardly* clear. Its language is capable of being understood by people who hear it. Even the rankest of unbelievers can understand the message contained in

> John 3:16. I have heard men speak who had an extraordinary knowledge of the Bible. However, they did not believe what it said. It is only the Holy Spirit who can work an *inner* clarity in the heart, which the Bible calls enlightenment (Eph 1:18). Thus, the Bible is simple enough for a child to understand, but so deep that a theologian can puzzle over it.
>
> The Bible is clear in what it says. This does not mean, however, that every statement will be understood by us. Peter related that some things in Paul's writings were difficult to understand (2 Peter 3:16). . . .
>
> Where we face difficulties like this, the problem is not in the clarity of Scripture. The problem lies with our sin-clouded understanding of Scripture.
>
> Since the Bible is clear in its presentation of sin and grace, law and gospel, salvation and sanctification, we reject the idea that other revelations are necessary to interpret or shed light on the Bible. (Italic added.)[30]

Defenders of Catholic teaching on Scripture and Tradition have been denying the clarity of Scripture ever since the time of Martin Luther and the Reformation. When, for example, the famous Dutch humanist Desiderius Erasmus wrote in support of the Catholic Church against Luther's teachings on the spiritual bondage of the human will, one of the arguments Erasmus used against Luther's use of Scripture was that the Bible is an unclear book. Erasmus said that one must defer to "the church"—the popes and church councils—for clear teaching. Contemporary Catholic apologists continue to deny the clarity of Scripture. They teach that people need "the church" to teach the "real" meaning of Scripture.

Lutherans also confidently hold to *sola Scriptura* because the Bible is without error. Formal terms referring to this are *inerrant* and *infallible.* Because Scripture is the verbally inspired Word of God and because God cannot lie (Numbers 23:19; Titus 1:2; Hebrews 6:18), every word of Scripture is true. This was the view of Jesus toward the Old Testament Scriptures (John 17:17). It includes not only the general message of Scripture but every word of it (John 10:35). It includes not only matters pertaining directly to the teachings of the gospel and salvation but also to matters of history, geography, science, etc. Jesus accepted as literally true the Bible's account of creation (Matthew 19:4-6), Noah and the flood (Matthew 24:37-39), and Jonah (Matthew 12:39,40). Lutherans refer to this truth as the plenary (full) inerrancy of Scripture, as opposed to just a partial inerrancy limited only to matters of "the gospel" or salvation.

Confessional Lutherans reject what are called the higher-critical methods of Bible interpretation, which assume that the Bible is only the word of fallible human beings and not the inerrant, infallible Word of a perfect God. Lutherans reject the theories which hold that many of the accounts presented in Scripture as historical events are only myths, fables, legends, sagas—"stories" of things that never actually happened.

How the Catholic view of Scripture has changed

Concerning the sufficiency and clarity of Scripture, Lutherans and Catholics have always been divided. That was not always the case, however, regarding the divine, verbal inspiration and inerrancy of Scripture. Historically, the Catholic Church affirmed the inspiration and inerrancy of all of Scripture. There were many theological differences between Lutherans and Catholics at the time of the Reformation in the 16th century, but both sides agreed that the Bible is unequivocally the Word of God and without error. When many proponents of modern science and Enlightenment philosophy started attacking the miracles and divine nature of Scripture in the 1700s and 1800s, the popes rejected such attacks. Popes such as Pius IX (reigned 1846–1878), Leo XIII (reigned 1878–1903), and Pius X (reigned 1903–1914) all issued encyclicals and other official decrees that clearly rejected Modernism (including evolutionism), as it was called, and its attacks on the truth of the Bible.

However, the crackdown on Modernism in the Catholic Church, especially by Pope Pius X, did not drive Modernism out of the Catholic Church as much as drive it underground. There it stayed pretty much until after the two world wars. The most obvious evidence of its resurgence came around the time of the Second Vatican Council (1962–1965). The more liberal-minded theologians who had been regarded with suspicion by the Roman curia and some who had been officially censured during the reign of Pius XII (reigned 1939–1958) for suspected Modernist tendencies were exonerated by Pope John XXIII (1958–1963) and even appointed to be official "theological experts" at the Second Vatican Council.

That a seismic shift in attitude toward scriptural inerrancy was taking place in the Catholic Church became evident in the early sessions of the council. Some of the more theologically conservative members of the Roman curia had drafted a document on Scripture for the council to consider. It contained indisputable language affirming the full inerrancy of Scripture and rejected various Modernist theories of the past. The council fathers rejected this document by a large majority. A committee of bishops was appointed to come up with something entirely different. The final result was the Vatican II document, "Dogmatic Constitution on Divine Revelation."

The new document was clearly a compromise. Much of what it says about the nature of Scripture sounds like historic Catholic teaching. But a key sentence contains ambiguous language:

> Since, therefore, all that the inspired authors, or sacred writers, affirm should be regarded as affirmed by the Holy Spirit, we must acknowledge that the books of Scripture, firmly, faithfully and without error, teach that truth which God, for the sake of our salvation, wished to see confided to the Sacred Scriptures.[31]

The question raised in this statement is whether everything written in Scripture is "without error" or only those things contained in Scripture "for the sake of our salvation." In other words, is Scripture completely inerrant or only partially inerrant?

Some scholarly studies have made a strong case that full inerrancy was still being advocated in the Vatican II dogmatic constitution.[32] On the other hand, the history of Scripture interpretation in the Catholic Church since Vatican II suggests otherwise.

In the Catholic Church today, very few bishops and theologians, even among the more theologically conservative ones, hold to the full inerrancy of Scripture. Higher-critical methods of Bible interpretation that were once condemned are now openly practiced by nearly all Catholic theologians. Anti-scriptural doctrines such as evolution (including the denial of Adam and Eve as historical persons and as the first parents of the human race) were condemned in the past but now are being taught openly. The denial of biblical miracles as historical facts was also condemned in the past, but no longer. It took liberal Protestant theologians almost two hundred years to tear down the divine authorship and authority of Scripture in many Protestant denominations and seminaries. Catholic theologians, on the other hand, managed to do the same in their church body in only a couple decades.

One prominent example of just how thoroughly modern Catholic biblical studies have adopted the higher-critical approach to Scripture interpretation is *The New Jerome Biblical Commentary*. The editors of this commentary include Raymond Brown and Joseph Fitzmeyer, who are regarded as two of the foremost and most highly respected Catholic Scripture scholars in the second half of the 20th century. Here are samples of statements or summaries of comments from this Bible commentary:

- Moses did not write the Pentateuch (the first five books of the Bible) (pp. 4,61).
- The book of Joshua "is a kind of historical or theological fiction" (p. 112).

- "Fundamentalists naively and uncritically equate the Christ of the Gospels with the historical Jesus" (p. 1318).
- "Surety about [Mary's] virginal conception [of Jesus] comes from church teaching rather than from scientific exegesis [interpretation of the Bible]" (p. 1319).
- God did not create the world out of nothing (p. 1293).
- The earth is 4.5 billion years old. Adam and Eve never existed (p. 1220).[33]

Such higher-critical views of Scripture are taught not only by Catholic theologians in their personal writings; these views have also been embraced and advocated by some at the highest official levels of the Vatican. As an example, in 1979 through 1980 in his weekly Wednesday papal audiences, Pope John Paul II delivered a series of lectures on the first three chapters of Genesis. The lectures were replete with the higher-critical theories, which deny that Moses is the inspired author of Genesis (contradicting Jesus—Matthew 19:4-8). Rather, Genesis was supposedly cut and pasted together over several centuries by several authors and editors from several different documents (labeled with the initials J-E-D-P) that contradict one another.[34]

In 1993 the Pontifical Biblical Commission of the Vatican issued an official document entitled "The Interpretation of the Bible in the Church." This document contains an opening address by Pope John Paul II, in which he frankly admitted to the "radical change in perspective" of the Catholic Church between the late 1800s and the 1940s, from what he called the *nonscientific* approach to the Scriptures in the past to the modern *scientific* approach of today. The document leaves no doubt as to what the scientific approach entails:

> The historical-critical method is the indispensable method for the scientific study of the meaning of ancient texts. Holy Scripture, inasmuch as it is the "word of God in human language," has been composed by human authors in all its various parts and in all the sources that lie behind

them. Because of this, its proper understanding not only admits the use of this method but actually requires it.[35]

The document warns against using the various critical methods of interpretation in ways that could lead to denying dogmas of the Catholic Church. The only method of Bible interpretation that is categorically condemned is what the document calls the fundamentalist approach, which "had its origin at the time of the Reformation, arising out of a concern for the fidelity to the literal meaning of Scripture." The document labels this approach as naïve, "dangerous," and one that "invites people to a kind of intellectual suicide." Fundamentalism, it says, fails to recognize that the Bible was written by "human authors possessed of limited capacities and resources." It "places undue stress upon the inerrancy of certain details in the biblical texts, especially in what concerns historical events or supposed scientific truth" and "does not take into account the development of the gospel tradition, but naïvely confuses the final stage of this tradition (what the evangelists have written) with the initial stage (the words and deeds of the historical Jesus)." Fundamentalism also "accepts the literal reality of an ancient out-of-date cosmology simply because it is found expressed in the Bible."[36]

Lutheran seminary professor John Brug offers his analysis of these statements of the Vatican document:

> These and other similar statements make it clear that it is not merely the excesses of "fundamentalism" which are being rejected here. It is the traditional view of verbal inspiration once held also by Rome. Also being discarded are the Gospels' version of the words and deeds of Christ, the historicity of the events recorded in the Scriptures, and the biblical doctrine of creation. Roman theology has swallowed the historical-critical approach "hook, line, and sinker."[37]

How does such teaching affect the average Catholic in the pew? This question must be considered in the context of how much exposure the Catholic person has to the Bible and Bible study material in his or her parish. Catholics are more exposed to Scripture than they were in the past. Over a three-year period Catholics who attend church regularly hear a large portion of Scripture read in the Sunday services. And that's a good thing. Readable modern translations of the Bible, based on the original Greek and Hebrew languages of the Bible, are readily available today, which is also a good thing. Prior to Vatican II, many Catholics viewed Bible reading primarily as a Protestant form of piety and tended to avoid it. But today, Bible reading seems to be somewhat more encouraged among Catholics than in the past. And Catholics in more literate countries, such as the United States, probably read the Bible somewhat more than they did in the past. Again, this is good.

Various Catholic sources indicate that perhaps one-third of Catholic parishes in the United States offer some form of formal Bible classes for members. Some parishes offer laity-led "small group" meetings for members in their homes, where they use materials prepared by the parish. The materials often incorporate a Bible reading, time for personal reflection in which a rather subjective approach ("What does this passage mean to me?") is used, and prayer. But a real danger lies in the interpretive notes included in Catholic editions of the Bible that are based on higher-critical theories about the Bible. Catholics no longer view the Bible as completely without error, as they once did. Widespread acceptance of the historical-critical views of the Bible among Catholics can only undermine their trust in God's Word, making their reliance on "the church" (the pope and the bishops) as necessary as ever.

Overall, it seems that Catholics in general know their Bibles less than Protestants. Here is the opinion/observation of one Catholic author: "Relatively few Catholics read and study the Bible regularly. Relatively few know what 'our book' teaches as well as many other Christians do."[38]

Probably the most obvious way that confessional Lutherans and Roman Catholics show their differing attitudes toward religious authority is how they introduce their teachings. Lutherans are trained to ask, "What does the Bible say? Where does Scripture teach that?" and to expect the response, "This is what God says in the Bible." Catholics are much more likely to ask, "What does the church say about this?" and to hear the response, "The church teaches . . ." By those simple formulas, Lutherans and Catholics reveal much about what they consider the highest religious authority in their lives.

Evolving Catholic views of Sacred Tradition

Earlier in this book we examined the role of Sacred Tradition in the Catholic Church. Has there been any change in recent years in this area?

As said previously, Catholics believe that God's revelation (his Word) does not come to us only in the written Scriptures but also in unwritten Tradition (capital *T*) through the succession of bishops. This Tradition includes all Catholic doctrines that are not explicitly taught in the Bible. The traditions (small *t*) include church regulations, such as laws about fasting and abstinence, which language to use in the liturgy, and certain other outward forms of the liturgy. Even priestly celibacy is considered a tradition—not a doctrine—of the Western rite of the Catholic Church. Catholics hold that traditions (small *t*) can change, while Tradition does not change.

Increasingly, however, many in the Catholic Church are coming to believe that Sacred Tradition (capital *S* and *T*) can indeed change. Let's trace this shift as it has occurred since the Council of Trent.

Catholic theologians at the time of the Council of Trent in the 16th century operated with a kind of definition of *Tradition* as the "unanimous consent of the Fathers." It was assumed and maintained that Christ taught the fullness of Christian Tradition (God's Word) to his apostles. The apostles committed some of that teaching to writing in the New Testament and some of it they passed on to the next generation of bishops in an unwritten manner by word of mouth. Second generation bishops, in turn, passed it on to the next generation of bishops, and so on, in an unbroken succession up to the time of the Council of Trent in the mid 1500s. It was assumed that whatever was Catholic doctrine at that point in time had been taught by Christ to the apostles and passed down unchanged by all the bishops and church fathers (teachers) of the early church. This was Trent's way of countering Reformation teaching, trying to make the Reformers' teachings appear as something new and different that broke with the past, while Rome's teachings enjoyed the unbroken and unanimous consent of all orthodox teachers since the days of the apostles. Roughly three centuries later, the First Vatican Council reaffirmed the "unanimous consent of the Fathers" view.

This view of Tradition has been all but abandoned by present-day Roman Catholicism. Why? Honest historical research has shown that there is no such thing as the "unanimous consent of the Fathers." Most Catholic theologians today honestly admit that current Catholic teachings on Mary and the papacy were simply not taught in the early church. They admit that it took centuries for such doctrines and others to develop into what they had become by the time of the Reformation.

This lack of consensus with the ancient past led Rome to embrace a new theory of Tradition to explain its distinctive teachings. John Henry Newman proposed one theory in the 1800s. The theory is known as the "development of doctrine." To try to explain the difference between the New Testament and early Christian church with the Roman Catholic Church of his day, Newman compared an acorn with an oak tree. An acorn and an oak tree appear to be two different things, but what will grow into an oak tree is already present in the germ of an acorn. The acorn simply cannot grow into anything else but an oak tree. Likewise the church and the Word of God is supposedly a single living entity that grows and develops, led and guided by the Holy Spirit. According to Newman, the church of the apostles could grow and develop throughout the New Testament only in one way, namely, into the Roman

Catholic Church of today. Or to put it another way, all Catholic doctrines are implicitly taught in the New Testament Scriptures, but not all are stated explicitly in their present form; these doctrines have needed time to develop.

Superficially, Newman's theory of doctrinal development might sound appealing to human reason. Lutherans and other Protestants, however, have pointed out that the New Testament knows nothing of any such supposed development of "implied" teachings; and on the basis of Scripture, they maintain that the entire revealed will of God is clearly found in the inspired written Word of God in the Old and New Testaments. They certainly concede that doctrinal terminology—words such as *Trinity,* for example—has been coined and has developed in meaning over time and that the outward forms of creeds have developed in how they present Scripture's teachings. But they maintain that the truths, which such coined words stand for and which early creeds summarize, are contained in their entirety and clearly stated in the Scriptures.

Newman's theory of doctrinal development posed difficulties for Catholic theology. It simply did not square with the "unanimous consent of the Fathers" theory, which had been enshrined in the supposedly infallible decrees of the councils of Trent and Vatican I. In the 20th century, Rome refined the theory of development and promoted a new concept of Tradition. Like Newman's original theory of doctrinal development, the current theory does not square with the "unanimous consent" teaching of Trent and Vatican I. But in our day, Rome no longer feels any need to show that a particular doctrine was taught by the early church and has dropped any pretense of validating its teachings on the basis of unwritten teachings given by Christ and passed down historically through the succession of bishops.

Catholic historians today readily admit, for instance, that the dogmas of the assumption of Mary and papal infallibility were unknown in the early church. All seven of the Catholic sacraments were not necessarily directly instituted by Christ during his earthly ministry. But it makes no difference! The Catholic Church, led by the pope and the bishops in communion with him, is an infallible authority in itself. Whatever the Church teaches, even without biblical or historical precedence, is infallibly true. Consider how Catholic apologist Karl Keating defends the Catholic doctrine of Mary's bodily assumption into heaven, solemnly defined as a dogma by Pope Pius XII in 1950:

> Still, fundamentalists ask, where is the proof from Scripture? Strictly, there is none. It was the Catholic Church that was commissioned by Christ to teach all nations and to teach them infallibly. The mere fact that the Church teaches the doctrine of the Assumption as definitely true is a guarantee that it is true.[39]

The 20th century saw the Catholic concept of Tradition evolve in still another way. A French Catholic philosopher named Maurice Blondel proposed what is described as a more "personalistic" view of Tradition. Describing Blondel's theory of Tradition, Catholic theologian Avery Dulles explains that Blondel felt that previous theories of Tradition had identified

> knowledge too closely with conceptual thought and formal declaration. Since the content of Christian faith is mystery, it is never fully reducible to explicit statement, it always remains to some degree unspecifiable. Hence Christianity cannot be transmitted wholly or even primarily by explicit teaching and systematic argument. Tradition, according to Blondel, is able to transmit the lived reality of the past.
>
> Tradition, then, is the bearer of what is tacitly known and thus of what cannot be expressed in clear, unambiguous statements. . . . More important than the question how God's words have been remembered is the question how Jesus has left us the means of legitimately supplementing

> what he did not say. Tradition, for Blondel, is the church's continuing capacity to interpret, to discern, to penetrate. Far from being a confining or retrograde force, it is a power of development and expansion.[40]

In other words, instead of static, fixed formulas of dogmatic definitions or implicit teachings that gradually developed into more explicit teachings, Blondel emphasized a more experiential aspect of Catholic Tradition, experienced within the Catholic community, a concept called tacit knowledge. It isn't so much intellectual knowledge as experiential know-how, like learning to ride a bicycle. You don't learn how to ride a bicycle by reading an academic treatise on how to ride a bicycle. You learn, rather, by having someone who already knows how show you and help you. You keep trying and practicing to ride a bicycle, gradually feeling more comfortable and confident at doing it, until it becomes second nature. So also with Catholic Tradition: it is not so much a list of infallibly defined dogmas as it is a way of life that is experienced. Like Newman's theory of development, this theory has a certain reasonable ring and nonthreatening appeal to it. But it is still foreign to the way God's prophets in the Old Testament and Christ and the apostles in the New Testament addressed the subject of authority in the church.

We have spent some time looking at these various evolving theories of Sacred Tradition in the Catholic Church because aspects of both Newman's and Blondel's theories are reflected in the documents of the Second Vatican Council. This is what Vatican II explicitly teaches about doctrinal development:

> The Tradition that comes from the apostles makes progress in the Church, with the help of the Holy Spirit. There is a growth in insight into the realities and words that are being passed on. This comes about in various ways. It comes through the contemplation and study of believers who ponder these things in their hearts (cf. Lk. 2:19 and 51). It comes from the intimate sense of spiritual

> realities which they experience. And it comes from the preaching of those who have received, along with their right of succession in the episcopate, the sure cherish of truth. Thus as the centuries go by, the Church is always advancing towards the plenitude of divine truth, until eventually the words of God are fulfilled in her.[41]

For many of the bishops at the council and other Catholics who had been used to hearing and thinking only in terms of the more static and traditional terms of the "unanimous consent of the Fathers," "eternal Rome," and "Rome always the same," the ideas expressed in the above quotation seemed revolutionary at the time they were written.

Other aspects of Sacred Tradition in the Catholic Church definitely have not changed. A few paragraphs later in the same document, the council made it clear in no uncertain terms where the ultimate religious authority and power still reside in the Catholic Church:

> But the task of giving an authentic interpretation of the Word of God, whether in its written form or in the form of Tradition, has been entrusted to the living teaching office of the Church *alone*. Its authority in this matter is exercised in the name of Jesus Christ.
>
> It is clear, therefore, that, in the supremely wise arrangement of God, sacred Tradition, sacred Scripture and the Magisterium of the Church are so connected and associated that one of them cannot stand without the others. Working together, each in its own way under the action of the one Holy Spirit, they all contribute effectively to the salvation of souls. (Italic added.)[42]

Vatican II, even as it adopted and adapted some of the more recent theories of Sacred Tradition, nevertheless made it abundantly clear where authority resides in the Catholic Church. It resides in what it calls the "living teaching office" (Latin: *magisterium*). The *magisterium* refers to the pope and the bishops in communion with the pope. The pope and the bishops *alone* possess the Scriptures and the right to interpret them. The pope and the bishops with him still claim to be the final arbiters of truth in the Catholic religion.

So, has the understanding of Tradition in the Catholic Church changed? In certain respects, yes, but not in the essential, infallible right of the Catholic Church to establish such teachings as if they were from God.

The difference between Catholic and Protestant Bibles

When non-Catholic Christians try to engage Catholic acquaintances on some religious topic, Catholics sometimes will try to deflect the conversation by saying, "Well, we Catholics have a different Bible from you Protestants." Are they right?

What they are referring to are books included in the Catholic Bible called the Apocrypha, or what Catholics call *deuterocanonical* books. There are 11 books or portions of books included in Catholic Bibles as part of the Old Testament. Their names are:

Judith
Tobit
Additions to the book of Esther
Ecclesiasticus, or the Wisdom of Jesus, the Son of Sirach
Wisdom of Solomon
Baruch
Prayer of Azarish and the Song of the Three Young Men
Susanna
Bel and the Dragon
First Maccabees
Second Maccabees

For brief descriptions of the contents of the books, see Lyle Lange's *God So Loved the World*, listed in the section "For Further Reading" at the end of this chapter. Professor Lange briefly explains what is known about the origins of the apocryphal books:

> After the time of Malachi (400 B.C.), a number of books were written that neither Jesus nor his apostles accepted

as part of the canon of the Old Testament. These books were included in copies of the Septuagint, a Greek translation of the Old Testament begun about 270 B.C. The early Greek-speaking Christians took over the Septuagint from the Jews of Alexandria. Some of the church fathers of the East quoted from the Apocrypha as did some from the West.[43]

The apocryphal books were never a part of the Hebrew Old Testament Scriptures. The Bible of Jesus' day contained exactly the same Old Testament books as are found in Protestant Bibles. The only difference is that the Hebrew Scriptures arranged some of the books differently than today's English Bibles do. In the Bible of Jesus' day, there were three groups: the *Law of Moses* (the first five books, as in modern Bibles), the *Prophets* (which included several of the historical books and most of the major prophets), and the *Writings* (the poetical books, starting with Psalms, the minor prophets, Daniel, and some of the historical books). When Jesus referred to the Old Testament Scriptures as "the Law of Moses, the Prophets and the Psalms" (Luke 24:44), he was referring to the whole Old Testament according to these three groups. The apocryphal books were not among them.

So how did these other books originate? We don't know exactly, but Jewish contemporaries of Jesus, such as the historian Josephus and the philosopher Philo, show from their writings that they were aware of the Apocrypha as books that had already been written in their day but were not regarded as inspired Scripture by the people living in Palestine. And they were not considered as Scripture by the Jews living in Alexandria, Egypt, where these books were translated into Greek. (Some were perhaps originally written in Greek.)

The apostles quote from the Greek Septuagint Bible in their New Testament writings but never from the Apocrypha. Many early Christian teachers and church fathers clearly regarded the Apocrypha as worth reading but not as inspired

Scripture. That includes Scripture scholars such as Origen and Jerome, both of whom knew both Greek and Hebrew, and the church father Athanasius. When Jerome translated the Hebrew Scriptures into Latin, he included the Apocrypha, but he made it clear that these books were not part of the inspired Old Testament. Some church fathers such as Augustine, who did not know Hebrew, assumed that the apocryphal books were part of the inspired Scriptures. This difference of opinion among church teachers and bishops, including popes, existed down to the 16th century. In fact, right up until the Council of Trent, there were Catholic theologians who did not hold the Apocrypha to be inspired. When Luther and his coworkers translated the Bible into German, they included the Apocrypha in a section between the Old and New Testaments with a note indicating the longstanding tradition that these books were worth reading but were not inspired Scripture.

Luther and other 16th-century church reformers, along with Lutheran and Protestant scholars since then, rejected the Apocrypha for several biblical and historical reasons. Here is a partial list of reasons as compiled by William Webster in his book *The Old Testament Canon and the Apocrypha*:[44]

- The Jews who were entrusted with the inspired Scriptures did not accept the Apocrypha as part of the canon of Scripture.
- Jesus, in particular, did not quote from the apocryphal books. He stated that the canonical Scriptures were comprised of the threefold division of the Law of Moses, the Prophets, and the Psalms.
- Many of the early church fathers followed the Jewish canon, which refused to give canonical status to the Apocrypha.
- The majority view of the leading theologians from the 5th century up to the time of the Reformation followed Jerome in denying full canonical status to the Apocrypha.

- Gregory the Great, as the papal bishop of Rome (A.D. 600), taught that the Apocrypha was not canonical. The official biblical commentary of the Middle Ages used for the training of all theologians taught that the Apocrypha, while useful for reading and edification, was not considered canonical and had no authority for establishing points of doctrine.
- It was not until the Council of Trent in the 16th century that the canon was officially and authoritatively established for the Roman Catholic Church. Included in that canon were the apocryphal books.
- The internal discrepancies that abound in certain books of the Apocrypha disqualify it as truly inspired and canonical.

The last point refers to various historical and theological teachings recorded in the Apocrypha that contradict the rest of inspired Scripture. For example, 2 Maccabees 12:42-45 speaks approvingly of praying for the dead and about the possibility of offering sacrifices for the dead in order to help them receive a more favorable judgment from God on the Last Day. Also, passages such as Sirach 29:11-13; Tobit 4:7-9; and Wisdom of Solomon 6:18 teach that salvation can be earned by doing the good work of giving alms. These teachings contradict the way of salvation that is taught in the inspired, canonical Scriptures.

In spite of the false teachings found in the apocryphal books, Catholics who assume that all the doctrinal differences between Lutherans and Catholics can be explained by the acceptance versus nonacceptance of the Apocrypha are simply misinformed. The main differences stem from the fact that Lutherans accept Scripture alone as the inspired Word of God and as the source and basis of all Christian doctrine and Catholics do not. The latter rely on Scripture *and* Sacred Tradition as interpreted by the papal magisterium as the source and basis of their teachings.

When discussing these matters with Catholics, depending on the situation and if they are open to it, Lutherans might suggest that together they read and discuss the Scriptures they do hold in common. Books such as John's gospel or Paul's letter to the Romans are good choices. Both books focus so beautifully on the saving love of God and his plan of salvation for sinners through his Son, Jesus Christ.

For Further Reading

Martin Chemnitz, *Examination of the Council of Trent,* Vol. 1 (St. Louis: Concordia Publishing House, 1971), pp. 35-313.

Lyle W. Lange, *God So Loved the World: A Study of Christian Doctrine* (Milwaukee: Northwestern Publishing House, 2005), pp. 35-96.

Raymond F. Surburg, "The Radical and Revolutionary Changes Occurring in Roman Catholic Biblical Studies Between 1893 and 1993," *Christian News,* March 14, 1994, pp. 12-14.

David J. Valleskey, "The Holy Scriptures—The Source and Norm of All Doctrine," *Wisconsin Lutheran Quarterly,* Vol. 90, No. 2 (Spring 1993), pp. 97-117.

William Webster, *The Old Testament Canon and the Apocrypha* (Battle Ground, WA: Christian Resources, Inc., 2002).

5 JUSTIFICATION

We now turn to the second key doctrinal topic over which Lutherans and Catholics have been divided ever since the 16th century: the doctrine of justification. How can sinners hope to stand before a just and holy God? How do we sinners receive God's forgiveness of sins? On what do sinners base their hope of eternal salvation? Lutherans believe that the Scriptures give clear, consistent answers to these questions.

Lutheran teaching of justification

It is not by our own efforts and works that we are saved, not even by our inner spiritual renewal (sanctification). Rather, we receive God's forgiveness—his declaration that "we are righteous in his sight," which is what justified means—only because of the suffering, death, and resurrection of Jesus Christ. Jesus is the Lamb of God who has taken away the sins of the world (John 1:29). Sinners are justified by his shed blood (Romans 5:9), and his resurrection guarantees it (Romans 4:25). Only through believing in Jesus, who was righteous for us as our substitute, are we sinners able to stand before a just and holy God.

Lutherans draw their teaching directly from many clear passages of Scripture. In his letter to the Romans, the apostle Paul wrote:

> All have sinned and fall short of the glory of God, and are justified freely by his grace through the redemption that came by Christ Jesus. God presented him as a sacrifice of atonement, through faith in his blood. . . . He did it to demonstrate his justice at the present time, so as to be just and the one who justifies those who have faith in

> Jesus. . . . For we maintain that a man is justified by faith apart from observing the law. (3:23-28)

In Bible times, the word *justify* was a legal, courtroom term (a "forensic" term). It described the action of a judge when he declared a defendant not guilty. Justification involved a person's legal status in a court of law, based on the judge's declaration of acquittal. Yet there is a difference between human courts and God's court. Unlike human courts and systems of justice, where a defendant's legal status is rightly determined only by his own guilt or innocence, the status of sinners before God, the heavenly judge, is determined on the basis of the righteousness of another, namely, God's Son, Jesus Christ. Jesus served as every sinner's substitute before God (see Isaiah 53:4-6). His suffering and death satisfied the demands of God's holy law—that every sin be punished (Galatians 3:10; Ezekiel 18:20). His holy, perfect life fulfilled the righteous requirements of God's law for every sinner. Paul states that sinners now personally receive God's verdict of righteousness (not guilty, forgiveness for all sins) not by *doing* anything but only through *believing,* that is, trusting that God's promise of forgiveness achieved by Christ for all people is true.

Paul presents the same message in his letter to the Galatians:

> We who are Jews by birth and not "Gentile sinners" know that a man is not justified by observing the law, but by faith in Jesus Christ. So we, too, have put our faith in Christ Jesus that we may be justified by faith in Christ and not by observing the law, because by observing the law no one will be justified. (2:15,16)

And in his letter to the Ephesians, Paul teaches the same way of salvation: "It is by grace you have been saved, through faith—and this not from yourselves, it is the gift of God—not by works, so that no one can boast" (2:8,9).

Whenever Scripture speaks of justification and salvation by God's grace, it is referring to the undeserved love that God has for sinners for Christ's sake. It is closely related to the concept of God's mercy. In this context, grace (or mercy) is not a divine quality that God puts into people (what Catholics call *infused grace*), which helps them do good works. Grace is God's act of saving sinners and bringing them to faith in the One who won forgiveness for us. Paul draws a clear distinction between God's gracious forgiveness in Christ and the Christian's subsequent life of doing good works (sanctification): "If [we were chosen] by grace, then it is no longer by works; if it were, grace would no longer be grace" (Romans 11:6). Here Paul clearly tells us that the way of salvation that comes by grace, on the one hand, and any proposed way of salvation that involves human works, cooperative efforts, or contributions of any kind, on the other, are mutually exclusive.

The teaching that forgiveness of sins and eternal salvation come only through believing in Christ is not limited to the writings of the apostle Paul. Jesus himself taught it clearly in the gospel:

> Just as Moses lifted up the snake in the desert, so the Son of Man must be lifted up, that everyone who believes in him may have eternal life. For God so loved the world that he gave his one and only Son, that whoever believes in him shall not perish but have eternal life. For God did not send his Son into the world to condemn the world, but to save the world through him. Whoever believes in him is not condemned, but whoever does not believe stands condemned already because he has not believed in the name of God's one and only Son. (John 3:14-18)

This is also the teaching of the Old Testament, as Paul shows in Romans chapter 4. He cites the examples of Abraham and David, quoting from Genesis 15:6 and Psalm 32:1,2:

> What does the Scripture say? "Abraham believed God, and it was credited to him as righteousness." Now when a man works, his wages are not credited to him as a gift, but as an obligation. However, to the man who does not work but trusts God who justifies the wicked, his faith is credited as righteousness. (Romans 4:3-5)

Notice how Paul uses the words *justify* and *credits* (also forensic, declaratory terms) interchangeably. Note also how the word *faith* is used in the sense of trusting in an unconditional promise.

Paul follows this up by showing that David in Psalm 32 also taught that sinners are justified (declared righteous, forgiven) by faith without first doing good works of any kind to merit it:

> David says the same thing when he speaks of the blessedness of the man to whom God credits righteousness apart from works: "Blessed are they whose transgressions are forgiven, whose sins are covered. Blessed is the man whose sin the Lord will never count against him." (Romans 4:6-8)

Notice especially how Paul regards *justification by faith* as synonymous with *receiving the forgiveness of sins* from God.

We can briefly summarize the Lutheran teaching of justification as follows:

- Justification is forensic (God's declaration of forgiveness).
- It is complete, since Christ earned God's forgiveness on the cross for every sin of every sinner.
- It involves a change in the sinner's *status* before God (from being condemned to being forgiven) and not a change in the sinner's *nature*.
- It is a gift that God promises, offers, and gives freely and unconditionally through the preaching of the gospel and administration of the sacraments and is received through faith alone.

The basic confessional statement of the Lutheran teaching on justification is found in Article IV of the Augsburg Confession, which reads:

> Our churches teach that people cannot be justified before God by their own strength, merits, or works. People are freely justified for Christ's sake, through faith, when they believe that they are received into favor and that their sins are forgiven for Christ's sake. By His death, Christ

made satisfaction for our sins. God counts this faith for righteousness in His sight (Romans 33:21-26; 4:5).[45]

Catholic teaching of justification

The Roman Catholic Church has always rejected the Lutheran teaching on justification and adamantly holds that sinners are justified by faith *and* by doing good works. While the Scriptures speak over and over of salvation as God's work alone for sinners, the Catholic Church views salvation as a lifelong *cooperative process* between God and the sinner, by which the sinner gradually becomes more and more inwardly righteous by doing good works. Grace is redefined as God's helping power ("infused grace") that is poured into the human soul, which helps a person do good works so that he or she gradually becomes more and more holy.

The Catholic Church at the Council of Trent solemnly cursed all Lutherans for their teaching that justification consists of God's declaration of forgiveness of sins received by God's grace alone through faith alone in Christ alone and not through any human merits or good works. Since the canons and decrees of Trent still stand as official Catholic dogma against Lutherans, we will quote a few of them (italic has been added for emphasis):

> Justification . . . is not only a remission of sins but also the sanctification and renewal of the inward man through the voluntary reception of the grace and gifts whereby an unjust man becomes just. (Chapter VII)

> If anyone says that the sinner is justified by faith alone, meaning that nothing else is required to *cooperate* in order to obtain the grace of justification, and that it is not in any way necessary that he be prepared and disposed *by the action of his own will*, let him be anathema. (Canon 9)

> If anyone says that men are justified either by the sole imputation of the justice of Christ or by the sole remission of sins, to the exclusion of the grace and the

> charity which is poured forth in their hearts by the Holy Ghost, and remains in them, or also that the grace by which we are justified is only the good will of God, let him be anathema. (Canon 11)
>
> If anyone says that justifying faith is nothing else than confidence in divine mercy, which remits sin for Christ's sake, or that it is this confidence alone that justifies us, let him be anathema. (Canon 12)
>
> If anyone says that after the reception of the grace of justification the guilt is so remitted and the debt of eternal punishment so blotted out to every repentant sinner, that no debt of temporal punishment remains to be discharged either in this world or in purgatory before the gates of heaven can be opened, let him be anathema. (Canon 30)[46]

At the Council of Trent, the Roman church not only cursed and condemned the Lutheran *doctrine* of justification, which is drawn directly from Holy Scripture, it also cursed *every Lutheran* person (and other Christian, for that matter) who believes in justification as Scripture teaches it.

The Catholic Church has never rescinded these canons of the Council of Trent that curse and damn Lutherans. What is more, Vatican II, in spite of its nice-sounding ecumenical appeals to Protestants as "separated brethren," did not rescind Trent's anathemas. The *Catechism of the Catholic Church* reiterates the Catholic doctrine of justification by faith *and* works:

> Justification is not only the remission of sins, but also the sanctification and renewal of the interior man. (n. 1989)
>
> Justification establishes *cooperation between God's grace and man's freedom*. On man's part it is expressed by the assent of faith to the Word of God. (n. 1993, emphasis original)
>
> Moved by the Spirit, we can merit for ourselves and for others all the graces needed to attain eternal life. (n. 2027)

Justification and the certainty of salvation as taught by Lutherans

The differing teachings of Lutherans and Catholics over justification result in differing views on whether or not a Christian can be certain of his or her eternal salvation. Can I know for certain that when I die I will go to heaven because of what Christ did to save me and what God promises in his Word? Or must I always remain in doubt because I can never be sure that I have done enough good works?

The Lutheran church teaches that believers can indeed be certain of their salvation because Scripture teaches it. God-given certainty of salvation goes hand in hand with faith in Christ. Christ did everything to accomplish salvation for every sinner. His saving work is finished and complete and gives us God's full and free forgiveness of all our sins. It is promised in the gospel message—it's a free gift without any condition sinners need to fulfill before it becomes theirs. And it is received by God-given faith, created and sustained by the power of the Holy Spirit working through this gospel message. As the apostle Paul states: "I am not ashamed of the gospel, because it is the power of God for the salvation of everyone who believes" (Romans 1:16).

Paul expressed this Christian hope and certainty of salvation like this:

> I am not ashamed, because I know whom I have believed, and am convinced that he is able to guard what I have entrusted to him for that day.
>
> Now there is in store for me the crown of righteousness, which the Lord, the righteous Judge, will award to me on that day—and not only to me, but also to all who have longed for his appearing. (2 Timothy 1:12; 4:8)

Every believer in Christ shares this God-given faith and certainty. Every believer can be certain of salvation, not because their faith is always strong but because of the nature of the gospel: "Therefore, the promise comes by faith, so that it may be by grace and may be guaranteed to all Abraham's offspring—not only to those who are of the law but also to those who are of the faith of Abraham" (Romans 4:16).

The certain hope of salvation is also taught in the gospels. Jesus promised, "Whoever believes in the Son *has* eternal life" (John 3:36) and "I tell you the truth, whoever hears my word and believes him who sent me *has* eternal life and will not be condemned; he has crossed over from death to life" (John 5:24).

When Lutherans speak of being sure of their salvation, they base their hope of going to heaven on God's promises in Christ, not on their own good works, their feelings, not even on how strong their faith may be at a particular time. God's Word and promises are always true and sure; that alone makes our Christian hope certain.

Scripture's teaching about the certainty of salvation does not mean, however, that believers cannot possibly fall away and lose their faith. Jesus warns us against falling away in his parable of the sower. The seed of God's Word sometimes takes root in the hearts of people as it brings them to faith, but then that faith is choked out of their hearts by the cares and concerns of this life. (See also 1 Timothy 6:6-10.) The apostle Paul warned the Galatian Christians that if they came to trust in their own good works and efforts at keeping God's law as the hope of their salvation instead of trusting in Christ alone, they would in fact become alienated from Christ and fall away from grace (Galatians 5:4).

So here we have two teachings of Scripture: God's promise that "he who began a good work in you will carry it on to completion until the day of Christ Jesus" (Philippians 1:6) and Scripture's warning to be careful so that you don't fall from faith (1 Corinthians 10:12). To human reason these two truths seem to contradict each other, but Lutherans allow both truths to stand (without trying to reconcile them according to human logic) because Scripture teaches both.

Justification and the certainty of salvation as taught by Catholics

The Catholic Church emphatically denies that a believer in Christ can be sure of his or her eternal salvation. In fact, all who believe and teach the Lutheran, scriptural doctrine were condemned and cursed by the Council of Trent: "If anyone says that he will for certain, with an absolute and infallible certainty, have that great gift of perseverance even to the end, unless he shall have learned this by a special revelation, let him be anathema."[47]

The Catholic denial of the certainty of salvation logically follows from its teaching that sinners are saved by faith *and also* by doing good works. Since people can never be sure they have done enough good works to merit eternal life, they can never know for sure if they are going to heaven when they die. They always have to remain in doubt, because their salvation depends not only on God's grace and Christ's saving work but also on their own works and efforts. The Lutheran church's scriptural teaching of salvation by God's grace alone through faith alone in Christ alone is the only teaching that provides true comfort to sinners who struggle with personal doubts and with feelings of guilt over their sins. To troubled souls, the Catholic teaching can only say, "Stay in the Catholic Church. God promises grace to help, but you have to keep trying hard to be as good as you can. So you can never know for sure in this life if you will enter heaven when you die."

That is not to say there aren't individual Catholics who trust in Christ's death and resurrection alone for their salvation. But if they do, it is in spite of their church's false teaching, not because of it.

Catholic basis of justification

Lutherans may wonder how the Catholic Church can teach that salvation comes both by faith and by doing good works when the Scriptures teach so clearly that our salvation is entirely God's work and that no human works, efforts, or cooperation is involved in our salvation. This section will briefly answer that question.

For one thing, Catholic theologians redefine key biblical words, as we have already pointed out. *Grace* is changed from meaning "God's undeserved love in Christ" to "God's power infused into the human soul," which helps people do good works to merit eternal life. *Justification* is changed from the biblical meaning of "declaring righteous" to "making righteous through a lifelong process of inner renewal." *Faith* is changed from "trust of the heart" created by God's Holy Spirit to a person's "intellectual assent" to the historical facts of the gospel. In each case, the change in meaning represents a shift from what *God does for us* in Christ to what *humans do,* or at least what God does in humans with their cooperation.

The Catholic teaching of salvation goes beyond just redefining key biblical terms to force them to fit their teaching. Catholics have a different view of the law and the gospel than do Lutherans. Every Lutheran remembers being taught a memory device in catechism class, using the initials S-O-S: God's law—S-O-S—Shows (us) Our Sin; the gospel—S-O-S—Shows (us) Our Savior. Another brief way Lutherans summarize the difference between God's law and his gospel is this: The law tells us *what we must do* (and not do) to be holy. The gospel tells us *what God has done* in Christ to save us from our sins.

Catholics reject this distinction and hold that the law and the gospel are basically the same: both give people lists of rules to keep so that by doing good they gradually become good, that is, righteous before God. Moses was the lawgiver in the Old Testament and Jesus, they say, is the new lawgiver in the New Testament. The *Catechism of the Catholic Church* teaches this:

> The New Law or the Law of the Gospel is the perfection here on earth of the divine law, natural and revealed. It is the work of Christ and is expressed particularly in the Sermon on the Mount. It is also the work of the Holy Spirit and through him it becomes the interior law of charity. (n. 1965)

In other words, the law and the gospel are the same thing. The law is law and the gospel is law. Both teach people what to do to be good. The Catholic teaching of "the law of the gospel" perverts the unconditional promises of the gospel—

the free forgiveness of sins won by Christ, promised in the gospel, and received through faith—into just another law with conditional promises, conditioned on human performance. This robs sinners of their hope in Christ as their Savior and leaves them without any true comfort as they struggle with their sins and spiritual weaknesses.

In support of their teaching of salvation by faith and works, Catholics will often point to the epistle of James, chapter 2. In this chapter, James seeks to correct the false understanding of faith as mere intellectual assent of biblical facts (sometimes called mere *head knowledge*). Along with correcting this wrong understanding of faith, James corrects another wrong idea: that as long as a person has this kind of "faith" (mere head knowledge), he doesn't have to do good works. James teaches that such "faith" is no real Christian faith at all. Christians will show their genuine faith in Christ by doing good works. Good works are not optional for Christians; doing them is God's holy will for his people. When Christians outwardly demonstrate their faith to others by doing good and helping them, they are justified by their works, James says. But note carefully: he is speaking of being justified before other people. "Show me," he says (verse 18). He is not speaking of the sinner's justification before God, that is, how sinners receive God's forgiveness for their sins. Justification in James is still a declaratory act, as it is in Paul's letters. Paul speaks of the sinner being justified by God, based on Christ's blood and righteousness. James speaks of Christians being justified (declared righteous) by *other people,* based on their good works, which they do as a result of their faith in Christ. James does not teach people to base their hope of forgiveness of sins and eternal salvation on their good works.[48]

To support their work-righteousness teaching, Catholics will, for instance, point to Jesus' words to the rich young ruler about keeping the Ten Commandments (Matthew 19:16-21; Mark 10:17-21; Luke 18:18-22). The rich young man asked Jesus what he had to do to inherit eternal life. Jesus referred the man to the Ten Commandments and told him that if he could keep them, he would have eternal life. "See!" Catholics will say. "Salvation comes by doing good works! Otherwise, why would Jesus have said that?"[49]

A very good question! Scripture clearly tells us what God's purpose is for giving sinners his law:

- "Through the law we become conscious of sin" (Romans 3:20).
- "The law was added so that the trespass might increase" (Romans 5:20).
- "I would not have known what sin was except through the law. For I would not have known what coveting really was if the law had not said, 'Do not covet'" (Romans 7:7).

Yes, God attaches temporal and eternal promises to his law. But when a promise is attached to the law, it is conditional. When the promise is eternal life, the condition is that you have to keep the law—all of it—perfectly all the time. And everyone who fails to keep God's law perfectly falls under the curse of the law. God gave his law to sinners to teach them to despair of trying to earn salvation by being good, because sinners can never be good enough. The apostle Paul set forth this view of the law in Galatians 3:10-14:

> All who rely on observing the law are under a curse, for it is written: "Cursed is everyone who does not continue to do everything written in the Book of the Law." Clearly no one is justified before God by the law, because, "The righteous will live by faith." The law is not based on faith; on the contrary, "The man who does these things will live by them." Christ redeemed us from the curse of the law by becoming a curse for us, for it is written: "Cursed is everyone who is hung on a tree." He redeemed us in order that the blessing given to Abraham might come to the Gentiles through Christ Jesus, so that by faith we might receive the promise of the Spirit.

Now back to Jesus' conversation with the rich young man. Jesus' reason for reminding the man of the law's conditional promises of life and then telling the man that he still needed to give up his wealth was to show the man that in spite of his outward piety and self-confidence that he had kept the law, he had not even begun to keep the First Commandment, which told him to love God above all things. The man loved his money more than God. In his heart he was an idolater. He desperately needed a Savior to rescue him from his utter failure to keep the law and be holy as God is holy. He first needed to be convinced of his need for a Savior before he could value the Savior he so much needed. He needed to be emptied of his own righteousness before he could put his faith in the righteousness Jesus had won for him.

Catholics will also point to Scripture's call for people to repent of their sins and to believe the gospel as proof that we must cooperate with God if we are to be saved.[50] They will say that God would not tell people to do such things if they didn't have the power and capability to do them, and by doing them they are cooperating (working) with God's grace (helping power). Lutherans respond: Yes, God tells us to repent and believe, but just because he speaks to us with "command" words doesn't mean sinners have the innate power to respond—any more than Lazarus had the power to come out of the tomb when Jesus commanded, "Lazarus, come out!" (John 11:43). Lazarus was dead; his resurrection was entirely the work of Jesus, as he exercised his almighty divine power through his Word to bring Lazarus to life. The same is true for sinners who by nature are "dead in . . . transgressions and sins" (Ephesians 2:1). Sinners, who are spiritually dead, have no more power and ability to cooperate with God's Word than physically dead Lazarus did.

"But because of his great love for us, God, who is rich in mercy, made us alive with Christ even when we were dead in transgressions—it is by grace you have been saved" (Ephesians 2:4,5). Notice who Paul says is doing all the work in our salvation—God alone in Christ. It is not that God is working and we are working along with him. Our salvation is altogether a miracle of God's grace—his undeserved love and mercy—and of his almighty power, just as was his raising of Lazarus from the dead.

Mixing works and human cooperation into justification has inevitable results. We have discussed one of those tragic results, the loss or denial of God-given hope and certainty of final salvation. Another result is the downplaying of the seriousness of sin, especially original sin.

Original sin downplayed

Scripture teaches that sin includes not only committing evil acts contrary to God's law but also failing to do the good and loving acts that God commands. Scripture also teaches that ever since Adam and Eve fell into sin, *the way we are* by nature is sinful. Adam and Eve were created in the image of God (Genesis 1:26,27), which means they were completely righteous and holy (Ephesians 4:24; Colossians 3:10). When they fell into sin, they lost the holy image of God (Genesis 5:3) and fell under God's condemnation and sentence of eternal death, which they passed on to the entire human race (Romans 5:12,15-19). The result is that all people now are born with a nature completely corrupted by sin. By nature all people are:

- *spiritually blind.* "The man without the Spirit does not accept the things that come from the Spirit of God, for they are foolishness to him, and he cannot understand them, because they are spiritually discerned" (1 Corinthians 2:14).
- *spiritually dead in sin.* "You were dead in your transgressions and sins" (Ephesians 2:1).
- *enemies of God.* "The mind of sinful man is death. . . . The sinful mind is hostile to God. It does not submit to God's law, nor can it do so" (Romans 8:6,7).

All our thoughts, inclinations, desires, and feelings are corrupted by sin and are evil in God's sight. Genesis tells us that before the great flood, "the LORD saw how great man's wickedness on the earth had become, and that every inclination of the thoughts of his heart was only evil all the time" (Genesis 6:5). After the flood, the condition of mankind's fallen nature has remained the same: "Every inclination of his heart is evil from childhood" (Genesis 8:21).

Lutherans carefully note how Scripture speaks so categorically about original sin. The Lutheran confession called the Formula of Concord states:

> [The Holy Scriptures] testify that original sin is an unspeakable evil and such an entire corruption of human nature that in it and all its inward and outward powers, nothing pure or good remains. Everything is entirely corrupt, so that because of original sin a person is truly spiritually dead in God's sight [Ephesians 2:5]. All a person's powers are dead to what is good.[51]

The biblical teaching of original sin means that sinners by nature are not just spiritually weakened but are spiritually dead in sin. We sinners are not just impaired in spiritual matters, needing a little help to find the path of good works; rather, we are spiritually blind. We need a miracle that is 100 percent God's doing to rescue us from our natural sinful condition.

The Roman Catholic Church officially teaches a doctrine of original sin—that all people are born with a nature that is corrupted by sin, which has been passed down to them since the fall of Adam (with the exception of Christ and his mother, Mary), which inclines them toward evil. And yet, when we look closely at Catholic teaching, we see that Catholics deny the scriptural teaching of *total depravity*. They hold that free will remains intact so that with God's help, people can cooperate with him in becoming righteous.

The *Catechism of the Catholic Church* states:

> [Original sin] is a depravation of original holiness and justice, *but human nature has not been totally corrupted:* it is wounded in the natural powers proper to it; subject to ignorance, suffering, and the dominion of death; and inclined to sin—an inclination to evil that is called "concupiscence." Baptism, by imparting the life of Christ's

grace, erases original sin and turns a man back toward God, but the consequences for nature, weakened and inclined to evil, persist in man and summon him to spiritual battle. (*Catechism,* n. 405, italic added.)

The first Protestant reformers, on the contrary, taught that original sin has radically perverted man and destroyed his freedom; they identified the sin inherited by each man with the tendency to evil (concupiscentia), which would be insurmountable. (*Catechism,* n. 406.)

Catholicism downplays the depth and depravity of original sin, opening the door for people to cooperate with God and for being justified by a combination of God's grace and human works.

The Catholic work-righteousness way of salvation has worked itself out in many of their teachings. Two of these teachings figured prominently at the beginning of the 16th century during the Reformation and are still part of official Catholic teaching today: *purgatory* and *indulgences.*

Purgatory

According to Scripture, all people will face the judgment seat of God at the end of their lives and on the Last Day: "Man is destined to die once, and after that to face judgment" (Hebrews 9:27). This judgment will be confirmed in a public way when Christ returns on the Last Day and raises all the dead. According to Scripture, there will be only two classes of people, believers and unbelievers, and only two destinations, heaven and hell. Believers in Christ will go to eternal life in heaven, and all those who die without faith in Christ will go to eternal punishment in hell (Matthew 25:31-46; Mark 16:16). When a person dies, his or her soul goes to its eternal destiny, either to heaven or to hell (Luke 16:22-24). Scripture does not teach any intermediate destination. When believers die, they will be "in paradise" with Jesus, as he promised the penitent thief on the cross (Luke 23:43). Paul says the same. When believers die, they will be with the Lord (2 Corinthians 5:8; Philippians 1:23).

According to Catholic teaching, when Christians die, their souls do not immediately go to heaven to be with Christ, where he "will wipe every tear from their eyes" and where there is no more "mourning or crying or pain" (Revelation 21:4). Quite the contrary! Unless they had already in this life reached a state of perfection, before they can go to heaven to be with the Lord and be comforted, they must first go to purgatory, where they are purged of their sinful tendencies and suffer any temporal punishments they still owe on account of their sins.

The Catholic Church has not officially defined the exact nature of the punishment of purgatory, but up until modern times, most Catholic theologians have taught that the punishment is some type of fire. Catholic theologians used to debate how hot the fires of purgatory burned. One of the common theories was that purgatory's fire burns just as hot as the fire of hell, the only difference being that hell's punishments last forever, while purgatory will be emptied when Christ returns on the Last Day. The details of purgatory have remained only theories, but Catholics were taught to expect years, centuries, or even millennia of unimaginable suffering after death to cook and burn away their sinfulness. They were taught to believe that Christ, when he said, "It is finished," on the cross (John 19:30), had not actually suffered as their substitute the punishments and penalties for all their sins; and for this reason, they themselves must suffer what Christ left undone.

For many Catholics today, the whole notion of purgatory, which leaves them bereft of any Christian comfort, is pretty much ignored. Catholic priests today seem seldom to make any mention of it in their funeral homilies.

Nevertheless, purgatory remains an integral part of official Catholic teaching and fits in with their idea that justification is a lifelong process of doing good works to try to make up for one's sins. It is obvious that most people, even by human standards, do not reach a state of perfection in this life, completely rid of all sinful tendencies, and therefore are not ready to enter God's perfect heaven immediately, where only perfect saints can live. The "making righteous process" has to continue after death. Completely lacking is the gospel teaching of the full and free forgiveness of sin's guilt and punishment and that God considers the believer to be righteous through faith in Jesus and a citizen of heaven now and into eternity.

So the awful teaching of purgatory remains on the official books because it has been defined as a dogma by popes and church councils. Nevertheless, even the *Catechism of the Catholic Church,* without denying that purgatory is a place or state of suffering and punishment, chooses to place the emphasis on purgatory as "final purification," reminding Catholics of the "comfort" they will have when they find themselves in purgatory and not in hell because they can be certain that eventually they will get to heaven (nn. 1030-1032).

While the teaching of purgatory as a place of terrible pain and suffering is not emphasized as much as it was in the past, it is still there. It is implied in such practices as prayers and masses for the dead, which are offered for the departed loved ones in purgatory.

Indulgences—when forgiveness goes "on sale" and still is not free

Purgatory is linked with indulgences, another huge flash point at the beginning of the Reformation. Lutherans are familiar with the account of how the Reformation started over the practice of selling indulgences in 1517. As Luther was doing pastoral work among the people of Wittenberg, he discovered that some of his parishioners thought they did not need to repent of their sins anymore and receive Christ's forgiveness from his ministers because they had paid money for pieces of paper called indulgences. These indulgences, under the pope's seal, said that all the temporal punishments the people would have to suffer in purgatory had been remitted by the pope's "indulgence." What's more, people had been persuaded by the indulgence sellers to purchase indulgences for their dead relatives to buy their way out of purgatory too.

Luther, the pastor, recognized that this practice was a perversion of the forgiveness of sins won by Christ and was undermining the church's true ministry of calling sinners to repentance and proclaiming the forgiveness of sins through faith in Christ. As a professor of theology, Luther publicly addressed the issue at the University of Wittenberg by publishing his now famous "Ninety-five Theses or Disputation on the Power and Efficacy of Indulgences," which is often regarded as the beginning of the Reformation. Churches everywhere that embraced the Protestant Reformation quickly rejected the claims and validity of papal indulgences.

But what happened with indulgences among Catholics after the beginning of the Reformation? The Council of Trent worked to clean up the more crass abuses, for example, giving people the impression that forgiveness could be bought with money, but the work-righteousness theology behind papal indulgences has remained to this day.

At the time of the Second Vatican Council, the bishops discussed what place, if any, indulgences should have in the church in the future, but they deferred to the pope to make a decision.[52] In 1967, Pope Paul VI issued an official decree called the "Apostolic Constitution on the Revision of Indulgences," which called for retaining indulgences in the Catholic Church. The wording of Pope Paul's decree was incorporated into the revised *Code of Canon Law* of 1983 and is also quoted in the *Catechism of the Catholic Church*.[53]

The catechism defines papal indulgences this way:

> An indulgence is a remission before God of the temporal punishment due to sins whose guilt has already been forgiven, which the faithful Christian who is duly disposed

> gains under certain prescribed conditions through the action of the Church which, as the minister of redemption, dispenses and applies with authority the treasury of the satisfactions of Christ and the saints.
>
> An indulgence is partial or plenary according as it removes either part or all of the temporal punishment due to sin. The faithful can gain indulgences for themselves or apply them to the dead. (n. 1471)

The catechism goes on to explain that according to Catholic teaching, sin incurs guilt and punishment. Punishment is twofold: eternal punishment in hell and temporal punishment in purgatory. Sin's guilt and eternal punishment are removed in the sacraments of Baptism and Reconciliation (Penance), but temporal punishments must be satisfied either in this life or in purgatory. At the same time, the Catholic Church claims to possess a "treasury of merits," or "treasury of the church," which consists of the meritorious works done by the virgin Mary and the saints over and above what was needed for them to get to heaven. Through papal indulgences these extra "merits" are applied to the living and to the dead in purgatory to shorten their time of suffering there.

Indulgences may be either full (plenary) or partial. Certain conditions stipulated by the church have to be met for an indulgence to be effective. Conditions for receiving a full indulgence, which remits all temporal punishment in purgatory either for oneself or for a dead person, include being free from all attachment to sin and performing the proper works—going to the Sacrament of Reconciliation (Penance) and receiving Holy Communion, giving alms to help the poor, offering certain prescribed prayers, and submitting to Roman Catholic Church authority, in particular to the authority of the pope by recognizing him as the successor to Peter and the possessor of the keys to heaven.[54]

In 1998, Pope John Paul II, as part of the preparations for celebrating the Jubilee 2000 anniversary of Christianity, issued a special jubilee indulgence. Included in the list of conditions for obtaining the plenary, or full, indulgence were the following:

> The plenary indulgence of the Jubilee can also be gained through actions which express in a practical and generous way the penitential spirit which is, as it were, the heart of the Jubilee. This would include abstaining for at least one whole day from unnecessary consumption (e.g., from smoking or alcohol, or fasting or practicing abstinence according to the general rules of the Catholic Church and the norms laid down by the Bishops' Conferences) and donating a proportionate sum of money to the poor, supporting by a significant contribution works of a religious or social nature (especially for the benefit of abandoned children, young people in trouble, the elderly in need, foreigners in various countries seeking better living conditions), devoting a suitable portion of personal free time to activities benefiting the community, or other similar forms of personal sacrifice.[55]

Suffice it to say, not much has changed in Roman indulgence theology over the centuries. Modern Roman indulgences still give the impression that forgiveness occasionally goes on sale and that forgiveness of punishment for sin is not free to the sinner. As ever in Catholic theology, God's forgiveness is a conditional promise, in this case, conditioned on the purchase of someone else's merits. If present-day Catholics in general are buying indulgences less than they were in the 16th century, it is probably because they are more secularized in their worldviews today than they were five hundred years ago. God is much less feared today as a judge who will punish sin than he was in the past. So matters like purgatory and indulgences are not as much of a concern to many modern Catholics.

But this modern attitude robs Christ of his glory as our Savior no less than did the false teaching about justification in the 16th century. When the demands of God's law and the depth of sin are downplayed, the all-sufficient nature of

Christ's atoning sacrifice for sin is also downplayed. Christ is robbed of his glory as Savior.

The Joint Declaration on the Doctrine of Justification

Ever since Vatican II opened the way for Catholics to participate in the modern ecumenical movement, liberal Lutherans and Catholics have engaged in formal dialogues on various levels, seeking to reduce the doctrinal differences between them. These interchurch dialogues culminated to a certain extent when members of the Lutheran World Federation (LWF) and Vatican officials announced in the late 1990s that they had reached an accord—kind of an agreement—on the doctrine of justification. In a document titled *Joint Declaration on the Doctrine of Justification* (JDDJ), LWF Lutherans and Roman Catholics claimed that the issue over which they had differed and remained divided for almost five hundred years was no longer a source of division between the two churches. The *Joint Declaration* said that the Lutheran *Book of Concord*'s condemnation of Catholic false teaching on justification no longer applied to Catholics and that the Catholic Trent's anathemas no longer applied to Lutherans who signed on to the *Joint Declaration*.

With great media fanfare, representatives of the Lutheran World Federation and the Vatican celebrated the document in a public ceremony on Reformation Day, October 31, 1999, in Augsburg, Germany. Even though it has been reported endlessly by both the secular and church news media that LWF and Vatican officials signed the *Joint Declaration*, they in fact did not sign the document as it was originally drafted. What was signed in Augsburg was a kind of proxy document called the *Official Common Statement* (OCS). According to eyewitnesses, it was hardly a time of celebration. The Lutheran and Catholic representatives reportedly grimaced as they each signed. There was no customary handshake, much less any mutual embrace.[56]

What was this about? Going back several months, in 1998 Cardinal Edward Cassidy, at the time the head of the Vatican's Pontifical Council for Promoting Christian Unity, announced in a Vatican news conference the drafting of the *Joint Declaration on the Doctrine of Justification*. Shortly afterward, the Vatican's Congregation for the Doctrine of the Faith under Cardinal Joseph Ratzinger issued a "response" to the declaration. It suggested that the alleged agreement between Catholics and Lutherans was artificial. Serious doctrinal differences remained. This "response" specifically took issue with the Lutheran teachings (1) that a baptized Christian is at the same time both a sinner and a saint and (2) that justification is the central teaching of the Christian faith. The "response" also affirmed salvation by faith and works and that the condemnations of Trent remained in force.

LWF Lutherans were stunned and furious at how the rug had been pulled out from under them. Ratzinger was publicly vilified in the German press for his role in the seemingly mixed messages coming out of the Vatican. Responding to the criticism and outcry, Ratzinger sought to salvage the *Joint Declaration* by gathering a small group of Catholic and Lutheran theologians who reworked it. The final version actually includes three documents: the actual *Joint Declaration,* the *Official Common Statement,* and an *Annex,* which included further clarifications. The *Annex* affirms salvation by faith and works, that God's grace does not exclude human action, and that the doctrine of justification is merely a "touchstone" for the Christian faith.

Confessional Lutherans around the world have rejected the *Joint Declaration* as a betrayal of the Lutheran Confessions. They correctly point out that it does not resolve any of the doctrinal issues on justification that have historically divided Lutherans and Catholics. The document lets Lutheran-sounding statements and Catholic statements stand side by side, as if one were as true and valid as the other.

The *Joint Declaration* also made no attempt to define key theological terms such as *grace, faith,* and *justification.* As a result, Lutherans and Catholics can both say, "We believe we are saved by grace through faith," yet mean different things. The document does not resolve the differences between Lutherans and Catholics on the doctrine of justification. What's more, the Vatican has clarified that when the document says that Trent's anathemas no longer apply, the anathemas were lifted only from the Lutherans who signed the document. In other words, Rome's curses still apply to all *confessional* Lutherans.[57]

Shortly after the signing, Rome showed just how much respect it really had for such "accords" with Lutherans on justification. When Pope John Paul II issued the decree for the upcoming Jubilee 2000 indulgence, he did so within days of the signing of the *Joint Declaration* in Augsburg. To add insult to injury, less than a year later the Vatican's Congregation for the Doctrine of the Faith, under Ratzinger's signature and with Pope John Paul II's approval, issued the document *Dominus Iesus* (Lord Jesus), which declares that Protestant churches, including Lutheran churches, are not real Christian churches because they do not accept the authority of the pope.

Rome and the salvation of non-Christians

A good case can be made that Rome's doctrine of justification has not only *remained unchanged* since the time of the Reformation but has, in fact, gotten worse. The Second Vatican Council opened the possibility for the salvation of non-Christians and even atheists in a way that the Catholic Church had never done before. Here is one of Vatican II's key sections on the optimistic hope of salvation of non-Christians:

> Finally, those who have not yet received the Gospel are related to the People of God in various ways. There is, first, that people to which the covenants and promises were made, and from which Christ was born according to the flesh (cf. Rom. 9:4–5): in view of the divine choice, they are

> a people most dear for the sake of the fathers, for the gifts of God are without repentance (cf. Rom. 11:28–29).
>
> But the plan of salvation also includes those who acknowledge the Creator, in the first place amongst whom are the Moslems: these profess to hold the faith of Abraham, and together with us they adore the one, merciful God, mankind's judge on the last day. Nor is God remote from those who in shadows and images seek the unknown God, since he gives to all men life and breath and all things (cf. Acts 17:25–28), and since the Saviour wills all men to be saved (cf. 1 Tim. 2:4).
>
> Those who, through no fault of their own, do not know the Gospel of Christ or his Church, but who nevertheless seek God with a sincere heart, and, moved by grace, try in their actions to do his will as they know it through the dictates of their conscience—those too may achieve eternal salvation.
>
> Nor shall divine providence deny the assistance necessary for salvation to those who, without any fault of theirs, have not yet arrived at an explicit knowledge of God, and who, not without grace, strive to lead a good life. Whatever good or truth is found amongst them is considered by the Church to be a preparation for the Gospel and given by him who enlightens all men that they may at length have life.[58]

Allowing for the possibility of salvation for Jews and Muslims (who consciously reject Jesus Christ as the Son of God and Savior) and even for the salvation of atheists (who deny the very existence of God) requires a crass doctrine of salvation by doing good works. It is a denial of the Christian gospel and robs Christ of his saving glory. While the teachings of purgatory and indulgences may have faded some from the beliefs and practices of many modern Catholics, the pluralistic and almost universalistic views of salvation for non-Christians seem to be widely taught and believed by many in the Catholic Church.[59]

Various surveys of Catholic religious beliefs confirm the sad fact that the Catholic Church's work-righteousness teaching of salvation is what most Catholics actually believe. As just one example, Peter Kreeft, a Catholic college philosophy professor, has made it his practice to ask the students in his classes how they hope to be saved and go to heaven. Kreeft tells of his findings:

> I find, incredibly, that 9 out of 10 Catholics do not know this [that Jesus saves us; we do not save ourselves]. . . . Well over 90% of students I have polled who have had 12 years of catechism classes, even Catholic high schools, say they expect to go to Heaven because they tried, or did their best, or had compassionate feelings to everyone, or were sincere. They hardly ever mention Jesus. Asked why they hope to be saved, they mention almost anything except the Savior.[60]

Confessional Lutherans and Roman Catholics remain as divided as ever over the central article of the Christian faith. The work-righteousness nature of Rome's doctrine of justification has not changed. It continues to affect Catholic teaching of other doctrines as well, as the next three chapters will show.

For Further Reading

Robert Preus, *Justification and Rome* (St. Louis: Concordia Publishing House, 1997).

Martin Chemnitz, *Examination of the Council of Trent,* Vol. 1 (St. Louis: Concordia Publishing House, 1971), pp. 455-611.

THE SACRAMENTS—*Part 1*

One of the hallmarks of the Catholic Church is its use of sacraments. It celebrates several of them within liturgical services, often with elaborate ritual and solemnity. While Protestants in general may speak of attending religious services to "worship God" or to "hear a sermon" and Lutherans speak of public worship in terms of "God serving his people with Word and sacrament," Catholics will often speak of their corporate worship as "celebrating the sacraments," indicating what a central role the sacraments play in the service.

Probably the most obvious proof that the Catholic Church places a heavy emphasis on "celebrating sacraments" in their worship is that they have seven sacraments. This chapter and the next will look briefly at the Catholic Church's teaching on sacraments in general and then at each of its seven sacraments.

Sacraments in general

What is a sacrament, and how many are there?

The word *sacrament* does not occur in the Bible. It is a church term that was used by early church teachers as a word for the sacred acts that had been instituted by Christ, which he commanded his church to observe.

Baptism and the Lord's Supper are the two sacred acts of Christ that were always recognized as sacraments. They were usually recognized as being in a class by themselves. This is because the New Testament clearly records that Christ explicitly instituted them and commanded Christians to use them. Both involve the use of earthly, visible elements together with Christ's words and his promise of the forgiveness of sins attached to their use.

Yet some early church teachers came to give the term *sacrament* a wider meaning. When the Scripture scholar Jerome produced his Latin translation of the Bible, called the Vulgate (about A.D. 400), he used the Latin word *sacramentum* to translate the Greek word for *mystery* that is used in several passages of Scripture, for example, in Ephesians 5:32: "This is a profound mystery [*sacramentum*]—but I am talking about Christ and the church." *Mystery* refers to the broad range of truths kept hidden in previous generations but revealed by Jesus to his church. And so, in line with Jerome's translation, along with Baptism and the Lord's Supper various sacred acts—"mysteries"—came to be called sacraments.

A common definition of *sacrament* in the early church was "a visible sign of an invisible grace." With such a broad and unspecific definition, it can be easily understood how there could be varying opinions about exactly what was meant by a sacrament and how many there were.

The use of the word *sacrament* varied somewhat in the early Christian centuries. It was not until the 12th century that the influential theologian Peter Lombard made the case for recognizing seven sacraments, and the number stuck. It was only at the Council of Florence in 1439 that the Catholic Church made the seven sacraments an official church teaching—less than one hundred years before the Reformation.

The *Catechism of the Catholic Church* lists the following seven Catholic sacraments:

The sacraments of Christian initiation

1. Baptism
2. Confirmation
3. Eucharist

The sacraments of healing

4. Penance and Reconciliation
5. Anointing of the Sick (formerly called Extreme Unction, also called Last Rites)

The sacraments at the service of communion

6. Holy Orders (Ordination)
7. Matrimony

The Lutheran reformers, while not making a doctrine out of the definition for the word *sacrament,* came to recognize only Baptism and the Lord's Supper as Christian sacraments.[61]

In response, the Catholic Church at the Council of Trent reiterated the medieval list of seven sacraments. Trent declared them all as divinely instituted and commanded by Christ and anathematized (cursed) all those who disagreed with its definition:

> If anyone says that the sacraments of the New Law were not all instituted by our Lord Jesus Christ, or that there are more or less than seven, namely, baptism, confirmation, Eucharist, penance, extreme unction, order and matrimony, or that any one of these seven is not truly and intrinsically a sacrament, let him be anathema.[62]

By contrast, Lutherans clearly make a distinction between sacraments instituted by Christ (Baptism and the Lord's Supper) and other early Christian customs that are mentioned in the New Testament but have no clear institution and command of Christ. Examples of these include the laying on of hands, or ordination (1 Timothy 5:22; 2 Timothy 1:6), and anointing the sick with oil (James 5:14). Lutherans also observe the custom of confirmation, which is not expressly mentioned in the New Testament. Lutherans hold that such customs, which are neither commanded nor forbidden in the Bible, fall into the realm of Christian freedom (adiaphora). On the other hand, Lutherans reject the Catholic teaching of elevating such human customs and rites to the same level as Baptism and the Lord's Supper, as if they were instituted and commanded by Christ and had his promise of the forgiveness of sins connected to them.

What makes a sacrament valid (real)?

Lutherans hold that it is not the faith or moral character of either the administrant or the receiver of the sacraments that makes them real or valid, but it is solely the Word, institution, command, and promise of our Lord Jesus Christ. Lutherans have taken over an axiom of Saint Augustine: "When the Word is joined to the element or natural substance, it becomes a sacrament."[63] If the words that Jesus commanded his church to use are omitted, it is not a sacrament. If the earthly elements are not used as Jesus commanded, it is not a sacrament. Lutherans also hold that the validity of the sacraments does not depend on some special divine power conferred on the clergy at the time of their ordination, as Catholics teach. (There is more about this in connection with ordination.) Christ's words and promises are true and powerful to do and give what they say. Sacraments do not receive their validity because of some divine power the Catholic Church instills in its priests, as taught in Catholicism.

According to Catholic teaching, the validity of the sacraments depends on the ordained clergy in another way: "The minister must voluntarily carry out the intention of the church. He . . . must intend what the church intends."[64] Making the validity of the sacraments depend in some way on the intention of the minister introduces doubt into the sacraments. What if the minister is a hypocrite and doesn't intend what the church intends? By contrast, Lutherans confess in the Augsburg Confession: "Both the Sacraments and Word are effective because of Christ's institution, even if they are administered by evil men."[65] The validity of the sacraments is dependent on Christ and his powerful words and institution and not on the sincerity of the ordained clergy. The church's ministers are Christ's called servants who merely speak the Lord's words and administer the sacraments according to Christ's institution.

What blessings does God offer and give in the sacraments?

The answer to that question is clear from what the Bible says. Concerning Baptism, the apostle Peter said to the crowd on Pentecost: "Repent and be baptized, every one of you, in the name of Jesus Christ for the forgiveness of your sins. And you will receive the gift of the Holy Spirit" (Acts 2:38). The disciple Ananias said to Saul at the time of his conversion: "What are you waiting for? Get up, be baptized and wash your sins away, calling on his name" (Acts 22:16). Through Baptism, God promises and gives the forgiveness of sins. Along with forgiveness also comes the promise of salvation. "Whoever believes and is baptized will be saved, but whoever does not believe will be condemned" (Mark 16:16; see also 1 Peter 3:21).

Jesus' words of institution for the Lord's Supper clearly promise the forgiveness of sins in this sacrament. "Then he took the cup, gave thanks and offered it to them, saying, 'Drink from it, all of you. This is my blood of the covenant, which is poured out for many for the forgiveness of sins'" (Matthew 26:27,28).

On this basis, Luther's Small Catechism teaches:

> What does Baptism give or profit?
>
> Answer: It works forgiveness of sins, delivers from death and the devil, and gives eternal salvation to all who believe this, as the words and promises of God declare.[66]

And concerning the Lord's Supper, the Small Catechism states:

> What is the benefit of such eating and drinking?
>
> Answer: That is shown us in these words, "Given for you" and "shed for you for the forgiveness of sins." This means that in the Sacrament forgiveness of sins, life, and salvation are given us through these words. For where there is forgiveness of sins, there is also life and salvation.[67]

Scripture makes no distinction between the blessings of forgiveness, eternal life, and salvation whether received through the Word, in Baptism, or in the Lord's Supper. It is the same forgiveness of sins that Christ won for all people by his suffering and death on the cross and that God freely offers to people in these means of grace.

Again the Catholic Church at the Council of Trent condemned the scriptural Lutheran teaching in no uncertain terms: "If anyone says that these seven sacraments are so equal to each other that one is not for any reason more excellent than the other, let him be anathema."[68]

In Catholic theology, each sacrament gives people a different "grace." Rome has not officially defined exactly what each of these seven different sacramental graces are, so individual Catholic theologians are still free to speculate about them. Here are the two different lists of "graces" from two medieval Catholic theologians, Bonaventure and Thomas Aquinas. Notice that Bonaventure viewed the sacramental graces as a "negative" (help *against* something); and Aquinas, as a "positive" (help *for* something).[69]

Sacrament	**Bonaventure**	**Aquinas**
Baptism	vs. original sin	regeneration
Confirmation	vs. weakness	strengthening
Eucharist	vs. willful sins	nourishment
Penance	vs. mortal sins	spiritual healing
Unction	vs. venial sins	spiritual and bodily healing
Orders	vs. ignorance	spiritual building up of the church
Matrimony	vs. lust	physical building up of the church

Behind this teaching of a different grace in each sacrament is the Catholic work-righteousness view of grace as God's helping power infused into the soul to help people do good works to attain their salvation (discussed in chapter 5).

How do we receive the spiritual blessings of the sacraments?

Still another major difference between Lutherans and Catholics is the teaching on how a person receives the blessings of the sacraments. The gift or blessing that God gives in the sacraments is his promise of the forgiveness of sins, eternal life, and salvation. Lutherans teach that these gifts are received through faith by believing that God's promises are true. As Paul says in Romans 4:16: "Therefore, the promise comes by faith, so that it may be by grace and may be guaranteed to all Abraham's offspring—not only to those who are of the law but also to those who are of the faith of Abraham. He is the father of us all." Concerning Baptism, Jesus promised, "Whoever believes and is baptized will be saved" (Mark 16:16). In his Word and sacraments, the Lord *offers* and *gives* his saving blessings. Through faith, we *receive* those blessings and personally benefit from them.

Again, in the interest of its work-righteousness teachings, the Catholic Church rejected and condemned the Lutheran teaching at the Council of Trent:

> Canon 5. If anyone says that these sacraments have been instituted for the nourishment of faith alone, let him be anathema.
>
> Canon 8. If anyone says that by the sacraments of the New Law grace is not conferred *ex opere operato,* but that faith alone in the divine promise is sufficient to obtain grace, let him be anathema.[70]

Canon 8 employs the technical Latin phrase *ex opere operato,* which means "from or by virtue of the work performed." In other words, the sacraments give their graces to people even apart from faith, simply through their outward participation in the sacrament. In fact, for centuries most Catholics participated in their sacraments without understanding a word of what was said (because they were conducted in Latin). By merely being present, they thought they were receiving sacramental "graces" simply "by the work performed" by the priest.

This teaching has led to the outward ritualism and formalism that exists in the Catholic Church. While still affirming *ex opere operato,* since Vatican II, the Catholic Church has tried to address what apparently even Catholics have come to view as an overemphasis on external ritual. Vatican II called for a liturgical renewal that involves the Catholic faithful in a "full, conscious, and active participation" of liturgical celebrations, which includes the use of several of the sacraments.[71] The liturgical rites, including the sacraments, are now usually celebrated in the language of the people so that they can understand what is being said.

At the same time, the simple, clear, straightforward language of "faith in the forgiveness of sins" is still almost entirely missing in the Catholic teaching on the sacraments.

Other changing emphases in the sacraments

Starting about the middle of the 20th century, under the influence of modern philosophy and historical-critical ways of thinking, some Catholic theologians started moving away from some of the emphases that had been in place since the Middle Ages and are currently taught in the documents of Vatican II, the Catholic catechism, and the official writings of recent popes. They no longer insisted that Jesus actually instituted all seven Catholic sacraments. Reflecting such views, modern Catholic theologian Richard McBrien approaches the subject as follows:

> Were the sacraments "instituted" by Christ? Here again the question is to be answered in its larger ecclesiological context. Just as the Church was not "founded" by Christ in the sense that he immediately and directly established a new religion, with specific organizational structure, doctrines, moral codes, and so forth, neither do the sacraments issue from some precise mandate of the Lord. . . . The rapidity with which Catholic theology, under the impact of recent developments in ecclesiology, in Christology, and in biblical studies, is moving away from the standard textbook treatments of the institution and the number of sacraments is very remarkable.[72]

In other words, Christ himself did not necessarily institute the seven Catholic sacraments. Like the church's organizational structure and creedal statements, the seven sacraments were later developments of church tradition.

Operating with the very broad definition of *sacrament* as a sacred "sign," Catholic theologians say that stories about Jesus are a "sign" of God's love in the world. They speak of the "human Jesus" as the "primordial sacrament." At the time of Vatican II, it was very popular to refer to the Catholic Church as the "basic sacrament" and as the "universal sacrament of salvation." This later designation was incorporated into Vatican II's teaching on the church.[73]

The official teaching of the Catholic Church still maintains seven sacraments, but the new openness to a broader usage of the word *sacrament* remains popular in the Catholic Church. So also has a more humanistic or human-centered emphasis as to what happens in the sacraments. The long-standing official teaching is that the sacraments are indeed "means of grace," that is, that in the sacraments, *God* is actively doing something, giving his grace to the recipients. The more modern emphasis is on what people are doing as they celebrate the sacraments. Here are quotations from two modern Catholic theologians, Mark Searle and Thomas Bokenkotter, which speak of this new human-centered emphasis:

> Undoubtedly the leading indicator if not the cause of this transformation is the abandonment of the questions and vocabulary of Scholasticism in favor of more existentialist and personalist approaches to understanding what the sacraments are and how they function in the Christian life. What began as a recovery of the ecclesial dimension of the sacraments quickly led to further shifts: (1) from speaking of sacraments as "means of grace" to speaking of them as encounters with Christ himself; (2) from thinking of them primarily as acts of God to thinking of them mainly as celebrations of the faith community; (3) from

> seeing the sacraments as momentary incursions from another world to seeing them as manifestations of the graced character of all human life; (4) from interpreting them as remedies for sin and weakness to seeing them as promoting growth in Christ.[74]

> Previously, theologians both Catholic and Protestant emphasized the transcendent aspect of the sacraments as efficacious signs of the mysterious working of God in the human heart. Today, many Catholic theologians and educators tend to focus on the human aspect of the sacraments as celebrations of what is most meaningful and precious in human experience. The sacraments are viewed as festive rites that celebrate the love of God as experienced and related to our own story.[75]

The views presented in these quotations could rightly be described as almost non-supernatural or anti-supernatural. According to this modernistic view, God isn't really present or doing anything at all in the sacraments, only the people are. In this regard, modern Catholic theology is nearly identical with modern liberal Protestant views of the sacraments, as the author of the second quote above acknowledges.

The following sections will give brief examples of this humanistic, non-supernatural emphasis, particularly in Baptism and the Eucharist.

Baptism

The institution of Baptism

The Catholic Church correctly teaches according to Scripture that Baptism is a sacrament instituted and commanded by Christ during his earthly ministry (Matthew 28:19). Following Christ's institution, Catholics administer Baptism by applying water in the name of the Holy Trinity, using the words Christ commanded ("in the name of the Father and of the Son and of the Holy Spirit"). Like Lutherans, Catholics baptize babies as well as people of all other ages. Also like Lutherans,

Catholics do not prescribe any one particular mode of applying the water. The water may be applied by immersion, sprinkling, or pouring. Both churches also teach that Baptism is to be applied only once in a person's life; it is not to be repeated like the Lord's Supper. Catholics and Lutherans recognize as valid the baptisms performed in each other's churches.

The blessings of Baptism

Catholics also teach that Baptism is a divine means of grace. Through Baptism, God gives his grace, forgiveness of sins, and creates new spiritual life.

Regarding the blessings of Baptism, however, Lutherans do take issue with some aspects of Catholic teaching. Catholics teach that the "grace" given in Baptism is not, as Lutherans teach, the undeserved kindness and love of God by which he forgives all sins for Christ's sake. Rather, it is God's helping power infused into the soul, which enables people to cooperate with God in achieving their salvation by doing good works.

Regarding the forgiveness of sins, Catholics teach that God not only pardons the baptized of all sin (original sin and actual sins committed prior to Baptism) but that he also eradicates the sinful nature so that there is no more sinful nature remaining in the baptized person. He or she is as inherently righteous and holy as Adam and Eve were before the fall into sin, although the effects of sin, such as mortality and concupiscence, remain in the Christian. (Concupiscence is the tendency or desire to sin, which Catholics say is not a sin even though the Bible calls it a sin. See chapter 5, "Original sin downplayed.") This teaching contradicts what Scripture teaches about the sinful nature remaining in the Christian even after he or she has come to faith, resulting in the continual battle between the sinful nature (the flesh or old Adam) and the Christian's new spiritual nature (the spirit or new man; see Romans 7:14-25) and the Christian's daily need for forgiveness.

Regarding the blessings of Baptism, the Catholic Church also errs by teaching that Baptism imprints an indelible "character" on the soul. Concerning this character, the Council of Trent teaches: "If anyone says that in three sacraments, namely, baptism, confirmation and order, there is not imprinted on the soul a character, that is a certain spiritual and indelible mark, by reason of which they cannot be repeated, let him be anathema."[76]

The *Catechism of the Catholic Church* reaffirms this teaching:

> Incorporated into Christ by Baptism, the person baptized is configured to Christ. Baptism seals the Christian with the indelible spiritual mark (*character*) of his belonging to Christ. No sin can erase this mark, even if sins prevent Baptism from bearing the fruits of salvation. (n. 1272)

The doctrine of the baptismal character has led to the teaching that anyone who is baptized in the Catholic Church remains a member of the Catholic Church forever, even if that person later renounces the Catholic faith. Catholic theologian John Hardon explains the teaching of the character as follows:

> *What is the baptismal character?*
> The baptismal character is a permanent, irremovable change produced by the sacrament of baptism. It imparts to those who receive it a likeness to Christ in his priesthood, grafts them onto Christ, the Vine, so that they participate in a unique way in the graces of his humanity. It imprints on their souls an indelible seal that nothing, not even the loss of virtue or faith itself, can eradicate.
>
> *Does a baptized person always remain a Christian?*
> A baptized person always remains a Christian because the baptismal character confers a permanent relationship with Christ.
>
> *Is a Catholic always a Catholic?*
> Yes, once a Catholic a person always remains a Catholic in the fundamental sense of having the baptismal character. One cannot cease to be a Catholic because, once baptized,

he cannot be unbaptized. The seal of baptism continues in this life and endures into eternity.[77]

By contrast, Lutherans teach from Scripture that a person can fall from grace through impenitence and unbelief. Such a person is no longer a member of the spiritual body of Christ, the holy Christian church (Matthew 18:15-18). If that person is brought to repentance and back to faith in Christ, then he or she is once again a Christian and a member of the holy Christian church.

Catholics also err regarding the blessings of Baptism when they deny the lasting power of Baptism to assure sinners of God's forgiveness, which he gives them in Baptism. According to the Council of Trent, "If anyone says that by the sole remembrance and the faith of the baptism received, all sins committed after baptism are either remitted or made venial, let him be anathema."[78] In others words, Baptism forgives sins only up until the time of Baptism. Any sins committed after Baptism can be forgiven only through the Sacrament of Penance.

The Catholic teaching that each sacrament gives a different kind of infused grace results in the Catholic view of Baptism as less than complete. It forgives sin, but a person has to wait for the Sacrament of Confirmation to receive the Holy Spirit more completely. "Confirmation perfects Baptismal grace; it is the sacrament which gives the Holy Spirit in order to root us more deeply in the divine filiation" (*Catechism,* n. 1316).

Lutherans, by contrast, hold that Baptism "works forgiveness of sins, delivers from death and the devil, and gives eternal salvation to all who believe this, as the words and promises of God declare."[79] Scripture also clearly teaches that along with these blessings, Baptism is a "washing of rebirth and renewal by the Holy Spirit" (Titus 3:5; see also John 3:5). Through Baptism, God gives *all* his treasures of salvation in full, not just some of them.

Liberalizing trends and emphases

The previous section on the sacraments in general noted the trend among liberal Catholics to downplay the sacraments as divine means of grace and to emphasize a human-centered view of them. This trend among more liberal Catholics is reflected in a conversation I once had with a Catholic priest. We were comparing notes concerning practices in our churches. The priest asked me at about what age we Lutherans usually baptize infants. I replied that almost always within the first month or so after a baby is born. To that the priest replied, "Oh, we Catholics used to baptize infants soon after birth, but we don't do that so much anymore. We don't want to give people the impression that we still believe some old medieval notion of original sin and that if a baby dies before being baptized, the baby's soul might be in danger of going to hell. We wait until the children are a little older now. Since Vatican II, we view Baptism more as a celebration of the joy we have in welcoming a new member into the community."

This conversation is, of course, only anecdotal. But it does reflect the modern, liberal Catholic human-centered view of the sacraments instead of emphasizing sin, our need for God's forgiveness, and the forgiveness God gives us in this sacrament. Lutherans certainly view Baptism as a celebration of joy over a person being brought into God's family of believers. But Lutherans never want to lose sight of the other fundamental spiritual blessings of Baptism: "It works forgiveness of sins, delivers from death and the devil, and gives eternal salvation to all who believe this, as the words and promises of God declare." God's blessings are operative in Christians' lives not only at the time of Baptism but every day throughout their lives. As such, Baptism is a source of continual, ongoing joy, comfort, and strength for Christians.

Confirmation

Confirmation is the second of the sacraments of initiation in the Roman sacramental system. According to Catholic teaching, God gives grace in Baptism to enable a person to begin the Christian life. In Confirmation, God is said to give the person grace to strengthen (or *confirm*) his or her new life in Christ.

Confirmation supplements Baptism by giving the Christian another sacramental grace—a character imprinted on the soul that cannot be erased or removed under any condition or circumstance.[80] That is, Confirmation is *indelible.* According to Catholic teaching, in Baptism God forgives all sins (committed up until the time of Baptism) and gives a small measure of the Holy Spirit—enough to start the Christian life. But in Confirmation, God gives the Holy Spirit in full to help the baptized person live a mature Christian life.

Lutherans reject the teaching that Confirmation is a sacrament. There is no evidence in Scripture that Christ instituted a rite of Confirmation during his ministry on earth, parallel to how he instituted Baptism and the Lord's Supper. The rite of Confirmation lacks Christ's institution; therefore it has no divine command, no earthly element to apply, no words of Christ to speak, and no promise of Christ of his grace, Spirit, and forgiveness.

What Catholics call their Sacrament of Confirmation originated as a human, church custom attached to the Sacrament of Baptism. After the Baptism was performed, the administrant anointed the head of the baptized with oil *as a symbol* that the baptized person had received the Holy Spirit *in Baptism*.

Over the centuries, the distinction between what Christ had specifically instituted and what was merely a church custom gradually became lost. In the Western, Latin-rite church, Baptism and Confirmation became separate sacraments. Bishops began to reserve the administration of Confirmation for themselves, while presbyters (priests) continued to administer Baptism. The Catholic teaching of Confirmation as a sacrament was officially finalized at the Council of Florence in 1439 and confirmed at the Council of Trent.

In the Catholic Church today, bishops still administer the rite of Confirmation to children after a period of instruction. Adults who wish to become Catholics are received into the church after a period of instruction, usually at the solemn Easter Vigil service. If an adult has not been baptized, he or she receives Baptism and then receives Confirmation and first Communion all at the same time, in the Easter Vigil service. For the Easter Vigil confirmations, bishops give special permission to parish priests to administer the rite of Confirmation.

Today the rite of Confirmation consists of the bishop (or designated priest) applying oil to the candidate's forehead. The oil is olive oil mixed with balsam and has been specially blessed by the bishop. As the oil is applied, the bishop (or priest) says, "Be sealed with the gift of the Holy Spirit."

As previously said, Lutherans reject confirmation as a sacrament instituted by Christ. They point out that it lacks the institution of Christ. They also point out that any supposed promise of the Holy Spirit attached to a rite—a promise that God has not expressly attached to it—is a superstitious use of God's name and a sin against the Second Commandment. What's more, any supposed promise of the Holy Spirit in confirmation detracts from the genuine divine promise of the Holy Spirit in Baptism. Confirmation gives nothing that God has not already given and promised in Baptism, which include

- Lifelong forgiveness of sins (Acts 2:38; Ephesians 5:26,27)
- The new birth of faith (John 3:5; Titus 3:5,6)
- The Holy Spirit (John 3:5; Titus 3:5,6)
- Union with Christ (Romans 6:3-9); Galatians 3:26,27)
- The strength to live the Christian life (Romans 6:1-14)
- Salvation (Mark 16:16; 1 Peter 3:21)

While Lutherans reject that the Roman rite of Confirmation is a sacrament, we have retained it as a good and useful *church custom*. After adults and baptized children have been instructed in the basic truths of the Christian faith and are ready to publicly profess their Christian faith, they are confirmed. The Lutheran rite of confirmation consists of a reaffirmation of the promises of God's Word regarding Baptism, the confirmand's public profession of the Christian faith, and a promise to be faithful, with God's help, to the teachings of Christ found in the Bible. The pastor gives to each confirmand the promises found in God's Word, namely, that God will give them his grace and help them to remain faithful Christian confessors throughout their lives.

In case it seems to you that there isn't much difference between the Lutheran custom of confirmation and the Catholic Sacrament of Confirmation, consider how the Catholic Church responded at the Council of Trent to the Lutheran church's teaching and practice.

> Canon 1. If anyone says that the confirmation of those baptized is an empty ceremony and not a true and proper sacrament; or that of old it was nothing more than a sort of instruction, whereby those approaching adolescence gave an account of their faith to the Church, let him be anathema.
>
> Canon 2. If anyone says that those who ascribe any power to the holy chrism of confirmation offer insults to the Holy Ghost, let him be anathema.
>
> Canon 3. If anyone says that the ordinary minister of holy confirmation is not the bishop alone, but any simple priest, let him be anathema.[81]

Rome's curses on Lutherans and their teaching on confirmation still stand.

Eucharist

At the beginning of this chapter, it was noted that one of the hallmarks of the Catholic Church is the celebration of its seven sacraments. If this is true of the sacraments in general, it is especially true of the sacrament they call the Eucharist (what Lutherans also call the Lord's Supper, Holy Communion, or the Sacrament of the Altar). The Second Vatican Council describes the Eucharist as "the source and summit of the Christian life,"[82] and Rome's *Code of Canon Law* calls it "the most august sacrament."[83] In its preaching and teaching, the

Catholic Church constantly seeks to instill a Eucharistic piety in its people. Participating in the Eucharist is viewed as the highest expression of unity within the Catholic Church.

When we examine the official Catholic teaching on this sacrament today, we must come to the conclusion that Lutherans and Catholics remain as divided on this teaching as they were at the time of the Reformation. Our two primary objections to Catholic teaching on the Eucharist relate to (1) how Catholics try to explain the real presence of Christ's body and blood in the Sacrament (*transubstantiation*) and (2) how they turn the sacrament, which is Christ's gift of his body and blood to us for forgiveness of our sins, into a propitiatory sacrifice that people offer to God. Along with these two primary objections, two other Catholic teachings that Lutherans reject as unscriptural are (3) Communion in one kind (*concomitance*) and (4) worship of the Eucharistic elements. Let's examine each of these four differences.

Transubstantiation

Transubstantiation is the teaching developed during the Middle Ages that the *substances* (the essential characteristics) of bread and wine are *changed into* the substances of Christ's body and blood. According to Catholic teaching, after the priest consecrates the elements, only the *accidents* (the outward forms and appearances) of bread and wine remain. In other words, the elements look, taste, and feel like bread and wine, but that is only on the surface. Their *substance* has actually been changed into Jesus' flesh and blood.

Transubstantiation is a human attempt to use the philosophy of Aristotle to explain the humanly unexplainable—the miracle of the *real presence* of Christ's body and blood in the Sacrament. Lutherans reject transubstantiation as an unscriptural and unnecessary human speculation.

Scripture clearly affirms both the reality of the earthly, physical elements of bread and wine and says that they are present in the Lord's Supper in a natural way. The apostle Paul refers to the bread in the Lord's Supper as *bread:* "Is not the bread that we break a participation in the body of Christ?" (1 Corinthians 10:16b). And in reference to the cup of wine, Paul parallels its content with that of the bread. He told the Corinthians: "Whenever you eat this bread and drink this cup, . . . whoever eats the bread or drinks the cup, . . . ought to examine himself before he eats of the bread and drinks of the cup" (1 Corinthians 11:26-28).

Scripture also affirms that the body and blood of Christ are really present in the Sacrament in a supernatural way. Christ clearly affirmed this in the words of institution of his Supper: "Take and eat; this is my body. . . . Drink from it, all of you. This is my blood of the covenant, which is poured out for many for the forgiveness of sins" (Matthew 26:26-28).

Therefore, according to Scripture, Lutherans confess in the words of Luther's Small Catechism: "It is the true body and blood of our Lord Jesus Christ, under the bread and wine, for us Christians to eat and drink, instituted by Christ himself."[84] And in the words of another Lutheran Confession, the Smalcald Articles:

> Of the Sacrament of the Altar, we hold that the bread and wine in the Supper are Christ's true body and blood. . . . As for transubstantiation, we care nothing about the sophistic cunning by which they [Roman Catholics] teach that bread and wine leave or lose their own natural substance so that only the appearance and color of bread remain, and not true bread. For it is in perfect agreement with Holy Scriptures that there is, and remains, bread, as Paul himself calls it, "The bread that we break" [1 Corinthians 10:16].[85]

In spite of the fact that Scripture affirms the presence of bread and wine in the sacrament, Rome has declared transubstantiation to be a divine doctrine and damns all who reject its teaching. In the words of the Council of Trent:

> If anyone says that in the sacred and holy sacrament of the Eucharist the substance of the bread and wine remains conjointly with the body and blood of our Lord

> Jesus Christ, and denies that wonderful and singular change of the whole substance of the bread into the body and the whole substance of the wine into the blood, the appearances only of bread and wine remaining, which change the Catholic Church most aptly calls transubstantiation, let him be anathema.[86]

The dogma of transubstantiation has been reaffirmed by recent popes, Paul VI and John Paul II, after liberal Catholic theologians in the 1960s questioned whether the philosophical reasoning behind transubstantiation was valid and suggested alternative philosophical theories. The *Catechism of the Catholic Church* also reiterates Trent's teaching on transubstantiation.[87] Lutherans continue to reject any and all philosophical explanations as unnecessary and presumptuous because they either go beyond or deny clear Scripture.

The sacrifice of the Mass

The second main error in Catholic teaching on the Lord's Supper (or Eucharist) is their idea that the Lord's Supper is a sacrifice *people* offer to God. They call the sacrament the *sacrifice* of the *Mass* (Mass is another name for Eucharist).

When Jesus instituted his New Testament Supper, his words of institution made it clear that here he was giving his disciples a *gift,* namely, his true body and blood to eat and drink for the forgiveness of sins. Rome has turned this gift from God into a sacrifice, which is a meritorious *work,* that man does for God. According to the Council of Trent:

> Inasmuch as in this divine sacrifice which is celebrated in the mass is contained and immolated in an unbloody manner the same Christ who once offered Himself in a bloody manner on the altar of the cross, the holy council teaches that this is truly propitiatory.[88]
>
> Canon 1: If anyone says that in the mass a true and real sacrifice is not offered to God . . . , let him be anathema.
>
> Canon 3: If anyone says that the sacrifice of the mass is one only of praise and thanksgiving; or that it is a mere commemoration of the sacrifice consummated on the

> cross but not a propitiatory one; or that it profits him only who receives, and ought not to be offered for the living and the dead, for sins, punishments, satisfactions, and other necessities, let him be anathema.[89]

In Catholic teaching, Christ offered himself as a sacrifice for sin *in a bloody way* on the cross. In the Eucharist, the priest offers up Christ again and again as a sacrifice for sin but *in an unbloody way.* Catholics today mostly avoid saying that Christ is re-sacrificed in the Mass. They prefer saying that it is one and the same sacrifice that is re-presented (in the sense of "made present again") over and over again. Nevertheless, they hold that the sacrifice of the Mass is a true sacrifice for sin.

Vatican II and the *Catechism of the Catholic Church* have reaffirmed the sacrifice of the Mass as a propitiatory sacrifice for the sins of the living and the dead (in purgatory).

> As often as the sacrifice of the cross by which "Christ our Pasch [Passover] is sacrificed" (1 Cor. 5:7) is celebrated on the altar, the work of our redemption is carried out.
>
> Through the ministry of priests the spiritual sacrifice of the faithful is completed in union with the sacrifice of Christ the only mediator, which in the Eucharist is offered through the priests' hands in the name of the whole Church in an unbloody and sacramental manner.
>
> By the celebration of Mass they [priests] offer Christ's sacrifice sacramentally.[90]

Regarding the Eucharistic sacrifice, the *Catechism of the Catholic Church* states:

> The Eucharist is thus a sacrifice because it re-presents (makes present) the sacrifice of the cross, because it is its *memorial* and because it *applies* its fruit:
>
> [Christ], our Lord and God, was once and for all to offer himself to God the Father by his death on the altar of the cross, to accomplish there an everlasting redemption. But because his priesthood was not to end with his death, at the Last Supper "on the night when he was betrayed," [he

> wanted] to leave to his beloved spouse the Church a visible sacrifice (as the nature of man demands) by which the bloody sacrifice which he was to accomplish once for all on the cross would be re-presented, its memory perpetuated until the end of the world, and its salutary power be applied to the forgiveness of the sins we daily commit. (*Catechism,* n. 1366.)
>
> The sacrifice of Christ and the sacrifice of the Eucharist are one single sacrifice: "The victim is one and the same: the same now offers through the ministry of priests, who then offered himself on the cross; only the manner of offering is different." "And since in this divine sacrifice which is celebrated in the Mass, the same Christ who offered himself once in a bloody manner on the altar of the cross is contained and is offered in an unbloody manner. . . ." (*Catechism,* n. 1367.)

Rome's teaching about the Eucharistic sacrifice doesn't stop with re-sacrificing Christ (or making his sacrifice present again and offering it as a true sacrifice for sin). The personal sacrifices of the priest and the laity are mixed together with Christ's sacrifice, and in the Eucharist all of this together is offered up to God as a propitiatory sacrifice for the sins of the living and the dead. According to Vatican II's teaching: "Taking part in the eucharistic sacrifice, the source and summit of the Christian life, they [the people of God] offer the divine victim to God and themselves along with it."[91]

Expounding on this teaching, Catholic theologian James O'Connor states:

> The realization that the Mass is the sacrifice of Christ and of the church also helps toward an understanding of how each Mass is itself a sacrifice and not just an effective memorial of Calvary. To say that the Mass adds nothing to the sacrifice of the Cross is an imperfect understanding of how Christ effects our redemption. . . . By Christ's will, we bring more than Christ and his offering to the Father.

> As sacrificial offerings we also bring ourselves and our own lives with their joys and sufferings. Taken up into the sacrifice of Christ, these too become part of the sacrifice of praise and propitiation presented to the Father. Thus, each Mass is a sacrifice in which something new is being offered, the constant accumulation of what the members of Christ offer with and in him. In this way, in each sacrifice, *the members of the Body add their own merits to the merits of Christ.* (Italic added.)[92]

Lutherans have always rejected the Catholic sacrifice of the Mass in the strongest of terms.[93] Turning the Sacrament of the Altar into the sacrifice of the Mass denigrates and denies the "once for all" nature of Christ's sacrifice on the cross, which Scripture so emphatically declares:

> Such a high priest meets our need—one who is holy, blameless, pure, set apart from sinners, exalted above the heavens. Unlike the other high priests, he does not need to offer sacrifices day after day, first for his own sins, and then for the sins of the people. He sacrificed for their sins *once for all* when he offered himself. (Hebrews 7:26,27, italic added.)

> Christ did not enter a man-made sanctuary that was only a copy of the true one; he entered heaven itself, now to appear for us in God's presence. *Nor* did he enter heaven *to offer himself again and again,* the way the high priest enters the Most Holy Place every year with blood that is not his own. Then Christ would have had to suffer many times since the creation of the world. But now he has appeared *once for all* at the end of the ages to do away with sin by the sacrifice of himself. Just as man is destined to die once, and after that to face judgment, so Christ was sacrificed *once* to take away the sins of many people; and he will appear a second time, not to bear sin, but to bring salvation to those who are waiting for him. (Hebrews 9:24-28, italic added.)

The Catholic Church teaches that the Eucharist is a sacrifice for sins and then adds to this their denial that the principal benefit of this sacrament is that sinners receive the forgiveness of sins: "If anyone says that the principal fruit of the most Holy Eucharist is the remission of sins, or that other effects do not result from it, let him be anathema."[94] It is simply baffling that a church can say such a thing in spite of Jesus' clear statement at the Last Supper that his disciples were to receive the bread and wine/body and blood "for the forgiveness of sins."

What does Catholic theology teach about the blessings of the Eucharist? The *Catechism of the Catholic Church* states it this way: "As bodily nourishment restores lost strength, so the Eucharist strengthens our charity, which tends to be weakened in daily life; and this living charity *wipes away venial sins*" (n. 1394). Here again we see Catholic theology thoroughly tainted by its work-righteousness approach: the Eucharist gives God's "grace," that is, his helping power, which helps sinners do good works (charity), which helps them overcome their venial sins (those sins that aren't all that serious).

Lutherans have always rejected Rome's teaching of the sacrifice of the Mass as crass work-righteousness, which strikes at the very heart of the gospel of God's unconditional forgiveness of all our sins. In the Smalcald Articles, Luther states:

> The Mass in the papacy has to be the greatest and most horrible abomination, since it directly and powerfully conflicts with this chief article [the gospel]. Above and before all other popish idolatries the Mass has been the chief and most false. For this sacrifice or work of the Mass is thought to free people from sins, both in this life and also in purgatory. It does so even when offered by a wicked scoundrel. Yet only the Lamb of God can and will do this [John 1:29], as said above. Nothing of this article [the gospel of justification by faith] is to be surrendered or conceded, because the first article does not allow it.[95]

The previous two sections dealt with the two main errors that Lutherans identify in Catholic teaching about the Eucharist. Let's briefly look at two more errors.

Communion in one kind (concomitance)

Jesus clearly commanded that both the bread and the wine be distributed to his disciples: "Take eat; . . . Drink from it, all of you" (Matthew 26:26,27). Communion *in both kinds* was the practice of the apostles. "For whenever you eat this bread and drink this cup, you proclaim the Lord's death until he comes" (1 Corinthians 11:26). However, at the Fourth Lateran Council (1215), the pope and the bishops decreed that from then on the laity were to receive Communion in only one kind—the bread. The wine was to be reserved for the clergy alone, specifically for the priest celebrating the Mass.

To justify this practice in the face of Jesus' clear command to his disciples, Catholic theologians developed a theory called *concomitance,* according to which wherever Christ's body is present, his blood is also present in the body. Logical as such an explanation may sound, it doesn't get around the fact that withholding the cup from the laity disobeys Christ's express command and institution for his Supper. When Lutherans at the time of the Reformation restored Communion in both kinds to the laity, Rome responded as usual with curses and condemnations.[96] Communion in one kind for the laity remained the Catholic practice until Vatican II in the 1960s, which called for opportunities for the laity to once again receive Communion in both kinds. In doing so, however, the pope and the bishops still maintain that they and they alone have the authority in the church to decide such things and not the revealed Word of God in the Bible.[97]

Eucharistic worship (adoration)

The Catholic teaching of transubstantiation holds that after the priest consecrates the physical elements of bread and wine, these elements are no longer present; only Christ's body and blood are present on the altar. This has led to the Catholic practice of adoring (worshiping) the consecrated elements. A consecrated host (one of the bread wafers that in Catholic teaching has been turned into Christ's body) is enshrined in a special receptacle in Catholic churches. Catholics worship this wafer because they believe it isn't bread anymore but has been completely changed into Christ's body.

In the 1200s, the Roman church instituted the festival of Corpus Christi (Latin for "body of Christ"). In this festival the clergy, in a public procession, carry around a consecrated host that the people worship. Lutherans reject such practices as superstition. Regarding Corpus Christi processions and other similar practices, the Lutheran Confessions state:

> It is taught that the elements or the visible species or forms of the consecrated bread and wine must be adored. However, no one—unless he is an Arian heretic—can and will deny that Christ Himself, true God and man, is truly and essentially present in the Supper. Christ should be adored in spirit and in truth in the true use of the Sacrament, as He is in all other places, especially where his congregation is assembled.[98]

Lutherans certainly worship and adore Christ in the Sacrament, where he is truly present with his body and blood. We believe his Word, and on the basis of Christ's promises there, we eat and drink Christ's body and blood given and poured out for us for the forgiveness of sins. However, Lutherans reject such practices as saving the consecrated host in a special receptacle in church so that people can bow down and worship it.

Liberalizing trends

This section presents a brief note on a liberalizing trend in what some Catholics believe and teach about the Eucharist, which seems to depart somewhat from official teachings of the past. Recent popes have been reiterating transubstantiation and the sacrifice of the Mass. This is because various theologians have been downplaying, ignoring, or "reinterpreting" these doctrines. As was noted in the chapter on justification, some Catholics, reflecting modern secularizing influences, have been downplaying the doctrine of sin and any need for sin to be atoned for by a sacrifice—even Christ's sacrifice on the cross! They have downplayed the Eucharist as a propitiatory sacrifice, that is, a sacrifice offered for our sins. Liberal Catholics refer to it only as a sacrifice of praise and thanksgiving.

While some might think this brings Catholic and Lutheran views closer together, it does not. What seems to motivate liberal Catholics is not a desire to return to Jesus' clear words of institution recorded in Scripture but to evaluate the Eucharist using modern philosophy. Consider how one Catholic theologian sums up the modern view of the Eucharist:

> A key characteristic of sacramental theology in the second half of the 20th century has been the shift from thinking about the sacraments as objects that dispense grace to perceiving them as relational events of encounters between God and humankind. It was Edward Schillebeeckx who helped us to begin viewing the Church and its sacraments as genuine, human encounters with God in the Spirit of the Risen Christ. . . . Both Schillebeeckx and [Karl] Rahner as well as others who followed them opened the field of inquiry concerning sacramental liturgy to profound range and depth of human experience, including those embodied, symbolic ways in which we meet God through our relating with one another.[99]

(Edward Schillebeeckx and Karl Rahner were liberal Catholic theologians, from Holland and Austria respectively, who were very influential at the time of the Second Vatican Council and in the years following the council.)

It seems that such views are also being accepted at least to some extent among the Catholic laity, especially those who attend Mass less than every week. A 2008 nationwide survey of adult American Catholics' religious beliefs revealed that 43 percent of American Catholics believe that the Eucharistic bread and wine merely symbolize the body and blood of Christ. In other words, they do not believe that they are literally eating and drinking the true body and blood of Christ in the Sacrament, only bread and wine. Many American Catholic bishops have expressed alarm at this trend and acknowledge a crisis in catechetical training (or lack of it) of many Catholic laity in the years since the Vatican II council.[100]

THE SACRAMENTS—*Part 2*

Penance and Reconciliation

When we looked at Baptism in the previous chapter, we noted that according to Catholic teaching the only sins God forgives in Baptism are original sin and actual sins committed prior to Baptism. Baptism does not offer forgiveness for any sins committed after Baptism. Another sacrament is needed if the sins committed after Baptism are to be forgiven. The Sacrament of Penance and Reconciliation does this. Another common name for this sacrament is Confession, which is what Catholics are referring to when they speak of "going to Confession."

Lutheran confession and absolution

Catholics point to Matthew 16:19; 18:18; and John 20:23 as the place where Penance was instituted in Scripture. Lutherans believe that in these passages Christ entrusted his disciples with his gospel message of proclaiming God's forgiveness to sinners. Specifically, we are to announce God's forgiveness to all repentant sinners, that is, to those who are sorry for their sins and acknowledge that by breaking God's laws they deserve his wrath and his temporal and eternal punishment. But the church is to withhold the announcement of God's forgiveness from impenitent sinners, that is, from those who are not sorry for their sins. Because of their impenitence, they remain without God's forgiveness. The church proclaims Christ's gospel message of forgiveness when individual Christians comfort one another with the gospel. The church carries out this same gospel ministry in a public way when its called ministers announce God's forgiveness of sins in the Absolution and when they proclaim it in sermons. In order to receive absolution individually, Christians may also confess their sins privately to their pastor. Martin Luther found great comfort in this individual reception of forgiveness, as he also did in the Sacrament of the Altar. The Lutheran Confessions speak very favorably about retaining the practice of private confession in the church so that pastors can personally absolve parishioners of their sins.

The Lutheran teaching on confession and absolution, rid of the errors and abuses of the medieval church, is summarized in Luther's Small Catechism:

> **How the Unlearned Should Be Taught to Confess**
>
> *What is Confession?*
> Answer: Confession has two parts: the one is that we confess our sins; the other is that we receive absolution, forgiveness, from the confessor, as from God Himself, and in no way doubt, but firmly believe that our sins are forgiven before God in heaven by this.
>
> *What sins should we confess?*
> Answer: Before God we should plead guilty of all sins, even of those that we do not know, as we do in the Lord's Prayer. But before the confessor we should confess only those sins that we know and feel in our hearts.[101]

Catholic Penance—a human work

In contrast to the unconditional forgiveness that Christ commanded be proclaimed to repentant sinners, based on his full and complete payment for all sins on the cross, the Roman church has injected works into the Sacrament of Penance and made complete absolution dependent on human works. Specifically, a person must perform three works before he or she can be forgiven: *contrition, confession,* and *satisfaction*.

The *Catechism of the Catholic Church,* quoting from the Council of Trent, defines *contrition* as "sorrow of the soul and detestation for the sin committed, together with the resolution not to sin again" (n. 1451). The catechism goes on to make a distinction between "perfect" contrition and "imperfect" contrition. Perfect contrition is said to be based on love for God. Imperfect contrition is borne out of fear of punishment. "By itself, however, imperfect contrition cannot obtain the forgiveness of grave sins" (n. 1453). Notice how the condition for meriting forgiveness is transferred from Christ's perfect and complete saving work to the sinner's own efforts: Is my act of contrition good enough? Is my heart pure enough? What about my motives? Is my love for God pure enough?

The second work, or condition, required in the Roman Sacrament of Penance is *confession*. All mortal (very serious) sins must be specifically confessed to an ordained Catholic priest. While it is not necessary to confess all venial (less serious) sins to a priest in order to have them forgiven, it is still strongly recommended.[102]

The third work required as a condition for forgiveness is *satisfaction,* to use the Catholic technical term. According to the *Catechism of the Catholic Church*:

> Absolution takes away sin, but it does not remedy all the disorders sin has caused. Raised up from sin, the sinner must still recover his full spiritual health by doing something more to make amends for the sin: he must "make satisfaction for" or "expiate" his sins. This satisfaction is also called "penance." (n. 1459)

The priest imposes on the penitent what he deems to be an appropriate penance to make up for the sins confessed. Even though the priest pronounces absolution to the penitent before he or she has performed the required acts of penance, the absolution remains conditional, depending on the performance of the penance. What is usually included in penance? The *Catechism of the Catholic Church* states: "[The penance] can consist of prayer, an offering, works of mercy, service of neighbor, voluntary self-denial, sacrifices, and above all the patient acceptance of the cross we must bear" (n. 1460). Lutherans note that in all these various acts, nothing is mentioned of faith, which trusts God's promise of unconditional forgiveness in Christ.[103]

According to Catholic teaching, only a validly ordained priest in the Catholic Church or in one of the Eastern Orthodox churches can administer this sacrament because only those churches have valid and true ministries—the "apostolic succession" of bishops.[104] Accordingly, Catholics believe that when Lutheran Christians hear their pastors pronounce the words of absolution to them: "I forgive you all your sins in the name of the Father and of the Son and of the Holy Spirit," they are hearing only empty words that do not really give God's forgiveness.

Lutherans also note that besides promoting work-righteousness, the Catholic Sacrament of Penance is inherently legalistic in another way. The role of the priest in Confession is that of a judge, very similar to judges in civil courts of law. It is the priest's role in Confession, like the judge in a court of law, to examine the defendant, to find out all the details of the defendant's crimes, and to impose the appropriate punishment. In this regard the Council of Trent states:

> Although the absolution of the priest is the dispensation of another's bounty, yet it is not a bare ministry only, either of proclaiming the Gospel or of declaring that sins are forgiven, but it is after the manner of a judicial act, by which sentence is pronounced by him as by a judge.[105]
>
> If anyone says that that the sacramental absolution of the priest is not a judicial act but a mere service of pronouncing and declaring to him who confesses that the sins are forgiven, provided only he believes himself to be absolved, . . . let him be anathema.[106]

The Catholic Church has also decreed that it is a law that all Catholics must go to Confession at least once a year during the Easter season (anytime between Ash Wednesday and Trinity Sunday).

Penance since Vatican II

Vatican II called for the revision of all the liturgical and sacramental rites of the Catholic Church, including Penance. In the revised rites of Penance, more emphasis is placed on the priest being a merciful, fatherly, forgiving figure than a judge who imposes punishments to "expiate" for sins committed. The new rites have allowed for a corporate confession of sins, that is, when a group of Catholics confess their sins together. This has proven to be very popular among many Catholics. But the Vatican has stipulated that priests cannot pronounce the absolution to the group as a whole. A valid absolution can be pronounced only when an individual Catholic has confessed his or her specific sins to a priest in private.

Here is the rite of corporate confession that has been used at the beginning of the Catholic Mass in the United States since Vatican II:

I confess to almighty God,
and to you, my brothers and sisters,
that I have sinned through my own fault
in my thoughts and in my words,
in what I have done,
and in what I have failed to do;
and I ask blessed Mary, ever virgin,
All the angels and saints,
And you my brothers and sisters,
To pray for me to the Lord our God.

Notice how the prayer to God for forgiveness quickly lapses into prayers to Mary and the saints for help—all without any mention of Christ! The words of the priest then follow:

May almighty God have mercy on us,
Forgive us our sins,
and bring us to everlasting life.[107]

We notice here that the priest's words are not a pronouncement of God's unconditional forgiveness for Christ's sake but only a mere wish for God's forgiveness (again without any mention of Christ's saving work).

It is ironic that in spite of Rome's attempts after Vatican II to make the Sacrament of Penance more appealing to Catholics, the result has been just the opposite. Compared to participation in the Sacrament of Penance prior to Vatican II, participation since Vatican II has drastically declined. According to "Sacraments Today," the report of the findings of the 2008 nationwide survey of US Catholic religious beliefs and practices, only 26 percent of adult Catholics go to Confession at least once a year. Thirty percent say they go to Confession less than once a year, and 45 percent say they never go. Furthermore, 62 percent of Catholics agree "somewhat" or "strongly" with the statement, "I can be a good Catholic without celebrating the sacrament of Reconciliation at least once a year."[108] Clearly, long gone are the days when "going to Confession" regularly, or even at least once a year, was a clear hallmark of practicing Catholics in the United States.

Anointing of the Sick

Lacking Christ's institution

According to Lutheran teaching about sacraments, a rite is not a sacrament just because the church says so. A genuine Christian sacrament has to have been clearly instituted by Christ during his ministry on earth. The institution requires Christ's explicit command to his church to use earthly elements along with his specific words that promise the forgiveness of sins. Lutherans reject the Catholic Sacrament of Anointing of the Sick because it lacks Christ's institution—the church as a whole is not commanded to use this rite, there are no words of institution, and the promise of forgiveness is lacking.

How then can Catholics claim Anointing of the Sick to be a true sacrament? Once again, the matter goes back to the basis on which the church determines doctrine. Is doctrine based on what the church says or is doctrine based on what God's Word says? Catholic theologian Joseph Martos, speaking about the historic differences between Catholics and Protestants on the sacraments, sums it up this way: "For Catholics, however, the ultimate authority was God's word spoken through the church; for the Protestants it was God's word spoken through the scriptures."[109]

How, then, did the Anointing of the Sick originate and develop into a Catholic sacrament? Rome points to Jesus' instruction to the apostles when he sent them out on what is sometimes called their first missionary tour, recorded in Mark 6:7-13. Jesus "gave them authority over evil spirits" (verse 7). And Mark tells us: "They went out and preached that people should repent. They drove out many demons and anointed many sick people with oil and healed them" (verses 12,13). Jesus spoke of anointing with oil and healing in his instructions to his disciples. However, no mention is made of Jesus instituting a permanent sacrament for the church of all time. Nor did he say that the anointing with oil necessarily conveyed supernatural healing power. The anointing with oil seems to have had a symbolic purpose similar, perhaps, to when Jesus healed a blind man by taking saliva and making a little muddy paste, which he wiped on the blind man's eyes. Then he instructed the man to wash in the pool of Siloam in Jerusalem, at which time his sight was restored (John 9:1-7). What is more, the book of Acts records many healing miracles performed by the apostles in the name of the Lord, but it never mentions the use of oil. None of the New Testament epistles mention a sacrament of healing instituted by Christ for his church for all times.

James tells the readers of his epistle:

> Is any one of you sick? He should call the elders of the church to pray over him and anoint him with oil in the name of the Lord. And the prayer offered in faith will make the sick person well; the Lord will raise him up. If

> he has sinned, he will be forgiven. Therefore confess your sins to each other and pray for each other so that you may be healed. The prayer of a righteous man is powerful and effective. (5:14-16)

James clearly states that any healing comes as a result of God hearing and answering prayers for a sick person, not from the anointing with oil as such.[110] Lacking corroboration in the gospels and other epistles, James seems to be referring to a *customary* use of oil by the church of his day rather than as a sacrament like Baptism or the Lord's Supper.

The historical development of anointing

How, then, did the Sacrament of Anointing develop to what it is today in the Catholic Church? Catholic theologian Richard McBrien admits that

> there is, for all practical purposes, no evidence in the early centuries for the actual rite of Anointing. . . . The first documentary item for the sacrament is provided by a letter of Pope Innocent I (d. 417) to Decentius, bishop of Gubbio. . . . This letter became a basic source for the later Roman and early medieval period, inasmuch as it was incorporated into the most important canonical collections and thus became the starting point for theological discussion of the sacrament. . . . Nowhere in the early tradition does one find mention of the Anointing as a sacrament of preparation for death.[111]

McBrien notes that by the 9th century the Anointing had "morphed" from a healing rite for the sick into "last rites" for the dying. By the 12th century, it was called Extreme Unction (*extreme* from the Latin word for "last" and *unction* from the Latin word for "anointing") and numbered as one of the seven sacraments. It infused a special "grace" to the dying Christian to forgive sins and to help keep him or her in a state of grace.

In the 16th century, Luther and the other reformers rejected Anointing as a sacrament because unlike Baptism and the Lord's Supper, it lacks Christ's institution. Likewise,

Scripture attaches no promise of grace and forgiveness to any such rite. At the same time, the reformers pointed out that the spiritual help and strengthening that God gives to believers facing sickness and death are the gospel promises contained in the Bible, which are clearly attached to Baptism and the Lord's Supper.

The Council of Trent reaffirmed the medieval Catholic doctrine of the Anointing and defined it primarily as the "last rites" for the dying. Only an ordained priest could administer the rite. The only oil allowed was olive oil, and the oil had to be blessed by a bishop for its use to be valid. The doctrine and practice prescribed by Trent remained in effect until the 1960s, when the Second Vatican Council revised the church's teaching.

Vatican II and changes in the Anointing of the Sick

The Second Vatican Council called for a change in Extreme Unction:

> "Extreme Unction," which may also and more fittingly be called "Anointing of the Sick," is not a sacrament for those only who are at the point of death. Hence, as soon as anyone of the faithful begins to be in danger of death from sickness or old age, the fitting time for him to receive this sacrament has certainly already arrived.[112]

This was not a simple name change, however, but a shift back to the earlier view reflected by Pope Innocent I in the 5th century. Richard McBrien describes the revised rite that was put into effect in 1972 by the authority of Pope Paul VI:

> The ritual elements include a greeting, words to those present, a penitential rite (Scripture, litany), the priest's laying on of hands, blessing of oil, prayer of thanksgiving, the anointing of the forehead and hands with oil with the words, "Through this holy anointing may the Lord in his love and mercy help you with the grace of the Holy Spirit;" and "May the Lord who frees you from sin save you and raise you up." There is a

prayer after anointing, the Lord's Prayer, Communion, and a blessing.[113]

This reflects a shift in emphasis. According to the *Catechism of the Catholic Church,* Anointing is "especially intended to strengthen those who are being tried by illness" (n. 1511). The specific "graces" given in this sacrament are now said to be the Holy Spirit, who gives strength and courage to bear one's illness; healing of the soul; healing of the body, if it is God's will; and the forgiveness of sins.[114]

The anointing helps the sick unite themselves with Christ's sufferings on the cross so that the suffering of the sick may "contribute to the good of the People of God."[115] In other words, this sacrament is supposed to help people make their suffering "redemptive," that is, a good work that contributes to their salvation.

On the surface, it seems that the new rite of Anointing is intended to serve as a more integral part of the church's pastoral care of souls than the old pre-Vatican II rite, which often appeared arcane and impersonal. It was spoken in Latin in a rote, impersonal, almost magical way and administered to people who often had already lost most of their faculties. The new rite is much more personal, and it seems to be well received among Catholics. According to the nationwide survey of US Catholics cited previously, 51 percent of the respondents (which includes both practicing and nominal Catholics) had requested Anointing either for themselves or for a family member. About three-fourths of Catholics polled said they consider it "somewhat important" to "very important" to receive Anointing at some point in their lives. Among active, practicing Catholics, 93 percent said that this sacrament is "somewhat" to "very" important for them.[116]

Matrimony

Marriage, a divine institution

Both Lutherans and Catholics teach that marriage is a divine institution, established by God in the beginning when he created Adam and Eve, as recorded in Genesis 1:26-28 and 2:18-24. (We are not taking into account here that most contemporary Catholic theologians and recent popes promote higher-critical views of Genesis, which deny that the first chapters of Genesis present historical events that actually happened.)

Both confessional Lutheran bodies and the Catholic Church teach that marriage, as God intended it, is a lifelong union between one man and one woman. The two are to live together in marital faithfulness to each other with God himself reserving the right to end the marital bond through the death of one of the spouses. Both church bodies also see divorce as contrary to God's will and therefore sinful. Both also teach as contrary to the Sixth Commandment all sexual activity outside the sacred bonds of marriage and reject as contrary to God's will such aberrations as polygamy and so-called homosexual marriages. Likewise, Lutherans and Catholics agree (to some extent) that God's purposes for marriage include:

- Companionship—"It is not good for the man to be alone. I will make a helper suitable for him. For this reason a man will leave his father and mother and be united to his wife, and they will become one flesh" (Genesis 2:18,24).
- Procreation, the producing of children—"Be fruitful and increase in number" (Genesis 1:28).
- Preservation of sexual purity for men and women—"It is better to marry than to burn with passion" (1 Corinthians 7:9).

I will show later why the agreement between Lutherans and Catholics on the purposes for marriage is only a partial agreement.

Is marriage a sacrament?

In spite of substantial agreement between confessional Lutherans and Catholics on marriage, there is also significant disagreement. The Catholic Church goes beyond Scripture when it claims that Christ elevated marriage to the level of a sacrament. While Christ was on earth, he taught about matters of marriage, adultery, and divorce (see, for example, Matthew 5:27-32 and 19:3-12) and confirmed that God instituted marriage for the human race in the beginning. However, Christ did not establish marriage as a sacrament of the Christian church. There are no words of institution; no command to use an earthly element along with God's Word; and no promise of the forgiveness of sins, eternal life, and salvation connected to marriage, even in regard to the marriage of Christians. Rome makes no attempt to find evidence in the gospels that Christ instituted a sacrament of marriage. It simply declares that Christ must have raised marriage to a sacrament because popes and church councils have declared it to be so. The Council of Trent, for example, declared:

> If anyone says that matrimony is not truly and properly one of the seven sacraments of the evangelical law, instituted by Christ the Lord, but has been devised by men in the Church and does not confer grace, let him be anathema.[117]

Marriage denigrated

At the same time that Trent exalted marriage by calling it a sacrament, it also denigrated marriage by affirming the medieval Catholic teaching that celibacy is a higher, more spiritual, and more holy way to live and serve God. Again, quoting from the Council of Trent:

> If anyone says that the married state excels the state of virginity or celibacy, and that it is better and happier to be united in matrimony than to remain in virginity or celibacy, let him be anathema.[118]

The exaltation of celibacy over marriage has a long history in the Catholic Church. In the centuries after the apostles, many people in the Mediterranean world, including many Christians, were influenced by the pagan philosophies of Stoicism and Neoplatonism, which looked down on the physical world, including the human body. Christians who were influenced by these philosophies viewed all physical pleasures as sinful. This contributed to the rise of *asceticism* in the church, that is, an emphasis on such things as constant fasting and self-denial. Living a celibate life came to be viewed as a more holy and spiritual—a more God-pleasing—way of life than marriage.

By the late 4th century, the very influential bishop Augustine of Hippo taught that the natural sexual desires between men and women, *even within marriage,* are all sinful. The sexual relation within marriage came to be viewed as little more than a necessary evil for producing children. Celibacy and virginity were the only morally pure, chaste, and holy estates. This led church councils and popes to make decrees forbidding the clergy to marry, and it also fueled the false teaching of work-righteousness. By the time of Luther in the 16th century, the institution of *monasticism* (spiritual associations of men and women who took various vows, among which was a vow of lifelong celibacy) pervaded Christendom.

One way in which this asceticism affected Catholic teaching on marriage involves what is called the *ends,* or purposes, of marriage. It was mentioned before that Scripture teaches various purposes, the primary purpose being that spouses provide a blessed companionship for each other, including sexual happiness. The producing of children is the second purpose of marriage.

Under the influence of asceticism and Augustine's theology for more than 15 centuries, Catholics have taught that procreation was *the* purpose of marriage. Vatican II seems to have shifted that emphasis slightly by including in its documents references to the unitive purpose of marriage along with the procreative purpose. However, the old emphasis of procreation as primary was not explicitly repudiated. As a result, Catholic theologians continue to debate exactly what has changed in the Catholic teaching on marriage and what has not.[119]

Birth control

Because of the amount of publicity it continues to receive in the news media, the Catholic teaching on birth control is widely known. The Catholic Church does not forbid married couples to space out or limit the number of children they have. What the church does absolutely prohibit is any and all artificial methods of contraception (barrier methods, chemical methods, sterilization, etc.) for family planning. The only method of birth control allowed is natural family planning, sometimes referred to as the rhythm method.

During Vatican II many Catholics were looking for the council to possibly reverse the church's position on contraception. Pope John XXIII, however, removed the topic of contraception from the council's agenda. He appointed a commission of experts to study the issues involved. His successor, Pope Paul VI, expanded the commission. When it became public that a majority of members of the papal commission recommended relaxing the ban on contraception, many Catholics, including many priests and theologians, truly expected that the pope would follow the advice of the majority of the commission. So when Pope Paul VI issued his encyclical on birth control in 1968, titled "On Human Life" (*Humanae Vitae* in Latin), many Catholics were shocked and bitterly disappointed.

The pope begins his encyclical by invoking his power as the vicar of Christ on earth to be the absolute teaching authority on all moral issues and the final interpreter of both God's written law in the Bible and the natural law implanted in all people's hearts by their Creator. The pope also restated the historic Catholic teaching on papal authority, namely, that the "faithful fulfillment" of the written and natural law, as taught by the pope, is "necessary for salvation."[120]

In the key sentence of the encyclical, the pope decrees: "Each and every marriage act must remain open to the transmission of life."[121] The pope goes on to say, "Similarly excluded is every action which, either in anticipation of the conjugal act, or in its accomplishment, or in the development of its natural consequences, proposes, whether as an end or as a means, to render procreation impossible."[122] Here the pope, in so many words, also forbids the husband to withdraw from sexual intercourse before ejaculation (*coitus interruptus*).

Pope Paul VI was only reiterating traditional Catholic teaching. Nevertheless, his encyclical caused a firestorm of protest in the Catholic Church. Catholic theologians all over the world signed public letters of protest and published them in several of the world's leading newspapers. Many Catholic priests simply refused to teach the pope's encyclical to the people in their parishes. Even many bishops were slow to come publicly to the pope's defense. Pope Paul VI never issued another encyclical, even though he reigned as pope for ten more years until his death in 1978.

Even though Pope Paul VI's encyclical did not teach anything new about birth control in the Catholic Church, the vast majority of Catholic married couples in western countries have chosen to ignore his statements. It has been estimated that about 80 percent of Catholics in the United States use artificial contraception as part of their family planning.[123] How do they justify this in view of the pope's teaching? More liberal, antiauthoritarian Catholics might say, "Celibate old men in Rome have no business telling me and my spouse what we can do or not do in our bedroom." More conscientious conservative Catholics might say things like "The pope's teaching is a good ideal to strive for, but my spouse and I aren't quite there yet."

It should be mentioned that Paul VI's encyclical makes no attempt to ground papal teaching in Scripture. The pope simply invokes his authority as the vicar of Christ on earth to interpret the natural law for the whole human race. It is certainly scriptural that God gave the gift of sex as a blessing and responsibility to be enjoyed within marriage. It also is God's will that his command to "be fruitful and increase in number" be carried out within the bonds of marriage. But it simply goes beyond Scripture to say that *every* sexual act between husband and wife must be *both* unitive (expressing marital love) *and* procreative (trying to conceive). To Lutherans, it seems that the Catholic teaching on birth control is much more focused on methods than motives, as it seeks to guide married couples in matters of family planning. (A full presentation on the moral issues involved in family planning and birth control is beyond the scope of this book.[124])

Divorce, annulment, remarriage

As noted previously, the Catholic Church, along with confessional Lutheran bodies, teaches that the marriage covenant is indissoluble. However, the Catholic Church's teaching on this truth does not line up with how Jesus teaches it. Jesus says, "What God has joined together, let man not separate" (Matthew 19:6). However, Scripture also recognizes that sinful humans have the power to act contrary to God's will and in the process break the marriage bond even before the death of a spouse. Adultery, by its very nature, breaks the marriage bond (Matthew 5:32; 19:9). Malicious desertion, by its very nature, also breaks the marital bond (1 Corinthians 7:10-15). Scripture teaches that a married Christian who innocently suffers the adultery or desertion of an unfaithful spouse may in such circumstances with a good conscience seek a divorce and some day enter into a second marriage.

The Catholic Church, on the other hand, teaches that humans not only *should not* break up marriages but that they *cannot* break them up. The Catholic Church does not recognize civil divorces. In the eyes of the church, a divorced couple is still married, even though the spouses may have split up, gone their separate ways, and even remarried.

Contrary to a common misconception, divorce in the Catholic Church is not regarded as an "unforgivable sin." Divorced Catholics remain "in the good graces" of the Catholic Church and may continue to receive Holy Communion. But if a divorced Catholic (even the innocent party in a previously broken marriage) remarries, he or she is banned for life from receiving Holy Communion.

The Catholic position on divorce and remarriage lays an unscriptural, torturous burden on the consciences of Christians who have innocently suffered a divorce because of the unfaithful action of their spouses. Its teaching imposes the same burden on unfaithful spouses who may later repent of their sin and as part of the fruit of their repentance seek God's help in living according to his will in a second marriage.

The way out of this situation for divorced Catholics who wish to remarry in the church is to seek an annulment for a previous marriage before a *tribunal* (a Catholic Church court), similar to what happens in civil courts. An annulment doesn't declare that "this marriage has ended." Rather, it declares, "This marriage never existed," even if the couple was married for many years and was blessed with children.

Up until about 1970, marriage annulments in the Catholic Church were very rare; a few hundred annulments were granted a year worldwide. Civil courts declare marriages annulled if one of the persons did not enter the marriage of his or her free and conscious consent and in cases of bigamy. In the 1970s, however, the Catholic Church started allowing "psychological reasons" as grounds for annulment. Catholic marriage annulments have skyrocketed, especially in the United States, where Catholic Church courts interpret "psychological reasons" very liberally. Divorced Catholics who wish to remarry and still remain in the good graces of the Catholic Church now seek annulments on the grounds that they were "psychologically or emotionally immature" at the time they got married. In the early 1960s, Catholic Church courts in the United States granted about three hundred annulments a year. By the 1990s, the number had grown to more than 60,000 a year.[125]

This drastic rise in annulments has led some people, including Catholics, to refer to the whole annulment business as "divorce Catholic style." It should also be pointed out that "easy annulments" is a particularly US Catholic phenomenon. By comparison to the Catholic Church in the United States, the Catholic Church in Italy (which has about the same number of Catholics as the United States) grants only about three hundred annulments a year. The situation has led recent popes and other high Vatican officials to complain repeatedly to the US Catholic bishops.

The Canon Law Society of America has reported that since 2006 both the number of applications for marriage annulments and the number of annulments granted has declined to about 35,000 a year.[126] Concerning the reasons for this recent downward trend in annulments, Catholic journalist John Allen states: "That may be partly because [Catholic Church] courts have become tougher. But it's probably more related to the fact that fewer Catholics are getting married in the church, and fewer of those who are bother to seek an annulment if their marriage breaks down."[127]

Lutherans certainly cannot claim immunity from marital sins any more than Catholics can. Lutherans, like Catholics, are influenced by the anti-Christian views that prevail in much of today's culture regarding sex, marriage, and having children. But God's people are led to repent of their marital sins, to be strengthened in their faith in Christ's forgiveness, and to live holy lives with God's help only through the faithful preaching and teaching of God's revealed Word in the Scriptures. To add man-made church laws that go beyond what God's Word teaches regarding marriage only burdens consciences.

Holy Orders (Ordination)

The final sacrament we want to consider in the Roman Catholic system is Holy Orders (sometimes loosely referred to as Ordination). We're considering it last because the entire Roman sacramental system and the spiritual power it exercises over people's souls is made to hang on the Roman view of the Sacrament of Holy Orders, which conveys this power to the ordained priesthood. The *Catechism of the Catholic Church* states:

> Holy Orders is the sacrament through which the mission entrusted by Christ to his apostles continues to be exercised in the Church until the end of time: thus it is the sacrament of apostolic ministry. It includes three degrees: episcopate, presbyterate, and diaconate. (n. 1536)

The catechism goes on to explain why this sacrament is called *Orders*. It is because this sacrament gives to a man a special "grace" that integrates him into the order of bishops, presbyters (priests), or deacons (nn. 1537,1538). In other words, Holy Orders places some men into a special spiritual class of people above regular church members.

Common versus ministerial priesthood

According to Catholic teaching, even though the Christian laity are said to make up a "baptismal or common priesthood," they have no actual spiritual power. They do not possess the gospel, and they cannot use the keys (Matthew 16:19; 18:17,18). They cannot tell penitent sinners that Jesus died to pay for all their sins and that therefore God forgives them for Jesus' sake. They cannot issue a public call to a minister of their own choosing to serve them. They cannot judge whether their priest is teaching according to God's Word or not because they do not possess God's Word. These powers belong exclusively to the bishops and priests, the ordained clergy, whom Catholics call the "ministerial priesthood." Only bishops and priests possess and can use the gospel. They, and they alone, serve as the mediators between God and sinners because only they, and they alone, can offer the sacrifice of the Mass for the sins of the living and of the dead in purgatory. They, and they alone, can offer the sacraments. They, and they alone, possess all spiritual power and authority in the church. Although one of the major themes of Vatican II was the importance of the Christian laity, the council clearly stopped short of saying that lay believers possess the keys (the gospel) and can use them. That authority remains solely with the priests and bishops.[128]

Indelible character

Catholics teach that Holy Orders gives priests and bishops an "indelible (permanent) character." This character is what gives them the power to transubstantiate bread and wine and to offer the sacrifice of the Mass for the sins of the living and the dead in purgatory. The indelible character conferred on a priest empowers him to perform five of the seven sacraments (not Confirmation, except with special permission from the bishop, and never Holy Orders). Bishops, who have the highest authority and power in the Catholic clergy hierarchy, claim that they alone have the power to perform the Sacrament of Holy Orders.

Catholics don't say it this way, but it would not be unfair to say that in the Catholic system the bishops are the means of grace. All of God's gifts of grace and salvation are funneled through them and secondarily through the priests.

The indelible character teaching means "once a priest always a priest." Once a man is ordained as a priest, his priesthood can never be taken away from him. This seems to be a contributing factor to the fact that the Catholic Church in the past has put much emphasis on trying to "rehabilitate" priests who have been guilty of great moral failings, including the crime of sexual abuse of children. Even if a priest is "laicized" (reduced to the status of a common church member) and completely stripped of all rights to conduct priestly functions, he is still a priest forever because of the indelible character he supposedly received at ordination. It is interesting to note that in spite of all the importance the Catholic Church places on the indelible character, it has never defined precisely what that character is.

Ordained deacons

Ordained deacons are the lowest rank of those who receive Holy Orders in the Catholic Church. Deacons, like priests and bishops, must be baptized adult males. Their sacramental role in the church, by comparison, is rather limited. They may perform baptisms, assist priests at the altar with the Eucharist, assist priests in marriage ceremonies, and they are allowed to preach in church. They cannot preside at Mass or hear confessions (including telling penitent sinners that their sins are forgiven for Christ's sake).

Priestly celibacy

As is well known, the Roman Catholic Church forbids its ordained clergy to marry, with few exceptions. According to Catholic Church law, bishops and priests must be single (celibate) at the time of ordination and remain celibate. If a man was married prior to being ordained a deacon, he may remain married. If he was single when he is ordained as a deacon, he must remain celibate. If a married deacon's wife dies after his ordination, he cannot remarry.

The history of celibate clergy in the Catholic Church is long and fairly complicated and beyond the scope of this book to present in detail. Suffice it to say that celibacy was not always the rule in the church. The New Testament speaks of married clergy as the norm. The apostle Paul stated that ministers, including himself and the other apostles, had the right to marry. Paul says that Peter was married (1 Corinthians 9:5). The gospels speak of Peter's mother-in-law (Matthew 8:14; Mark 1:29,30). In Paul's lists of qualifications for the church's ministers, he states that a minister is to be "the husband of but one wife" and "must manage his own family well" (1 Timothy 3:2,4,5,12). Although Jesus himself was not married, he never imposed celibacy on others, including the apostles.

There is no conclusive historical evidence that celibacy was practiced or imposed on the clergy in the period leading up to the Council of Nicaea in A.D. 325. A resolution to make celibacy obligatory for all clergy was proposed at the Council of Nicaea and rejected. In the centuries following that time, the bishops of Rome and various regional councils repeatedly tried to impose celibacy on the clergy. It wasn't until the time of Pope Gregory VII (1073–1085) and the First and Second Lateran Councils (1123 and 1139) that a concerted effort was made to impose celibacy universally in the Western (Latin) church on all priests and bishops.

The reasons for imposing mandatory celibacy also have a detailed history. Briefly, as we mentioned in the previous section on marriage, in the centuries after the apostles, the church became infected with strains of pagan philosophical thinking and an asceticism that denigrated marriage and the sexual union within marriage. Celibacy was viewed as a higher, more spiritual, more holy estate than marriage. In the time of Pope Gregory VII, moral corruption among the clergy was rampant. There was also the problem of the children of clergymen inheriting church land and property that the pope thought should not pass out of the ownership of the church. The pope's solution was an absolute and universal ban on married clergy, even to the point of forcing already married priests and bishops to abandon and drive away their wives and children.[129]

In recent times, the "sex is dirty—even in marriage" reason for clergy celibacy has been downplayed in favor of the reason that priests are less distracted from their callings as priests if they are celibate. Another, more theological-sounding reason is the bride-groom analogy. The church is the bride and Christ is the groom; since priests are Christ's representatives on earth—"stand-ins" for Christ—they should view themselves as married to the church, Christ's bride. Although this reason sounds a little more theological, the official Catholic position is that mandatory priestly celibacy is not a *doctrine* of the Catholic Church but only a *discipline*. This means the pope can change it at anytime he chooses. Recent popes have made special exemptions from the celibacy rule for married clergy from other Christian denominations who convert to Catholicism and then seek to become ordained Catholic priests. But so far, the general rule of mandatory clergy celibacy remains in force.

Male-only priesthood

While priestly celibacy is a mandatory discipline imposed by the pope, the ban on the ordination of women into the priesthood is considered to be a doctrine that cannot be changed. While it is possible that the present or some future pope might relax the celibacy rule, that does not seem likely in regard to women's ordination. If there was any question about this after Vatican II, Pope John Paul II seemed to slam the door shut on it when he issued a papal decree in 1994 called "*Ordinatio Sacerdotalis*: Reserving Priestly Ordination to Men Alone." This is the key sentence in the document:

> Wherefore, in order that all doubt may be removed regarding a matter of great importance, a matter which pertains to the Church's divine constitution itself, in virtue of my ministry of confirming the brethren (cf. Lk 22:32) I declare that the Church has no authority whatsoever to confer priestly ordination on women and that this judgment is to be definitely held by all the Church's faithful.[130]

The pope's strongly worded statement hasn't stopped all clamoring in the Catholic Church for equal rights for women to be ordained, but any such efforts appear at this time to be futile. What the Catholic Church has done in lieu of women's ordination is to allow women to serve in a great variety of administration and leadership roles in parishes and dioceses. Women today who serve as parish administers are in effect the pastors of parishes. They do everything short of presiding at the sacraments, which only a priest can do. The Catholic Church has no doctrine of the role of woman in the church based on the order of creation as taught in the Bible (Genesis 2:18-24; 1 Corinthians 11:3-16; 14:33-35; 1 Timothy 2:11-15).[131] Rome's main argument today for male-only priests is that when priests prepare sacraments, especially the Eucharist, they are acting "in the person of Christ." Since Christ was a male, his priests must also be males.

The Lutheran response to Holy Orders

Confessional Lutherans respond to Rome's teaching on Holy Orders by confessing, first of all, that the only ministerial, mediatorial priesthood in the New Testament is that of Jesus Christ himself. The book of Hebrews says:

> When Christ came as high priest of the good things that are already here, he went through the greater and more perfect tabernacle that is not man-made, that is to say, not a part of this creation. He did not enter by means of the blood of goats and calves; but he entered the Most Holy Place once for all by his own blood, having obtained eternal redemption. For this reason Christ is the mediator of a new covenant, that those who are called may receive the promised eternal inheritance—now that he has died as a ransom to set them free from the sins committed under the first covenant. (9:11,12,15)

See all of Hebrews chapters 7–10, which explains that the entire Old Testament ministerial priesthood and its entire repeating sacrificial system was fulfilled and completed once for all by Christ and his sacrifice on the cross. The Old Testament system was not replaced in the New Testament with another ministerial priesthood and repeating sacrificial system. In line with Scripture, Lutherans therefore reject the need for any ongoing mediatorial priesthood that has to offer the propitiatory sacrifice of the Mass over and over again.

The only human priesthood recognized in the New Testament is the royal priesthood of all believers in Christ. Writing to Christians, the apostle Peter says:

> You also, like living stones, are being built into a spiritual house to be a holy priesthood, offering spiritual sacrifices acceptable to God through Jesus Christ. But you are a chosen people, a royal priesthood, a holy nation, a people belonging to God, that you may declare the praises of him who called you out of darkness into his wonderful light. (1 Peter 2:5,9)

And in Revelation, speaking of all Christians, the apostle John writes: "To him who loves us and has freed us from our sins by his blood, and has made us to be a kingdom and priests to serve his God and Father—to him be glory and power for ever and ever! Amen" (1:5,6; see also 5:10 and 20:6). The only sacrifices that New Testament believers offer to God are the spiritual sacrifices of thanksgiving that consist of their entire lives dedicated to joyful service to their Lord in thankful response to his grace and salvation (Romans 12:1).

The church's public ministers of the gospel are never called priests in the New Testament. The New Testament speaks of a variety of offices, or forms, of the public ministry: apostles, prophets, evangelists, pastors, and teachers (Ephesians 4:11); overseers and deacons (1 Timothy 3:1,12); and elders (Titus 1:5). The church's ministry is a service of preaching the gospel and administering the sacraments, of calling sinners to repentance and preaching the forgiveness of sins in Jesus' name (Luke 24:47). The only spiritual authority and power in Christ's church is God's Word, and this spiritual authority belongs to the entire church of believers, not just to the apostles and their "successors." Paul wrote to the members of the church in Corinth, "All things are yours" (1 Corinthians 3:21). There are no divinely established ranks of authority among the church's ministers, only differences of responsibilities (Matthew 23:8-11).

The right and privilege to serve in the public ministry comes only from God through the church that calls ministers today (Romans 10:15), not through the right of a so-called apostolic succession (Acts 20:28).

The laying on of hands mentioned in Scripture is a Christian custom, dating back to the time of the apostles, not a divine sacrament commanded by Christ that gives the recipient an indelible character (1 Timothy 4:14; 5:22; 2 Timothy 1:6). The custom of laying on of hands at the ordination and/or installation of a pastor is the church's way of showing in a public and orderly way that a man has been called into the church's public gospel ministry. Lutherans continue to observe this fine church custom without associating any unscriptural meaning to it.

Sacramentals

Besides the seven sacraments, the Catholic Church encourages the devotional use of various physical objects and bodily actions that can supposedly bring special blessings to the people who use these objects or perform these actions in a devotional way. These objects and actions are called sacramentals. They include such things as holy water, crucifixes, candles, church bells, and rosaries, and making the sign of the cross, bowing, kneeling, genuflecting, and folding one's hands and bowing one's head in prayer.

Catholics do not claim that sacramentals were instituted by Christ or are commanded by God's Word. Rather, they were instituted by the church. Nevertheless, sacramentals are said to convey special "graces" and blessings to the people who use them properly.

The Question and Answer Catholic Catechism describes sacramentals this way:

> Sacramentals are objects or actions the Church uses in order to confer blessings on the faithful through the merits of the Mystical Body of Christ [the Roman Catholic Church]. . . .
>
> Unlike the sacraments in which Christ confers grace through the sacrament itself, they are forms of prayer that obtain grace through the merits of the Church and depend on the dispositions of the person who uses sacramentals. And, unlike the sacraments, they do not really produce the extraordinary and distinctive grace they signify but are the occasion for receiving some blessing from God through the Church because a person uses sacramentals with faith.[132]

Notice the element of work-righteousness in this definition ("through the merits of the Church and depend on the dispositions of the person who uses sacramentals"). What the exact blessings are for those who use sacramentals seem to be left deliberately vague because it all depends on the needs of the person using them.

Catholic teaching on sacramentals also holds that sacred objects (crucifixes, candles, rosaries, etc.) which are blessed by a priest or bishop convey certain blessings. "The blessing of the priest or bishop confers on the object blessed a special title of God's protection and assistance, or its being set aside for the exercise of divine worship."[133]

What makes Catholic holy water "holy" is the fact that it is not just plain water but water specially blessed by a priest or bishop. Once again, we notice the special mediatorial role of the priests and bishops in the Catholic religion.

What are Lutherans to make of Catholic sacramentals? Lutherans should not use sacred actions and objects that are so directly and deeply associated with unscriptural false teaching and superstition that they cannot be used without partaking in the error. Using rosary beads to pray the Rosary would be an example. On the other hand, Lutherans in their Christian freedom make use of church bells, crosses, crucifixes, candles, and religious pictures and statuary in good conscience without attaching any superstitious meaning to them. They use them as symbolic reminders of biblical teachings. The same is true for certain bodily actions, such as folding one's hands in prayer, bowing one's head, and making the sign of the cross. Such actions do not bring special blessings "through the merits of the Church." They express in a symbolic way the faith and religious devotion of the heart without in any way attaching superstitious beliefs to them.

When Lutherans discuss the use of sacramentals with their Catholic friends, they may find their friends expressing a variety of practices and beliefs, from an almost Lutheran view to a highly superstitious view. At the same time, it is probably also fair to generalize that the more Catholicism has pervaded the people of a particular region and culture, especially where there is no competition from Bible-teaching Protestants, such as in Latin America until recently, the more such practices and beliefs are shot through with superstition. This is generally true for formal church practices, but it is especially true in regard to the folk practices of piety that people carry on in private.

Talking with a Catholic friend about sacramentals may provide an opening for sharing your faith, but it can also lead to arguments about secondary matters. Better to steer the conversation toward Christ and his work of salvation—complete, full, free, and received by faith in Christ alone without condition or qualification.

For Further Reading

On Sacraments in General

Adolf Hoenecke, *Evangelical Lutheran Dogmatics,* Volume IV (Milwaukee: Northwestern Publishing House, 1999), pp. 49-80.

On the Seven Sacraments

Martin Chemnitz, *Examination of the Council of Trent,* Vol. 2 (St. Louis: Concordia Publishing House, 1978), the entire volume.

Lyle W. Lange, *God So Loved the World* (Milwaukee: Northwestern Publishing House, 2005), pp. 477-533.

On the Anointing of the Sick

Mark Jeske, *James, 1,2 Peter, 1,2,3 John, Jude,* in The People's Bible series (Milwaukee: Northwestern Publishing House, 2002).

David Kuske, "Exegetical Brief: James 5:14—'Anoint Him With Oil,'" *Wisconsin Lutheran Quarterly,* Vol. 102, No. 2 (Spring 2005), pp. 125-127.

Mark K. Rogers, "An Exegetical and Historical Study of the Anointing With Oil," *Lutheran Synod Quarterly,* Vol. 40, No. 4 (December 2000), pp 262-305.

On Holy Orders and the Priesthood

John F. Brug, *The Ministry of the Word* (Milwaukee: Northwestern Publishing House, 2009), pp. 253-276.

8 MARY *and the Saints*

The cult of Mary and the saints is tightly woven into the spiritual fabric of the Catholic religion. The word *cult* in this context does not refer to some exotic, non-Christian sect but to everything involved in how one venerates or devotes oneself to something, in this case, to Mary and the saints. In general, the cult of Mary and the saints involves asking them to intercede on behalf of the petitioner before God, believing that Mary and the saints play an active role in one's salvation.

Mary

Probably no Catholic doctrine and expression of Catholic piety provokes a more negative reaction from Lutherans than its Marian doctrine and spirituality. Lutherans see Catholics praying the Rosary and other prayers to Mary, asking her to intercede before God on their behalf. They hear Catholics heaping titles of honor on Mary, such as Our Mother, Queen of Heaven, Queen of the Universe, Mediatrix of All Graces, and Co-Redemptrix (*trix* is a Latin feminine ending, so the words mean "female mediator" and "co-redeemer").

Lutherans might ask their Catholic friends, "How can you believe and do such things that border on blasphemy and are tantamount to idolatry?" To which Catholic friends would likely reply with the same amount of surprise: "How can we not love and honor Mary? No one was (and still is) closer to Jesus than his own mother. Jesus loved and honored his mother, and so should we. If we love Jesus, how can we not also love and honor Mary for being Jesus' mother?"

The actual issues over which Catholics and Lutherans differ on Mary go much deeper than the way that a Catholic might typically express his or her pious feeling toward her. The Marian doctrines of Catholicism include the following:

Teachings on which we agree

Mary was a virgin when Jesus was born.
Mary is the mother of God.

One on which there is only partial disagreement

Mary has perpetual virginity.

Those Lutherans must completely reject

Mary had an immaculate conception and is sinless.
Mary ascended bodily into heaven.
Mary is the Mediatrix, Co-Redemptrix, and Mother of the Church.
Mary should be venerated (worshiped).

The virgin birth

Lutherans and Catholics agree on the teaching of the virgin birth of Jesus, the scriptural teaching that Jesus was miraculously conceived in the womb of the virgin Mary by the power of the Holy Spirit without a human father (Isaiah 7:14; Matthew 1:18-25; Luke 1:26-38). Lutherans agree with Catholics that Jesus was miraculously conceived and born of the virgin Mary, but not because popes and church councils have decreed it but because the Bible clearly teaches it.

Mary is the mother of God

The other teaching on which Lutherans and Catholics agree is that Mary is the mother of God. This statement grew out of discussions in the early church over Jesus' divine nature. While the title itself is not found in Scripture, it is used to convey a scriptural teaching about the *Christ*. The firstborn son of Mary was not just a human being but was also true God—God and man in one person from the very moment of his incarnation. Everything Jesus did for us as our Savior—including being born for us, living a perfect life for us, dying for our sins, rising from the dead—he did as the God-man, which gives infinite value to his saving work for us sinners. The baby boy that Mary carried in her womb and gave birth to is the second person of the Holy Trinity, the eternal Son of God, who had taken on human flesh.

Lutherans and Catholics agree that calling Mary the mother of God does not in any way mean that Mary was the source of Jesus' divinity, but that the son to whom Mary gave birth by the power of the Holy Spirit is God himself. The Lutheran Confessions affirm this scriptural teaching in the Formula of Concord: "We believe, teach, and confess that Mary conceived and bore not merely a man and no more, but God's true Son. Therefore, she is rightly called and truly is 'the mother of God.'"[134]

At the same time, Lutherans hold that Scripture never uses Mary's physical relationship with Jesus as a reason for exalting her in the ways the Catholic Church does. In fact, the Catholic exaltation of Mary goes counter to Scripture in any number of ways.

Perpetual virginity of Mary—"ever-virgin"

There are two matters to think about under this heading. First, the Catholic Church teaches that it is a divine doctrine that Mary's womb remained physically closed before, during, and after Jesus' birth. Second, it teaches that Mary remained a virgin and celibate her entire life and that Jesus' "brothers and sisters" were his cousins. I have placed a discussion of these teachings in the partial agreement category because Lutherans do not categorically reject that they *could have* happened.

According to the *Catechism of the Catholic Church*:

> The deepening of faith in the virginal motherhood led the Church to confess Mary's real and perpetual virginity even in the act of giving birth to the Son of God made man. In fact, Christ's birth did not diminish his mother's virginal integrity but sanctified it. . . . Against this doctrine the objection is sometimes raised that the Bible mentions

brothers and sisters of Jesus. The Church has always understood these passages as not referring to other children of the Virgin Mary. (nn. 499,500)

When Catholics refer to the virgin birth, they mean that when Mary gave birth, the baby Jesus miraculously left her womb without physically opening it (*utero clauso*), similar to how Jesus entered the room where the apostles were hiding on Easter evening, miraculously appearing in their midst even though the doors were closed and locked (John 20:19). Lutherans concede that Jesus, the God-man even as a baby, could have passed from his mother's womb in such a miraculous way. But Scripture is silent about the matter, and so the Catholic error is that they teach it as a divinely revealed doctrine.

The Catholic Church also teaches that Mary and Joseph had no sexual relations after Jesus' birth and, in line with this, that Jesus' brothers and sisters were his cousins. The error—and this is the principle objection that Lutherans have to this teaching—is that the Catholic Church by its own authority has decreed its interpretation of Jesus' brothers and sisters to be a doctrine. The most natural way to understand the references in the Bible to Jesus' brothers and sisters, however, is that they were in fact Jesus' literal half-brothers and half-sisters, children born to Joseph and Mary after Jesus (Matthew 12:46-50; 13:55,56; Mark 3:31-35; 6:3; Luke 8:19-21; John 2:12; 7:2-5; Acts 1:14).[135]

What seems to drive the Catholic doctrine of Mary's perpetual virginity goes back to the early centuries of the Christian church. The pagan religious philosophy of Gnosticism taught that the "spirit" is good and the ultimate reality. The physical "body" is bad, a prison for the spirit. Salvation consists of the spirit being liberated from the physical body. Such views wormed their way into many Christians' thinking. According to such thinking, it would have been more fitting for Jesus to be born in a way that was more "spiritual" and less "physical" or "bodily." And having sexual relations within marriage was considered to be inferior to a celibate relationship. Lutherans reject such teachings as coming from pagan religious philosophy and as foreign to the Scriptures.

The immaculate conception of Mary

The Catholic teachings about Mary that are considered from this point on are unscriptural, and so they are teachings on which Lutherans and Catholics disagree.

The *immaculate conception* refers not to Jesus' conception but to the Catholic teaching that Mary was conceived without original sin (the hereditary sinful corruption of human nature inherited from our parents since the fall of Adam and Eve). Not all Catholic theologians accepted this teaching, and so it was debated within the Catholic Church for many centuries, until finally in 1854, Pope Pius IX solemnly decreed it to be an infallible dogma of the Catholic Church. The decree is contained in these words:

> We declare, pronounce, and define that the doctrine which holds that the most Blessed Virgin Mary, in the first instant of her conception, by a singular grace and privilege granted by Almighty God, in view of the merits of Jesus Christ, the Savior of the human race, was preserved free from all stain of original sin, is a doctrine revealed by God and therefore to be believed firmly and constantly by all the faithful.
>
> Hence, if any shall dare—which God forbid!—to think otherwise than as has been defined by us, let him know and understand that he is condemned by his own judgment; that he has suffered shipwreck in the faith; that he has separated from the unity of the Church.[136]

Where in Scripture do Catholics claim to find this dogma? Simply, they don't claim to find it in Scripture! Consider the honest admission of the orthodox Roman Catholic theologian Ludwig Ott: "The doctrine of the Immaculate Conception of

Mary is not explicitly revealed in Scripture."[137] Instead, Ott and most other Catholic theologians state that the immaculate conception is *implied* in Genesis 3:15 and Luke 1:28. Genesis 3:15 proclaims God's first promise of the Savior after Satan had tempted Adam and Eve into sin. Speaking directly to Satan, the Lord said, "I will put enmity between you and the woman, and between your offspring and hers; he will crush your head, and you will strike his heel." The woman in this verse is clearly Eve. Her "offspring" ("seed" in Hebrew) who will crush the serpent's head, that is, destroy the devil's power over sinners, is Christ. The prophecy contains no direct reference to Mary. But that has not stopped Catholic theologians from this reasoning: Since Christ is mentioned, and no one was closer to Christ than his own mother, it follows that Mary was also involved with crushing the serpent's head and destroying Satan's power. Accordingly, Mary would not have been able to help Jesus destroy Satan unless she was perfectly free from sin, including the original sin inherent at birth—thus the immaculate conception! This is how Catholics "interpret" the Bible when it doesn't actually teach their doctrines. The doctrine is developed by Sacred Tradition (invented by men) and then read into Scripture passages that, by Catholics' own admission, don't actually teach it.

The other Scripture passage that Catholics constantly cite as the source of their Marian doctrines is Luke 1:28, the angel's greeting to Mary when he announced that God had chosen her to be the mother of the Savior: "The angel went to her [Mary] and said, 'Greetings, you who are highly favored! The Lord is with you.'" Catholics rely on Saint Jerome's (who lived roughly 342–420) somewhat faulty Latin translation "full of grace" (*gratia plena* in Latin). Then they read into the angel's greeting the medieval Catholic definition of *grace,* as God's power that helps people do good works—a life in which the person works with God to become better and better and in this way merits salvation. Since Mary was "full" of this power, she must have been holy her entire life, totally without sin, including original sin. In line with this reasoning, Luke 1:28 implies Mary's immaculate conception!

There is another common argument of human reason that Catholics often employ: How could Jesus have been without sin if his mother was sinful? For Jesus to have been conceived without sin, his mother must have also been without sin. Catholics continually use arguments like this in spite of the fact that many early church fathers (bishops and theologians) clearly taught from Scripture that Mary was a sinner like the rest of humanity and in need of a Savior. Catholics today are not bothered by these facts of history. They simply state that it took time for the church to develop the doctrine and incorporate it into the body of Sacred Tradition. Indeed, it took more than 18 centuries until it was infallibly defined by Pope Pius IX in 1854.

Lutherans reject the immaculate conception because Scripture declares that all human beings since Adam and Eve have been born sinful:

> We have already made the charge that Jews and Gentiles alike are all under sin. As it is written: "There is no one righteous, not even one; there is no one who understands, no one who seeks God. All have turned away, they have together become worthless; there is no one who does good, not even one." For all have sinned and fall short of the glory of God. (Romans 3:9-12,23)

When Scripture speaks in such absolute terms, there are no exceptions unless Scripture itself explicitly tells us there are. And it does. There is an exception, but only one—Jesus Christ (Hebrews 4:15). Every other human being is born a lost and condemned sinner in need of God's forgiveness for their sins. Mary herself recognized this scriptural truth and confessed her need of a Savior (Luke 1:47).

The bodily assumption of Mary

The *bodily assumption* of Mary simply means that at the end of her life she was taken directly to heaven. There is certain "logic" to the development of this Catholic doctrine concerning Mary. If Mary was conceived without sin and remained sinless her entire life, doesn't it seem reasonable that death, which is "the wages of sin" (Romans 6:23), would have had no hold over her?

It took many centuries before the doctrine of Mary's bodily assumption into heaven began to develop in the Catholic Church. And when it did, it was based on references in nonscriptural books written in the 5th and 6th centuries. This literature tries to pass itself off as coming from the apostles, but actually reflects a growing body of legends about Mary, which are not found in Scripture. Protestant theologian Elliot Miller describes this literature as follows: "The accounts are filled with fantastic, absurd miracles, are written in poor taste, and contain bad theology. Yet historians recognized them to be the source from which the doctrine of Mary's assumption arose."[138] Even some of the early bishops of Rome condemned this literature, called *transitus* literature (from the Latin word for *passing* to eternal life), as false and spurious.[139]

It took 18 centuries of "development" before the doctrine of the immaculate conception of Mary was infallibly defined by Pope Pius IX as a divinely revealed dogma. Ninety-six years later, in 1950, Pope Pius XII infallibly defined the dogma of the bodily assumption of Mary with these words:

> By the authority of our Lord Jesus Christ, of the Blessed Apostles Peter and Paul, and by our own authority, we pronounce, declare, and define it to be a divinely revealed dogma: that the Immaculate Mother of God, the ever Virgin Mary, having completed the course of her earthly life, was assumed body and soul into heavenly glory.
>
> Hence if anyone, which God forbid, should dare willfully to deny or to call into doubt that which we have defined, let him know that he has fallen away completely from the divine and Catholic Faith.[140]

But what *scriptural* proof do Catholics offer for this dogma? The answer is the same here as it was for the immaculate conception. Catholic apologist Karl Keating's answer to that question is revealing: "Strictly there is none. It was the Catholic Church that was commissioned by Christ to teach all nations and to teach them infallibly. The mere fact that the Church teaches the doctrine of the Assumption as something definitely true is a guarantee that it *is* true."[141]

The argument the pope's decree uses to establish the "truth" of the assumption is a deceptively attractive argument of human reason that Catholic theologians have used since the Middle Ages to establish doctrines not found in Scripture. It goes like this: (1) God can do all things; (2) it was fitting that he do it; therefore (3) God did it. Pius XII used this very line of reasoning when he stated in his decree: "Since it was within his [Christ's] power to grant her this great honor, to preserve her from the corruption of the tomb, we must believe that he really acted in this way."[142]

One other thing to note about the pope's decree is that he leaves unanswered whether or not Mary ever died—whether she died and then God raised her body from the dead, glorified it, and took it to heaven, or whether God took Mary, body and soul, directly to heaven at the end of her earthly life. Catholic theologians explain that the verdict is still out on that point of doctrine, waiting for further "development." Meanwhile, most Catholic theologians at this time seem to favor the idea that Mary's earthly life ended first with death, because that would follow the pattern of her Son.

Mary Mediatrix, Co-Redemptrix, Mother of the Church

The "logic" in Catholic teaching about Mary's exalted status also leads them to give her an active role in achieving and dispensing salvation for sinners. Not only does Mary "parallel" Christ as conceived without sin. Not only is she exalted body and soul to the right hand of her Son in heaven. She is also given a parallel role to Christ in the plan of salvation.

In Catholic teaching, Mary is called the *Mediatrix of All Graces*. *Mediatrix* is the Latin word *mediator* with a feminine ending. In English we might say that Mary is the "mediatress" of grace. Although Mary's son, Jesus, is truly a mediator of God's grace, Catholics tend to view him as an angry judge who needs to be placated. And who is in a better position to do that than his mother? Mary can intercede for sinners before her son because she is the perfect mother. And Jesus could never turn down his mother's intercessory requests to have mercy on sinners.

Some Catholic theologians and popes have gone so far as to call Mary the *Co-Redemptrix*. Again, note the feminine form of the Latin word *redemptor*. Mary is Co-Redeemer along with Christ. Christ made salvation possible for sinners by his suffering on the cross. And so did Mary! She stood at the foot of the cross with her son and suffered in her soul too. She added her redemptive suffering to Jesus' redemptive suffering, and together they redeemed and saved the world.

In fact, Catholics mark the beginning of Mary's redemptive work for the world at the point when the angel visited her in Nazareth and announced to her that God had chosen her to be the mother of the promised Messiah. They claim that this happened when Mary responded to the angel by saying, "Let it be to me" ("May it be to me" in the NIV, Luke 1:38). Catholics refer to this act as Mary's *fiat,* which is the Latin for "let it be." With her *fiat,* Mary began actively cooperating with God to earn mankind's salvation. Moreover, her saving work for sinners did not end with her suffering on Calvary. Mary continues working in heaven as mankind's mediator and intercessor before God.

Catholics emphasize that in her saving role, Mary is definitely secondary to Christ, the primary mediator, but she is a mediator nonetheless. Christ is the head and source of all saving graces, but Mary is the "neck" through which all saving graces must flow. For this reason, Mary is called the Mother of the Church. She is also called that because she is the perfect example of a person cooperating with God in doing good works and meriting salvation because of those good works.

Let's let some Catholics speak for themselves on Mary's role in salvation. Consider one of the classic Catholic books on Mary, *The Glories of Mary*, by Saint Alphonsus Ligouri (1696–1787). Ligouri is not only a saint in the Catholic Church, he has also been honored as one of the "Doctors (teachers) of the Church." His famous book has been translated into numerous languages and remains in print in several editions to this day. Here are some samples of Ligouri on Mary:

> As many creatures as there are who serve God, so many they are who serve Mary: for as angels and men, and all things that are in heaven and on earth, are subject to the empire of God, so they are also under the dominion of Mary! (page 3)

> Although Mary is indeed a Queen she is not a Queen of justice, intent on punishing the wicked but a Queen of mercy, intent only on winning pardon and peace for sinners. This is why the Church insists that we call Mary "the Queen of Mercy." (page 4)

> It is as if Christ, the King of Justice and Mercy, has given half the kingdom to Mary, reserving justice to Himself and mercy to her. Christ will come with His strict and avenging justice on the Last Day. It is Mary, anointed with the oil of gladness, who will temper that with mercy by her maternal intercession. (page 4)

> Since Jesus is the Father of our souls, Mary is also their Mother: for she, by giving us Jesus, gave us true life; and afterwards, by offering the life of her Son on Mount Calvary for our salvation, she brought us forth to the life of grace. (pages 7,8)

> Thus it is in every engagement with the powers of hell, we shall always certainly conquer by having recourse to the Mother of God, who is also our Mother, saying and repeating again and again, "We fly to your patronage, O

holy Mother of God: we fly to your patronage, O holy Mother of God." How many victories the faithful have gained by using this short but powerful prayer. (page 10)

St. Bernard exhorts all sinners to have recourse to Mary, invoking her with great confidence; for although the sinner does not himself merit the graces which he asks, yet he receives them because this Blessed Virgin asks and obtains them from God, on account of her own merits. (page 17)

Listen, all you who desire the kingdom of God: honor the most Blessed Virgin Mary and you will find life and eternal salvation. (page 21)

If at the hour of death we have the protection of Mary, what need we fear from all our infernal enemies? (page 31)

We may obtain mercy more quickly from Mary than from Jesus, because Jesus is also a judge who can punish, while Mary exercises mercy as a patroness. . . . Many things are asked from God and are not granted; they are asked from Mary and are obtained. Now why is this? Because God has thus decreed to honor His Mother. (page 48)

Not only is the most Blessed Virgin Queen of heaven and of all the saints, but she is also Queen of hell and all evil spirits: she overcame them valiantly by her virtue. From the very beginning God foretold the victory and empire that our Queen would one day obtain over the serpent, when he announced that a woman should come into the world to conquer him. (page 49. Here he takes Genesis 3:15 to be a prophecy about Mary.)

If we wish to relieve the holy souls in purgatory, let us do so by imploring the aid of our Blessed Lady in all our prayers, and especially by offering the Rosary for them, as that relieves them greatly. (page 87)

Our sins my cause us to fear to approach the Almighty, because it is His infinite majesty that we have offended.

> We must never fear to go to Mary, for in her we shall find nothing to terrify us. (page 97)
>
> Let us, then, devout reader, beg God to grant us, at the moment of death, that the last word on our lips may be the name of Mary. (page 102)[143]

According to *The Glories of Mary,* all authority in heaven and on earth, authority over all creatures including all angels and demons, has been given to Mary. Again, Christ for the most part is viewed as an angry judge who punishers sinners, so we should look to Mary for mercy and forgiveness of sins.

Another important Mariologist in Catholic thought is Saint Louis Marie de Montfort (1673–1716), a French priest and preacher who was roughly a contemporary of Alphonsus Ligouri. Louis Marie wrote a book titled *True Devotion to the Blessed Virgin,* which, like Ligouri's book, has been translated into many languages and is still in print. Pope John Paul II, widely recognized for his pronounced Marian piety, acknowledged that Louis Marie's book had a large influence in shaping his own Marian views and piety. As a young man, he wondered whether he was giving too much attention to Mary at the expense of Christ and whether he should focus more on Christ. Louis Marie's book led him to the conviction that the only way to Christ was through devotion to Mary.[144] Here are a few samples from *True Devotion to the Blessed Virgin:*

> God the Son imparted to his mother all that he gained by his life and death, namely, his infinite merits and his eminent virtues. He made her the treasurer of all his Father had given him as heritage. Through her he applies his merits to his members and through her he transmits his virtues and distributes his graces. She is his mystic channel, his aqueduct, through which he causes his mercies to flow gently and abundantly. (Section 24, page 9.)
>
> Devotion to our Blessed Lady is necessary to attain salvation. . . . Lack of esteem and love for the Virgin Mary is an infallible sign of God's disapproval. On the other

> hand, to be entirely and genuinely devoted to her is a sure sign of God's approval. (Section 40, page 16.)
>
> The salvation of the world began through Mary and through her it must be accomplished. Mary scarcely appeared in the first coming of Jesus Christ so that men, as yet insufficiently instructed and enlightened concerning the person of her Son, might not wander from the truth by becoming too strongly attached to her. This would apparently have happened if she had been known, on account of the wondrous charms with which the Almighty had endowed even her outward appearance. . . . But in the second coming of Jesus Christ, Mary must be known and openly revealed by the Holy Spirit so that Jesus may be known, loved and served through her. The reasons which moved the Holy Spirit to hide his spouse during her life and to reveal but very little of her since the first preaching of the gospel exist no longer. (Section 49, page 20.)
>
> What Lucifer lost by pride Mary won by humility. What Eve ruined and lost by disobedience Mary saved by obedience. By obeying the serpent, Eve ruined her children as well as herself and delivered them up to him. Mary, by her perfect fidelity to God, saved her children with herself and consecrated them to his divine majesty. (Section 53, page 23.)[145]

Pope John Paul's indebtedness to Louis Marie's book is evident in the fact that when John Paul was consecrated as a bishop, he took as his official motto *Totus Tuus,* a Latin phrase that means "Totally Yours," that is, "I am totally devoted to you, Mary." And such total devotion to Mary is the way to God.

At the time of the Second Vatican Council, many bishops thought it was time for the Catholic Church to infallibly declare Mary to be Co-Redemptrix. Several popes had used the title in their official speeches and messages, but up to this point it had not yet been decreed to be an infallible dogma of the Catholic Church. Other bishops made the argument that the "development" was not yet "mature" and needed more time. An additional concern was that a major emphasis of the council was for the Catholic Church to engage the modern ecumenical movement. The bishops were well aware that if the Catholic Church would make another infallible decree about Mary, of her being Co-Redemptrix no less, it would pour cold water on any possible ecumenical relations with Protestants and Eastern Orthodox Christians. So by a very narrow margin the majority of bishops at the council voted to include a more "tempered" approach to what the council would say about Mary.

Here are a few key sentences from the section on Mary in Vatican II documents:

> 58. The Blessed Virgin advanced in her pilgrimage of faith, and faithfully persevered in her union with her Son unto the cross, where she stood, in keeping with the divine plan, enduring with her only begotten Son the intensity of his suffering, associated herself with his sacrifice in her mother's heart, and lovingly consenting to the immolation of this victim which was born of her.
>
> 59. Finally, the Immaculate Virgin preserved free from all stain of original sin, was taken up body and soul into heavenly glory, when her earthly life was over, and exalted by the Lord as Queen over all things, that she might be the more fully conformed to her Son, the Lord of lords, (cf. Apoc. 19:16) and conqueror of sin and death.
>
> 60. In the words of the apostle there is but one mediator: "for there is but one God and one mediator of God and men, the man Christ Jesus, who gave himself a redemption for all" (1 Tim. 2:5-6). But Mary's function as mother of men in no way obscures or diminishes this unique mediation of Christ, but rather shows its power. But the Blessed Virgin's salutary influence on men originates not in any inner necessity but in the disposition

of God. It flows forth from the superabundance of the merits of Christ, rests on his mediation, depends entirely on it and draws all its power from it. It does not hinder in any way the immediate union of the faithful with Christ but on the contrary fosters it.

62. This motherhood of Mary in the order of grace continues uninterruptedly from the consent which she loyally gave at the Annunciation and which she sustained without wavering beneath the cross, until the eternal fulfillment of all the elect. Taken up to heaven she did not lay aside this saving office but by her manifold intercession continues to bring us the gifts of eternal salvation. . . . By her maternal charity, she cares for the brethren of her Son, who still journey on earth surrounded by dangers and difficulties, until they are led to their blessed home. Therefore the Blessed Virgin is invoked in the Church under the titles of Advocate, Helper, Benefactress, and Mediatrix. This, however, is so understood that it neither takes away anything from nor adds anything to the dignity and efficacy of Christ the one Mediator.

66. Mary has by grace been exalted above all angels and men to a place second only to her Son, as the most holy mother of God who was involved in the mysteries of Christ: she is rightly honored by a special cult in the Church. . . . This cult, as it has always existed in the Church, for all its uniqueness, differs essentially from the cult of adoration, which is offered equally to the Incarnate Word and to the Father and the Holy Spirit.

67. The sacred synod teaches this Catholic doctrine advisedly and at the same time admonishes all the sons of the Church that the cult, especially the liturgical cult, of the Blessed Virgin, be generously fostered, and that the practices and exercises of devotion towards her, recommended by the teaching authority of the Church in

> the course of centuries be highly esteemed. . . . But it strongly urges theologians and preachers of the word of God to be careful to refrain as much from all false exaggeration as from too summary an attitude in considering the special dignity of the Mother of God.[146]

In the years following the council, many Catholics, especially in Western countries, thought that the council called for putting Mary "on ice." Traditional Marian piety and devotions, such as praying the Rosary and *novenas* (a series of prayers said over nine days), were downplayed. But both Pope Paul VI and Pope John Paul II, who of course were the ultimate interpreters and teachers of the council, taught that in no way was Mary to be "put on ice." Pope John Paul II especially sought to reinvigorate Marian devotion and piety in Catholics in his official teaching documents and by his own personal example. While it is true that the council refrained from using the title "Co-Redemptrix" for Mary, it did not disavow it. In the council's view, Vatican II reaffirmed all previous Roman Marian dogmas, as well as Mary's active role in achieving salvation.

During the 1990s, leading up to the year 2000, a major effort was made among Catholics around the world to gather signatures on a petition asking Pope John Paul II to mark the jubilee anniversary of Christianity in 2000 by infallibly decreeing Mary to be Co-Redemptrix. Even though John Paul had made use of the term *Co-Redemptrix* about a half dozen times in his speeches and messages over the years of his pontificate, he did not issue any infallible decree. No doubt his reasons mirrored those of the majority of bishops at Vatican II, namely, that ecumenical relationships with various Protestant churches and especially the Eastern Orthodox church would suffer a serious setback. The pope's nonresponse to the petition drive wasn't so much a "no" as a "not yet."

Lutherans reject the teaching that Mary or anyone else worked and suffered along with Christ to achieve salvation for sinners. They reject the view that Christ is mostly an angry judge who punishes sinners and that sinners need Mary to intercede for them—to soften up Jesus' heart. Scripture teaches that "there is one God and one mediator between God and men, the man Christ Jesus, who gave himself as a ransom for all men" (1 Timothy 2:5,6). Jesus always invited sinners to trust in him as "the way and the truth and the life" and to confess that he alone is the way to God (John 14:6).

One time, when Mary presumed to interfere in her Son's ministry, Jesus gently but clearly rebuked her (John 2:4). Jesus also clearly rejected the notion that any human mother-son relationship gave Mary a special privileged position in his saving kingdom (Matthew 12:48-50). The letter to the Hebrews tells us:

> Since we have a great high priest who has gone through the heavens, Jesus the Son of God, let us hold firmly to the faith we profess. For we do not have a high priest who is unable to sympathize with our weaknesses, but we have one who has been tempted in every way, just as we are—yet was without sin. Let us then approach the throne of grace with confidence, so that we may receive mercy and find grace to help us in our time of need. (4:14-16)

Christ Jesus is our hope (1 Timothy 1:1), not Mary.

Veneration (worship) of Mary

Catholics often defend their veneration of Mary by saying, "We do not *worship* Mary, we only *venerate* her. Worship belongs only to God." What they are referring to is a fine distinction set up by the Catholic Church between two Greek words for worship: *latria* and *doulia. Latria* (worship), they say, belongs only to God; *doulia* (veneration) is given to the saints. Mary, they say, is to be venerated more than the saints. She is to be given *hyperdoulia* (super veneration). Scripture, however, knows nothing of these distinctions.

Catholic apologists, when explaining this distinction to Protestants, will say, "Oh, we don't pray *to* Mary and the saints; we pray to God *through* Mary and the saints." But the distinction between worship and veneration seems to be lost on most Catholics. Catholics commonly speak of praying to Mary and the saints. In fact, the many prayers to Mary and the saints that Catholics are taught by their church are worded in exactly that way. Here are a few of the long-standing Catholic prayers to Mary:

> *Hail Mary:* Hail Mary, full of grace, the Lord is with you! Blessed are you among women, and blessed is the fruit of your womb, Jesus. Holy Mary, Mother of God, pray for us sinners, now and at the hour of our death. Amen.

This prayer to Mary is the predominate prayer in the Rosary. Praying the Rosary consists of the introductory section, comprised of the Apostles' Creed, the Our Father (another name for the Lord's Prayer), three Hail Marys, and the Glory Be to the Father. That is followed by the First *Decade.* A decade consists of saying the Our Father, ten Hail Marys, and the Glory Be to the Father. Praying a complete Rosary consists of praying 15 decades, for a total of 150 Hail Marys. To keep track of how far along they are in praying the Rosary, Catholics use a set of prayer beads, fingering each bead in turn to keep track of how many prayers they have prayed. The set of beads is also called a rosary. Usually Catholics limit themselves to praying a Rosary of five decades.

Here are two more prayers:

> *Salve Regina:* Hail, holy Queen, Mother of mercy; hail our life, our sweetness and our hope. To you do we cry, poor banished children of Eve. To you do we send up our sighs, mourning and weeping in this valley of tears. Turn then, most gracious Advocate, your eyes of mercy toward us. And after this our exile, show us unto the blessed fruit of your womb, Jesus. O clement, O loving, O sweet Virgin Mary.

> *The Memorare:* Remember, O most gracious Virgin Mary, that never was it known that any one who fled to thy

> protection, implored thy help or sought thy intercession, was left unaided. Inspired by this confidence, I fly unto thee, O Virgin of virgins my Mother; to thee do I come, before thee I stand, sinful and sorrowful; O Mother of the Word Incarnate, despise not my petitions, but in thy mercy hear and answer me. Amen.

Examples of such prayers can be multiplied many times over. Lutherans reject them not only because of their content but because praying to anyone other than God is inherently sinful. Prayer is an act of worship (Luke 2:37). It should be reserved for God alone. To pray to a dead person has no foundation in Scripture. While Scripture is full of commands to pray to God, it contains not even a hint that God wants his believers to pray to Mary or the saints. Scripture is full of promises that God will hear and answer the prayers of his believers addressed to him in faith in Jesus' name. There is not even a hint in Scripture that dead people can hear the prayers of people on earth, much less answer them. Lutherans reject prayers to Mary and the other saints as idolatry, a sin against the First Commandment. It leads people away from God-pleasing trust in Christ as the one and only mediator between God and man to placing their faith and trust in Mary and the saints as their mediators, spiritual aids, and helpers.

While we Lutherans do not "venerate" or worship Mary, we do honor her in a biblical way. We teach about Mary what the Bible teaches, no more and no less. We speak of her, as the Bible does, as a humble believer. She was a recipient of God's grace, but she is not a foundation, a source, or a conduit of grace. We rightfully make her words at the wedding of Cana a fitting motto: "Do whatever he [Jesus] tells you" (John 2:5). With God's help, we follow the example that Scripture sets forth of Mary's humble submission to God's good and saving will for us (Luke 1:38). We do not hesitate to confess the miracle that the virgin Mary conceived the Savior by the power of the Holy Spirit, even though we cannot explain this miracle according to human reason (Luke 1:29-37). We speak of Mary as Scripture does and call her truly blessed by God, the blessed virgin Mary (Luke 1:48). Like Mary, we acknowledge that we are sinners in need of a divine Savior (Luke 1:47). And we follow Mary's example in the Bible of addressing our prayers and songs of praise to God alone (Luke 1:46-55).

Apparitions of Mary

Students of Catholic Church history take note of the fact that while Catholics have venerated Mary for centuries, the cult of the Virgin has grown dramatically in the 19th and 20th centuries. A major part of this growth has been the rise in the number of supposed apparitions of Mary. Catholics believe that not only can they communicate with the dead (Mary and the saints) but the dead (particularly Mary) can communicate back to them. This happens through miraculous apparitions. Mary, it is claimed, actually appears to individuals or groups of individuals and gives messages to them.

Visible appearances of Mary are always designated by the geographical place where the apparition occurs. Sites of apparitions become very holy places. Catholics build shrines or churches on them. Pious Catholics make religious pilgrimages to these places, often to pray to the virgin for special favors. Miraculous healings are associated with some sites. Some of the more prominent sites of Marian apparitions are Guadalupe, Mexico (1530); Lourdes, France (1858); and Fatima, Portugal (1917). In their devotion to Mary, Catholics refer to the Marian apparitions as "Our Lady of" followed by the place where she appeared: "Our Lady of Guadalupe," "Our Lady of Lourdes," and "Our Lady of Fatima." Millions of Catholic pilgrims visit these locations every year. A pope's visit to one of them becomes a major media event.

The Marian apparitions noted above have received official Catholic approval as being legitimate and *worthy of pious belief.* Other apparitions may not receive official approval (in other words, the verdict is still out). An example of this is

Medjugorje in Bosnia-Herzegovina. In the early 1980s, six children reported seeing apparitions of Mary and receiving messages from her on a regular basis. Even though the local bishop of Medjugorje never validated the apparitions, maintaining that he is not convinced that anything supernatural occurred, millions of Catholics from all over the world began making pilgrimages to Medjugorje. Travel to Medjugorije waned during the 1990s when Yugoslavia disintegrated and civil war ensued throughout the region. But since the end of the civil war, travel to Medjugorje has picked up again. The Vatican formed a commission to look into the phenomenon of Medjugorje, but it has yet to reach any conclusion.

What do Lutherans make of such so-called apparitions of Mary and all of the alleged miracles associated with them? We do not automatically dismiss all such phenomena by saying that nothing really happened. Scripture asserts that "Satan himself masquerades as an angel of light" (2 Corinthians 11:14). And regarding the Antichrist, Scripture says, "The coming of the lawless one will be in accordance with the work of Satan displayed in all kinds of counterfeit miracles, signs and wonders, and in every sort of evil that deceives those who are perishing" (2 Thessalonians 2:9,10). God, speaking through Moses, told his people Israel:

> If a prophet, or one who foretells by dreams, appears among you and announces to you a miraculous sign or wonder, and if the sign or wonder of which he has spoken takes place, and he says, "Let us follow other gods" (gods you have not known) "and let us worship them," you must not listen to the words of that prophet or dreamer. The LORD your God is testing you to find out whether you love him with all your heart and with all your soul. It is the LORD your God you must follow, and him you must revere. Keep his commands and obey him; serve him and hold fast to him. (Deuteronomy 13:1-4)

All of the messages and revelations claiming to have come from the Marian apparitions over the centuries have one thing in common: they encourage the Catholic cult of the virgin

Mary. But the Mary who is venerated and prayed to as Advocate, Helper, Benefactress, Mediatrix, Queen of Heaven, Mother of the Church, and so on, is not the Mary of Scripture, the genuine mother of Jesus. At heart, the veneration of Mary is linked to the Catholic belief that humans can cooperate with God to achieve union with the divine—salvation by doing good works.[147] For this reason, we can only conclude that the apparitions are from Satan, who is using them to keep people out of God's kingdom.

The saints

In the Catholic religion, the first qualification for becoming a saint is that a person has to be dead. The saints are all dead people. We call attention to this fact because that is not how the Bible uses the word *saint*. In the Bible, a saint is literally "a holy person." In their letters to Christians, the writers of the New Testament address all those who believe in Christ as saints—holy people—not holy in themselves but holy in God's sight because they have God's complete forgiveness for all their sins through faith in Christ. All believers in Christ are sinner-saints (Romans 1:7; 2 Corinthians 1:1; Ephesians 1:1; Philippians 1:1, etc.). Lutherans often refer to believers who have died as "saints triumphant." They are now enjoying in heaven the victory over sin, death, and hell that Christ won for them.

In the Catholic religion with its work-righteousness view of salvation, saints are those Catholics who lived holy enough lives so that when they died, their souls didn't have to first go to purgatory to suffer the temporal punishment for sin that went unpunished during their time on earth. They could skip purgatory and go directly to heaven. This requires not only a life of doing good works but also what Catholics call living a life of "heroic virtues."

The road to Catholic sainthood

The formal process of becoming a saint in the Catholic Church is an elaborate process that usually takes many years, sometimes even centuries. The Vatican carefully oversees and regulates the process. The details of the process have changed over the centuries. What we explain here is a summary of the current process, which has two main parts: the first leads to *beatification,* and the second culminates in *canonization* to full sainthood.

Normally, the process leading to beatification cannot begin until at least five years after the death of the candidate for sainthood. (Prior to 1983, the usual waiting period was 50 years.) The pope reserves for himself the right to waive the five-year waiting period if he chooses to do so. This was done in recent years with Mother Teresa of Calcutta and with Pope John Paul II, both widely known and popular among Catholics all over the world at the time of their deaths.

Usually the process is started by the bishop in the candidate's diocese, in consultation with other bishops and officials at the Vatican. The bishop appoints a panel of theological experts to examine all records pertaining to the candidate's life and interview people who may have personally known the candidate and who can testify to the candidate's virtuous life—all to determine whether the candidate did indeed live a life of "heroic virtue" or had died a martyr's death. The candidate also had to show complete fidelity to all the teachings of the Catholic Church.

After the candidate dies, it has to be demonstrated that another Catholic prayed to the candidate, asking him or her to intercede before God, and that God performed a miracle as a result of the candidate's intercession. Quite typically it is a miracle of healing. To be recognized as a genuine healing miracle, the healing has to be:

- complete—not just "feeling better" but a total healing of the illness or ailment
- durable—the condition does not return
- inexplicable—there can be no natural, medical explanation for the cure

A panel of medical and scientific experts are convened to examine all the evidence to see if the alleged miracle can be verified as authentic.

Once this investigation is complete, the "cause" is forwarded to Rome and thoroughly investigated by the Congregation for the Causes of Saints. After this congregation has completed its investigation, it makes a recommendation to the pope for beatification. After the candidate is declared beatified, another miracle is required and the investigation process by the Congregation for the Causes of Saints starts all over again, culminating finally in canonization, which is the formal and infallible declaration of the pope that the candidate is indeed a saint. Sainthood declares that the soul of the saint is indeed in heaven, enjoying the beatific vision (seeing God face-to-face), and that the saint can be prayed to (invoked) and asked to intercede before God on a person's behalf here on earth.

The beatification and canonization ceremonies take place within a solemn mass. Beatification masses are now usually performed by the local bishop. Masses of canonization are performed exclusively by the pope in an elaborate and solemn ceremony at St. Peter's Basilica in Rome.

After a person is canonized as a saint, he or she is assigned a feast day and churches and shrines may be dedicated to and named after the saint. The person may be designated as the patron saint of a country, a diocese, or a religious organization. Statues and images of the saint may be created, and relics of the saint may be venerated. And, of course, Catholics are encouraged to seek the saint's intercession before God.

As noted previously, the Catholic Church officially disclaims that the invocation of saints is the same as a prayer to God, but the distinction is lost on most Catholics. Catholics commonly refer to the invocation of saints as "praying to the saints," and they can be heard sayings things like, "Prayers to this or that saint are especially powerful."

The cult of the saints since Vatican II

After Vatican II, it seemed for a few years that the cult of the saints was in decline among Catholics (along with veneration of the virgin Mary). Pope John Paul II sought to correct that "misunderstanding" of Vatican II by beatifying and canonizing more saints during his pontificate than all previous popes combined (1,338 beatifications and 482 canonizations).[148]

The place that the veneration of the saints occupies in the lives and personal piety of individual Catholics varies considerably. Some Catholics claim that they seldom if ever address their prayers (invocations) to the saints and instead speak only to God, asking him directly for his help. For many other Catholics, veneration of the saints occupies a much more central place in their religious piety and practice. Generally speaking, in countries like the United States, where there is a large Protestant Christian influence, Catholic veneration of saints seems to be somewhat more restrained than in countries where Catholicism has a much longer history and is deeply entrenched in the culture.

Lutheran rejection of the veneration of the saints

Confessional Lutherans reject the Roman Catholic cult and veneration of the saints for the same reasons that they reject the veneration of Mary. Veneration of the saints is based on a work-righteousness view of salvation. As such it undermines trust in the gospel teaching that salvation is an unconditional gift of God, completely won for all by Christ. It is received freely through faith in Christ alone, without any human works, merits, achievements, disposition, "heroic virtues," etc. Possessing the righteousness and holiness of Christ by faith, all believers in Christ are holy (saints) in God's sight. At death, the souls of all Christians are taken to heaven where they enjoy the beatific vision, seeing God face-to-face. The Bible encourages all Christians to approach God's throne of grace in prayer through faith in Christ without the help or intercession of any other intermediaries (1 Timothy 2:5,6; Hebrews 4:16).

The invocation of the saints is based on the assumption that God hears and answers prayers not because of his mercy in Christ but because of how good the person is. That this is not just an unfair "Lutheran spin" on Catholic teaching can be seen by how Catholics themselves present the need for the invocation and intercession of saints:

> Most of us turn to prayer when we need something. . . . God can sometimes seem impersonal and distant, like the big boss. To approach him can sometimes feel intimidating. Saints are friends of God who have proven their sincerity and reaped the rewards of their good lives. They are in heaven and have the power to help us. It never hurts to have friends in high places, and it is often smart to have someone speak on your behalf. Saints offer intercession. Patron saints are believed to have influence over certain situations because of some special circumstances of their lives. . . . There are saints for many diverse matters. Some watch over funeral directors, gallstones, uncontrolled gambling, garage workers, gardeners, and glandular disorders. Some saints are remembered for particular causes. St. Anthony is the patron saint of lost objects; St. Jude is the saint for impossible cases.[149]

As we said regarding prayers to Mary earlier in this chapter, there is no command in Scripture to pray to the dead and no promise that the dead either hear or can answer anyone's prayers on earth. Lutherans do not rule out that demonic miracle-working powers are at work when people pray to the dead (2 Thessalonians 2:9). Catholics claim that they don't pray to the dead, they only invoke them to intercede on their behalf before God. Yet this is a distinction without meaning, and it seems lost on most Catholics. When Catholics describe how they venerate the saints, they frequently speak of *praying to* the saints and sometimes even of *worshiping* the saints.

What the Lutheran confessors said at the time of the Reformation about the Catholic veneration of the saints is still valid today:

> Our churches teach that the history of saints may be set before us so that we may follow the example of their faith and good works, according to our calling. For example, the emperor may follow the example of David [2 Samuel] in making war to drive away the Turk from his country. For both are kings. But the Scriptures do not teach that we are to call on the saints or to ask the saints for help. Scripture sets before us the one Christ as the Mediator, Atoning Sacrifice, High Priest, and Intercessor [1 Timothy 2:5–6]. He is to be prayed to. He has promised that He will hear our prayer [John 14:13]. This is the worship that He approves above all other worship, that He be called upon in all afflictions. "If anyone does sin, we have an advocate with the Father" (1 John 2:1).[150]
>
> The invocation of saints is also one of the Antichrist's abuses that conflicts with the chief article and destroys the knowledge of Christ [Philippians 3:8]. It is neither commanded nor counseled, nor has it any warrant in Scripture. Even if it were a precious thing—which it is not—we have everything a thousand times better in Christ.
>
> The angels in heaven pray for us, as does Christ Himself [Romans 8:34]. So do the saints on earth and perhaps also in heaven [Revelation 6:9–10]. It does not follow, though, that we should invoke and adore the angels and saints [Revelation 22:8–9]. Nor should we fast, hold festivals, celebrate Mass, make offerings, and establish churches, altars, and divine worship in their honor. Nor should we serve them in other ways or regard them as helpers in times of need. Nor should we divide different kinds of help among them, ascribing to each one a particular form of assistance, as the papists teach and do. This is idolatry. Such honor belongs to God alone. As a Christian

> and saint upon earth, you can pray for me in many necessities. But this does not mean that I have to adore and call upon you. I do not need to celebrate festivals, fast, make sacrifices, or hold Masses for your honor. I do not have to put my faith in you for my salvation. I can honor, love, and thank you in Christ in other ways. If such idolatrous honor were withdrawn from angels and departed saints, the remaining honor would be harmless and quickly forgotten. When advantage and assistance (both bodily and spiritual) are no longer expected, the saints will not be troubled, neither in their graves nor in heaven. No one will much remember or esteem or honor them without a reward or just out of pure love.[151]

For Further Reading

Martin Chemnitz, *Examination of the Council of Trent,* Volume 3 (St. Louis: Concordia Publishing House, 1986), pp. 353-507.

Lucien Dhalenne, "Antichristian Mariology," *Wisconsin Lutheran Quarterly,* Vol. 55, No. 3 (July 1958), pp. 167-192.

Elliot Miller and Kenneth R. Samples, *The Cult of the Virgin Mary: Catholic Mariology and the Apparitions of Mary* (Grand Rapids: Baker Book House, 1992).

Hermann Sasse, "Mary and the Pope: Remarks on the Dogma of the Assumption of Mary," *Logia,* Vol. XIX, No. 3 (Holy Trinity 2010), pp. 5-13.

James R. White, *Mary—Another Redeemer?* (Minneapolis: Bethany House Publishers, 1998).

9 PARISH AND *Worship Renewal*

In most chapters of this book, we have looked at Catholic teaching as presented in official church documents and we have compared those teachings with Scripture and the Lutheran Confessions. In this chapter on parish and worship renewal, I make some observations about a few aspects of Catholic parish life, especially changes that have come about since Vatican II. My observations are admittedly limited. However, they are based on years of visiting Catholic parishes, primarily in southeastern Wisconsin, talking to Catholic acquaintances, as well as ongoing reading of a variety of Catholic books, periodicals, and Internet blogs.

Priest sex abuse scandal

The last time I visited a Catholic parish, about a year ago, it was not to observe a Mass but to attend a public concert by a local community chorus and orchestra that were using the church's facilities. As I walked through the entry area, I passed by the parish office and noticed a sign posted in the office window. The sign stated that to help ensure that this was a safe environment for children, everyone on the staff of this parish and parish school had received special training with regard to sexual abuse. The sign also said that all children in the parish school had received training in how to recognize and properly react to any inappropriate sexual behavior attempted against them.

Catholics themselves say that since the time of the Reformation, no event has shaken the Catholic Church with greater force than the priest sex abuse scandals of the last couple of decades. The scandals started to receive public attention in the United States with a series of high profile criminal cases against several priests who were accused and charged with sexually molesting dozens, if not hundreds, of children over a number of decades. Naturally questions were raised regarding how such serial molesters could continue to offend over and over again for so many years in multiple Catholic parishes.

By 2002, almost every Catholic diocese in the United States was being sued by alleged victims of priest sexual abuse. Clearly the Catholic Church, at least in the United States, had a problem. The way the bishops had been treating allegations of priests' sexual abuse of children had been inadequate. Before 2002, such abuse was viewed primarily as a moral failing and a psychological problem and not as criminal behavior. The bishops' focus seemed to be more on rehabilitating the offending priests than on helping the victims. Often, when parents of abused children presented their allegations to the bishops, or when adults came forward themselves years after the alleged abuse, the bishops would make their own investigations without involving the legal authorities. If the allegations seemed credible, the priest would be removed from the parish and sent to a special clinic set up to give psychological treatment to suspected abusers. After receiving treatment, the offending priests would be declared "healed" and allowed to go back into priestly ministry at another parish, often to re-offend. The families of abused children were asked to keep quiet about the matter so that it wouldn't create a scandal in the church.

The growing size of the problem and the mounting legal costs of lawsuits and settlements finally helped the bishops realize they needed to change their approach. They came to recognize that sexual abuse of children is a crime that is much more harmful to children than they realized. In 2002, the United States Conference of Catholic Bishops (USCCB) adopted a zero tolerance policy and established guidelines for bishops and dioceses to deal with allegations of sexual abuse against minors. In 2004, the bishops put in place a National Review Board to oversee that dioceses and bishops are complying with the guidelines. The review board was comprised of prominent Catholic laypeople. Since these measures have been put in place, there have been very few new allegations of sexual abuse against minors. Almost all the new allegations are of incidents that occurred in the past—30 or more years ago.

As a result of the US bishops' vigorous response, the claim that some Catholics now make is probably true: there is probably no safer environment for children today than in a Catholic church or school. Nevertheless, two criticisms continue to be leveled. One is from victims' advocacy groups who say that while bishops have done much to address the problems of the past, more bishops should be losing their jobs or be punished in other ways for their failed oversight of offending priests.

The other criticism comes from prominent lay Catholics, such as William Donahue, the president of the Catholic League for Religious and Civil Rights, and others who claim that the bishops are not sufficiently addressing the issue of homosexuality among Catholic priests and its role in the sex abuse scandal. They point to the fact that 81 percent of all sexual abuse allegations against priests involve male children, 51 percent of them between the ages of 11 and 14, and 27 percent between the ages of 15 and 17—in other words, pubescent and adolescent males. The bishops seem reluctant to publicly address this aspect of the sex abuse scandal, perhaps because of the negative publicity it would create for them. It has been noted that while homosexuals make up approximately 2 percent of the general population, anywhere between 10 and 50 percent of Catholic priests are homosexuals.[152]

How much has the priest sex scandal affected the attitudes of practicing Catholics towards their church? Surprisingly—or perhaps not surprisingly—not much at all. According to a poll conducted in 2010 by CBS News and *The New York Times,* 77 percent of Catholics who attend Mass weekly say that "the Vatican's handling of recent child sex abuse reports" has had no effect on how they "feel about the Catholic Church." Eighty-eight percent of both practicing and nonpracticing Catholics claimed that the scandal has had no effect on their dealings with priests. According to 82 percent, the scandal has not had any effect on their attendance at Mass; 79 percent said it has had no effect on their church donations; and 87 percent said it has not had any effect on their children's involvement in church activities.[153]

While the number of new allegations of priest sex abuse has sharply declined in the United States, similar scandals have come to light more recently and are now being played out in a number of other countries, including Australia, Austria, Germany, Great Britain, Ireland, Mexico, and the Netherlands. Clearly the priest sex abuse scandal is not a uniquely American problem, as some Vatican cardinals first claimed it was.

Lutherans have no reason to react smugly to this scandal in the Catholic Church. Clergy misconduct is by no means unique to Roman Catholicism. No denomination, Lutherans included, is immune from its clergy falling into sins against the Sixth Commandment. It does seem, however, that Catholicism's ordination theology of "once a priest, always a priest" has made it difficult, at least in the past, for bishops to act more quickly to remove offending clergy from the active priesthood. Roman Catholicism, with its enforced rule of priestly celibacy, has also been a fertile breeding ground for a significant homosexual subculture within the priesthood.[154] While Lutheran pastors and other church workers do not have to contend with the theological baggage of Romanism, they still have to guard against the temptations of the sinful flesh and daily pray, "Lead us not into temptation" and "Deliver us from evil."

Parish schools

Parish schools have always been a hallmark of the Catholic Church in the United States. From early on, Catholics in America were a minority, often regarded with suspicion by non-Catholics. Public schools did not allow Catholic priests to come in to teach religion to Catholic students, as was a common practice in schools in Europe, where Catholics often represented the majority of people. In order to safeguard Catholic identity in their children in America, many Catholic parents made the sacrifices needed to support their parish schools. For many Catholic parents, it also meant encouraging one or more of their daughters to consider the vocation of becoming a religious sister, most of them serving as teachers in parish schools.

Worldwide, Catholic school education has seen a boom in the last 15 years. Between 1997 and 2008, the number of Catholic elementary schools worldwide rose from 86,505 to 93,315, along with a 20 percent increase in total student enrollment. Secondary Catholic schools have seen even larger growth, from 34,849 to 42,234 schools in the same period, with a 28 percent increase in student enrollment.[155]

While the Catholic Church worldwide has been experiencing significant growth, outpacing the growth of the world population in general, Catholic schools in the United States have suffered dramatic declines in enrollment. At their height in 1965, there were about 10,500 Catholic grade schools in the United States, with 4.2 million students. Today the number is just under 7,000 schools, with about 2 million students. Just during the years 2000 to 2010, the total number of students enrolled in Catholic grade schools and high schools declined 22 percent, from 2.6 million to 2 million.

Why has Catholic education seen this dramatic decline in the United States? There seem to be a number of contributing factors. Probably the largest factor is simple demographics. Catholic families today are generally smaller than only a couple generations ago. Another contributing factor has to do with the much lower number of men and women becoming religious brothers and sisters since Vatican II. In 1965 there were 179,000 religious sisters in the United States, with 104,314 of them (58 percent) serving as teachers in parochial schools. By 2010 the total number of sisters had decline to 57,544 with only 2.6 percent serving as teachers.[156] So, in a period of one generation, the US Catholic parish school system lost almost its entire workforce—a labor force, we might add, that had always worked for extremely low wages, keeping the cost of education very low.

To replace that workforce, Catholic parishes have had to hire Catholic laypeople who were professionally trained as teachers. While lay teachers may still sometimes work for lower wages than public school teachers, they require a living wage in order to support themselves. That has driven up the cost of education dramatically. Most parish schools fund their operations primarily by student tuition (and often with receipts from annual parish festivals). The average elementary school tuition in 2010 was $3,383, and the average high school tuition was $8,182. Many Catholic families simply can no longer afford to enroll their children in Catholic schools.

Another factor in the decline has to do with the erosion of Catholic identity experienced in the years after Vatican II. Religion curriculums published for Catholic parochial schools often were doctrinally very weak. Catholic lay teachers often did not have much formal training in Catholic theology, and the training many received from Catholic colleges after Vatican II was liberal. As a result, many Catholic schools lost much of their distinctive Catholic identity compared to the strong Catholic identity their parents had experienced in Catholic education before Vatican II. Parents noticed that Catholic schools just weren't teaching their children "how to be Catholic" anymore, so they came to the conclusion that the sacrifice needed to afford expensive tuition was no longer worth it. One of the reasons the pope and the bishops decided at a synod of bishops in 1985 to produce the *Catechism of the Catholic Church* was to provide an authoritative doctrinal benchmark that all Catholic religion curriculums and catechetical materials would have to agree with. In recent years, Catholic bishops have been clearly working to restore a sense of Catholic identity in their schools.

In spite of the overall decline in Catholic parochial school enrollment and the challenges Catholics face in funding schools, many parish grade schools, especially in middle-class suburban areas, seem to be thriving. In spite of relatively high tuition cost, they are experiencing full enrollments, with waiting lists of students.

Catholic bishops and other education leaders say that one of their biggest challenges with funding education in the future comes with the growing diversity of the Catholic Church in America. Thirty-five percent of all US Catholics today are Hispanic, but only 3 percent of Hispanic school-age children attend Catholic schools.[157] What can Catholic schools do to attract more Hispanics? How can they make their schools affordable to Hispanics? Catholics have not yet figured out all the answers, but they are working on it. In spite of the challenges, Catholics still seem to value the role that Catholic schools play in helping to raise their children.

Declining numbers of priests

In the previous section, I mentioned the precipitous decline in the number of religious sisters in the years after Vatican II and what impact that has had on Catholic school education. The priesthood experienced a somewhat similar decline in numbers in the United States and in most other Western countries after Vatican II. In the United States during the 1960s and 1970s, the total number of priests age 70 and younger was just under 60,000. By 2010, the number had dropped to just under 35,000. By 2020, it is expected to drop to about 15,000.[158] Meanwhile the Catholic population in the United States continues to rise, primarily through immigration. In fact, in the 20-year period from 1990 to 2010, the US Catholic population grew by nearly 50 percent, from 46 million to more than 69 million.[159]

The impact of this decline in the number of priests has been noticeable in nearly every Catholic parish across the country. Larger parishes that were once served by three or four priests at a time now have to make do with one or two, even if their membership has grown. Smaller parishes that used to have one resident priest now have to share a priest with one or more other parishes. Many smaller parishes have been forced to close or consolidate with other parishes. In the same 20-year period (1990–2010) in which the US Catholic population grew by 23 million, the number of parishes dropped by 10 percent, from 19,600 to 17,784.[160] In the 1960s, there were fewer than 600 parishes in the United States without a resident priest. By 2010, the number was close to 4,000 parishes without a resident priest. While Catholic laypeople have been trained to pick up much of their parish's administrative and educational duties, according to Catholic doctrine, only ordained priests can preside at the sacraments, which is the heart and core of Catholic worship and spiritual life.

The decline in the number of priests along with the rise in membership is probably the single greatest challenge for the Catholic Church in the United States today. This challenge will no doubt remain for many years to come, as many older priests retire in large numbers, while seminaries recruit far smaller numbers of younger men to train for the priesthood.

As a way to alleviate this problem, some groups have called for opening up the priesthood to women and/or for allowing priests to marry. However, Pope John Paul II made it clear in a very emphatic way in 1994 that opening up the priesthood to women was not going to happen because Catholic doctrine prohibits it.[161] Relaxing the rules that prohibit priests from marrying is not yet being considered in any significant way. Whether some future pope will allow priests to marry remains to be seen. In the meantime, one thing the US bishops have been doing to help alleviate the shortage is to bring in priests from countries in Latin America and Africa where there is a relative abundance of vocations to the priesthood. So it has become not at all uncommon for American parishes, especially in urban areas, to be served by priests who are native to countries such as Guatemala and Nigeria. As of 2002, about 16 percent of all priests active in US parish ministries come from countries outside the United States.[162] The importation of priests into the United States from other countries, however, is probably not a long-term solution, especially because the priest-to-Catholics ratios in Latin American and African countries are much higher than in the United States. The priest-to-Catholics ratio in the United States is about 1 to 1,200, while in Latin America it is about 1 to 7,000.

It was noticed back in the 1980s and 1990s that many of the seminaries in dioceses run by theologically liberal bishops were nearly empty, while some of the seminaries in dioceses run by more conservative bishops had no problem recruiting students. Young men attracted to the priesthood generally were admirers of Pope John Paul II and adhered to Roman orthodoxy. Liberal seminary faculties tended to weed out such candidates, leaving their seminaries largely empty.[163] That trend seems to be reversing somewhat, as older and more liberal bishops retire and are replaced with more conservative bishops who are working to make changes in their seminaries. However, even with some increases in seminary enrollments, the problem of a shortage of priests will continue to challenge the Catholic Church in the United States for many years to come.

Worship and liturgy

Probably no aspect of Catholic parish life has seen more change in the years since Vatican II than worship and liturgy. Prior to Vatican II, the language of the Mass and of all sacramental rites was Latin. The only active participants in the old Latin Mass were the priest and the altar boys who served him. Altar boys were trained to speak the congregation's liturgical responses in Latin. The people in the pews remained largely passive, other than sitting, kneeling, or standing at the proper moments during the Mass. For the most part, they remained silent and merely watched. The only places in the service where English (or another vernacular language) was spoken was after the Epistle and Gospel were read in Latin, when the priest would read the lessons in the vernacular. Perhaps the Creed was spoken by the people in the vernacular after the priest had recited it in Latin; likewise, with the Lord's Prayer. The sermon (or homily) was also preached in the language of the people. Except for the sermon and the vernacular Scripture readings, the priest conducted the entire service facing the altar with his back to the people.

In a Low Mass, there was little or no music at all. The entire service was spoken by the priest (and altar boys), much of it in a barely audible voice. In a High Mass, a choir sang the songs of the liturgy ("Kyrie," "Gloria Patri," "Credo," "Sanctus," "Agnus Dei"). Again the people did not participate in the singing; they remained mostly passive and merely watched the priest and choir do the worship.

The high point of the Mass was to watch the priest consecrate the bread and wine for the Eucharist and elevate the consecrated host and cup. In that part of the service, an altar boy would ring the *sacring bell* to alert the people that at that moment the transubstantiation of the elements had occurred and that the priest was now offering the holy sacrifice of the Mass.

Prior to Vatican II, the communicants received only the body of Christ and not the cup. They received Communion while kneeling at a Communion rail, with the priest placing the consecrated host directly on the communicants' tongues. Communicants never received the host with their hands; only the priests' hands were allowed to handle the consecrated host.

The entire service was highly ritualized, with everything intended to convey a sense of mystery, reverence, and awe. God was made to seem remote and aloof, to be approached "directly" by the ordained priests alone. The people in the pew were even encouraged to silently pray their own prayers and devotions, especially the Rosary, during Mass.

That was the Roman Catholic worship experience since the Middle Ages, largely unchanged since the time of the Council of Trent in the 16th century. Rome's answer to Protestant Reformation worship practices—services in the language of the people, preaching the Word of God, and encouraging active participation by the congregation, especially in singing congregational hymns—was to do just the opposite.

That was all to change. The Second Vatican Council called for the updating of all Roman sacramental and liturgical rites, calling for the "full, conscious, and active participation" of the people. In fact, the council stated rather emphatically: "In the restoration and promotion of the sacred liturgy the full and active participation by all the people is the aim to be considered before all else."[164] Some of the specifics the council called for included revising the lectionary to include more Scripture, introducing parts of the liturgy into the language of the people, and permitting local cultural diversity to be given some expression, only with the approval and under the careful supervision of the local bishops however. At the same time, Vatican II clearly called for keeping intact the core of the historic Western rite, which other historically liturgical churches (Anglicans, Episcopalians, Lutherans) also share.

Vatican II's document on worship set forth broad, general principles but few specifics. It was left to committees of "liturgical experts" in the Vatican and local bishops' conferences to work out the details. The end result was perhaps a more radical and faster change than most bishops at the council likely envisioned. Within a period of barely six years, the use of Latin was almost entirely swept away. Catholics going to Sunday Mass can now hear and understand the entire service in their own languages. The people can speak or sing their own liturgical responses. Hymn singing has been introduced in the worship, often to the accompaniment of a guitar.

The historic one-year lectionary, which consisted of Epistle and Gospel lessons, was replaced with a three-year lectionary, consisting of Old Testament, Epistle, and Gospel lessons, as well as a Psalm that is sung. Many Lutheran and other liturgical Protestant churches saw value in the new three-year Roman lectionary and adapted it for their own use.

Changes in church architecture and interior design were quickly affected by the worship renewal. Historic altars positioned against the wall were removed, or are no longer used, and were replaced by freestanding altar-tables. Priests now conduct the entire service facing the people. Communion rails were removed, and people can now receive Communion with their hands while standing. To some degree, Communion in both kinds has also been gradually restored. Side altars dedicated to Mary were often removed, as well as much of the old religious statuary.

Part of the implementation of the post-Vatican II worship reforms included enlisting laypeople to read the Scripture lessons (except the Gospel, which requires an ordained priest or ordained male deacon), cantors, and more recently female altar servers.

These are just some of the officially authorized changes in worship that came about in the years after Vatican II. Besides the changes authorized by the Vatican and bishops' conferences, many priests in local parishes did all kinds of unauthorized changing, tinkering, and experimenting with the liturgy. For example, in the 1970s, some Catholic priests performed "clown Masses." While some of the more silly experimentation has faded away, significant numbers of priests apparently continue to tinker with the liturgy, changing the official texts of the liturgy, as well as breaking other official worship rules that are prescribed by Rome. Almost every pope since Vatican II (Paul VI, John Paul II, Benedict XVI) has complained about and written official directives to the bishops to clamp down on all the unauthorized experimentation that apparently still goes on in Catholic worship.

How has all this change, most of which took place in barely ten years' time, been received by the Catholic rank and file? It seems, for the most part, quite well. The changes were difficult for some, especially at first, but most religious surveys of Catholics show that the vast majority of Catholics who regularly attend Mass today have accepted the changes. After 40 years, the "new" Mass is the only one that a whole generation of Catholics has ever known or experienced.

Nevertheless, concerns about the worship and liturgical reforms remain. Some Catholics have noticed that with the changes, the sense of sacred awe and reverence in the presence of God has definitely declined. This is sometimes described this way: the old way of viewing a church was as a house of *God;* since Vatican II, a church is viewed as a house of the *people* of God. In other words, the primary focus is more on the people and what they are doing than on God. This focus is reflected fairly often in *gathering songs* written for Catholics to sing at the beginning of their services, in which the lyrics often say little more than "We celebrate that we are the people of God." Notice where the primary focus is and where it *is not.*

Significant numbers of more traditionalist Catholics have asked for permission from church authorities to allow for more opportunities to hear the old Latin Mass. As a result, both Pope John Paul II and Pope Benedict XVI directed the bishops to make provisions for Mass to be celebrated according to the old Latin rite for those who desire it. Most bishops, while complying with the pope's directives to some degree, say they have not noticed much of a call for the old Latin Mass. A medium-sized archdiocese in the United States with, say, about four hundred or so parishes might have three or four venues that offer Sunday Mass according to the old Latin rite. The fact that the previous two popes issued at least three such directives (1988, 2007, 2011) shows that some bishops have resisted the pope's wishes. This is especially true of bishops in the United States and France.[165] In various communications to bishops and priests, Pope Benedict XVI also called for the "new" Mass to be conducted in a way that expresses more awe and reverence, specifically by following the official liturgical rules set forth by Rome.

In December 2011 when a new English translation of the liturgy was introduced, English-speaking Catholics experienced what some are calling another significant conservative turn in worship. Many progressives are bemoaning the new translation as a giant step backward and a "betrayal of Vatican II." More conservative Catholics have always been less than happy with the liberties that previous English translations took with Rome's official Latin text of the new Mass, claiming that it watered down orthodox Catholic doctrine. Liberals counter that the new English translation is too slavish to the official Latin text, making the English sound somewhat awkward in some places and its meaning more difficult to understand. The use or nonuse of inclusive language, not only as it applies to humans but also with reference to God, is a source of continuous contention among many Catholics.

While Pope Benedict XVI was in office, he was committed to worship reforms. At the same time, it was clear that he was more sympathetic to the more liturgically conservative elements in the Catholic Church than to the progressive elements. His approach seemed to be to try not to alienate too many of any factions in the worship wars, knowing that it would take a long time to "reform the reform." Benedict's successor, Pope Francis (2013–), has not given much indication as to where he stands on debated issues of Catholic worship. He seems to favor less ornate liturgical ceremonies than his predecessors. It is safe to say that the Catholic version of worship wars will continue into the future.

10 A FEW GLOBAL TRENDS *in Catholicism*

In this chapter we will look at trends that we can see going on now, and it would be reasonable to assume they will probably continue into the foreseeable future. For most of the information in this chapter, I relied primarily on a very helpful book, *The Future Church,* by Catholic journalist John L. Allen.[166]

World church and the global shift south

Up until the mid 20th century, it would have been accurate to say that Catholicism was centered in Europe. Most other continents (especially Africa, Asia, and Latin America) were viewed as mission areas. With very few exceptions, the popes were Italians, and the most prominent bishops and cardinals were Europeans. While the Catholic Church was a worldwide church, its focus and viewpoint could be described as noticeably Eurocentric. This Eurocentric outlook simply reflected the fact that most Roman Catholics lived in Europe. In 1900 there were about 266 million Catholics worldwide. Two hundred million Catholics lived in Europe; 66 million lived in the rest of the world. By 2000, there were about 1.1 billion Catholics worldwide. Now only 350 million are Europeans and North Americans. The vast majority of Catholics today—720 million—live in Latin America, Africa, and Asia. Four hundred million Catholics, more than one-third of all Catholics, live in Latin America.

Because of Catholicism's global demographic shift to the Southern Hemisphere, it seems reasonable to assume that their numbers will be represented in an increasing way in the Roman Curia and the College of Cardinals. In the last few decades we have, in fact, seen cardinals being appointed to key posts in the Vatican who have come from Africa and South America, as well as India. This does not mean, however, that we can expect Italian to cease being the daily working language of the Vatican any time soon. Many key positions are still held by Italians. And even though the Catholic population of Europe is declining, most of the money the Catholic Church receives still comes from Catholics who live in Europe and North America. Nevertheless, it is reasonable to assume that Rome will increasingly turn its attention to where most of its members live.

What might this mean in practical terms? To help answer this question, consider the profile of southern Catholicism (Catholicism roughly south of the equator) offered by John Allen. Here are a few features in his suggested profile:

- Morally conservative on family issues, abortion, homosexuality, and pornography.
- Politically liberal: skeptical of capitalism and globalization, open to a robust role for the state in the economy, pro-United Nations, anti-war, especially opposed to US military action.
- More open to miracles, miraculous healings, and the supernatural. In the Catholic South, the border between Catholicism and folk religion, magic, and spiritism has always been somewhat blurry. The Catholic leadership's concern in the future might be more focused on combating syncretism (blending different religions together) than with combating European-style religious skepticism.
- Supporting a strong political role for the church. The strict separation of church and state is not so much a part of the heritage in the countries of the Catholic South as it is in the United States and modern, secularized Europe.

- Much less focused on internal church issues (power of the pope and Roman Curia, ordination of women, liturgy wars, etc.) and more concerned about addressing societal issues (poverty, HIV/AIDS, war, etc.)[167]

It seems likely that this "southern" viewpoint will continue to be expressed and become even more prominent in the future. Various position statements from the Vatican and conferences of bishops have already addressed some aspects of this southern profile. Allen, for instance, imagines the possibility some day of a pope from Africa issuing an encyclical on the topic of demon possession and exorcism.

On that note, observers of the Catholic Church sometimes speculate about when we might see the first African pope. No one knows, of course, but it is significant that Cardinal Claudio Hummes from Brazil was often mentioned as a possible successor to Pope John Paul II. The papal conclave in 2005, of course, elected the German Joseph Ratzinger to fill that position. But the following year, Ratzinger (Pope Benedict XVI) appointed Cardinal Hummes to one of the top positions in the Vatican. A few decades ago such a move would have been hard to imagine. But the once unimaginable became a further reality in 2013 when Cardinal Jorge Mario Bergoglio of Argentina was elected as Benedict XVI's successor, taking the papal name Francis in honor of Saint Francis of Assisi.

Evangelical Catholicism

Evangelical Catholicism has no direct connection with Protestant Evangelicalism. Rather, the term is used by Allen and others to refer to the renewed sense of Catholic identity that many Catholics have picked up from Popes John Paul II and Benedict XVI.

Recall that in the years after Vatican II, a more liberal Catholicism was in vogue. The emphasis was for Catholics to be open to the modern world and to "dialogue" with it. As a result, many of the traditional distinctive religious practices that set Catholics apart from other Christians were discontinued or downplayed, including Friday fasting, bowing and kneeling in church, devotions to Mary, Eucharistic adoration, etc. Since the 1960s, Catholicism has gone from being a culture-shaping majority in many countries, especially in Europe, to being an embattled cultural minority.

Reacting to this shift, Popes John Paul II and Benedict XVI attempted to reestablish a solid Catholic identity by reaffirming traditional Catholic beliefs and practices. Many bishops have been following suit.[168] This emphasis is the label to which *evangelical Catholicism* refers.

Allen offers these three characteristics of evangelical Catholicism:

- A strong defense of traditional Catholic identity in both doctrine and practice
- Robust public proclamation of Catholic teaching
- Faith seen as a matter of personal choice rather than cultural inheritance[169]

Mother Angelica's Eternal Word Television Network (EWTN) is an expression of evangelical Catholicism. The Catholic World Youth Day events started by John Paul II and continued by Benedict XVI and Francis, with their direct appeal to young adult Catholics, are also an example of evangelical Catholicism. Some of the more recent rising stars among the American episcopate, such as Archbishop Timothy Dolan, formerly of Milwaukee and now in New York, and Archbishop Charles Chaput, formerly of Denver and now in Philadelphia, are examples of the evangelical Catholic style of bishop. Cardinal Francis George of Chicago also falls into this category of bishop. Significantly, Chicago, New York, and Philadelphia are considered to be among the most important archdioceses in the United States and, for that matter, in the world.

How might an evangelical Catholic bishop differ from a more liberal bishop? An example would be in how an evangelical bishop approaches the Catholic pro-life movement. Some of the more liberal bishops in the past gave very little, if any, public moral support to the Catholic pro-life groups. They might say things like, "Of course, I am pro-life, but I'm concerned that the pro-life groups are overly rigid and loveless." Evangelical Catholic bishops, by contrast, don't hesitate to give public moral support to the Catholic pro-life groups, including joining them out on the streets when they conduct marches for life and in other types of public expressions for the pro-life cause.

We might summarize the difference between evangelical Catholicism and liberal Catholicism as being the way in which the two approach culture. Evangelical Catholic bishops vigorously engage the culture, while liberal bishops accommodate themselves to it. Evangelical Catholics want to "engage the culture," not just dialogue with it. Past liberal bishops would probably dispute such a generalization, claiming that they also "engaged the culture," just on different issues. The fact remains, however, that liberal Catholics spent much of their energy trying to "reform the church," which often meant pushing for things like women's ordination and reducing the power of the pope and the Roman Curia. Today, due to the emphasis of John Paul II, liberal Catholicism is clearly in decline while evangelical Catholicism is on the rise.

Where does this leave the more liberal Catholics? For the most part, they are growing older and diminishing in numbers, power, and influence in the church. It is the evangelical Catholicism of John Paul II, Benedict XVI, and bishops like Chaput and Dolan, that is attracting and keeping younger Catholics.[170] Cardinal Francis George has gone so far as to publicly declare that the liberal Catholic experiment is dead. John Allen, by contrast, does not see Catholic liberalism disappearing altogether, but that in the future it will likely be confined more to certain Catholic "ghettos," such as academic institutions. But he acknowledges that Catholic liberalism is clearly no longer "setting the agenda" for the Catholic Church.

Just so there is no misunderstanding, confessional Lutherans should not mistake evangelical Catholicism for evangelical

Lutheranism. Evangelical Catholicism is unabashedly Catholic orthodoxy all the way, just presented in a more winsome way. Lutherans will not find the unconditional gospel of the forgiveness of sins preached by evangelical Catholics any more than it was by the more liberal Catholics a generation ago. A clear preaching of the genuine, apostolic, scriptural gospel of God's unconditional forgiveness of sins earned in full for all by Christ, proclaimed in the gospel, and received through faith in Christ alone remains tragically absent in today's Catholicism just as it was in the past. The Catholic view of salvation remains one of "grace" *and* human works.

Pentecostalism

While Catholicism is definitely not becoming more Lutheran, some segments of Catholicism are becoming more Pentecostal. This is especially true in the Catholic Global South, but certainly not limited to there.

John Allen presents the following facts. In the last half century, Pentecostalism has been far and away the fastest growing segment of Christianity. In the mid 1970s, it represented only 6 percent of the worldwide Christian church. By the year 2000, it represented almost 20 percent, about 380 million people. If considered as a group, this makes the Pentecostals the second largest division of Christianity in the world, second only to Roman Catholics. Two-thirds of all Pentecostals are found in developing countries, many of which are in Latin America and Africa south of the Sahara. This is the area of the world where Catholicism has seen significant growth during the same period.[171]

Allen notes some of the characteristics of Pentecostalism:

- Belief in miraculous gifts of the Spirit, especially speaking in tongues and healing
- A literal reading of the Bible
- Emphasis on the presence of evil spirits and demon possession, use of exorcism

- Imminent return of Christ, preceded by the rapture of believers to heaven
- Miracles, especially healings
- Christ believed to be the only way to salvation
- Conservative moral code, especially on sexual issues including homosexuality and abortion[172]

While some of these characteristics might seem opposed to Catholic teaching, Allen notes that there are certain theological parallels with Catholic teaching:

- A conservative moral code
- In addition to Scripture, seeking ongoing revelations of the Spirit, often taking precedence over Scripture
- A certain openness to folk religion
- Faith and works both included when talking about salvation

These parallels enable Pentecostal spirituality to fit nicely into traditional Catholicism. In fact, these parallels and others have led religion observer Harvey Cox to go so far as to describe Pentecostalism as "Catholicism without priests."[173]

Catholicism's relationship with Pentecostalism has been one of both competition and assimilation. In regard to competition, Allen notes that especially in Latin America, Pentecostalism's fantastic growth has not occurred in a vacuum. Almost all converts to Pentecostalism are ex-Roman Catholics. He sums it up this way: "In the Global North, dissatisfied Catholics usually become secularized; in the South, they usually become Pentecostals."[174] While this religious competition has irked Catholic leaders in Latin America, they have admitted that of those who have left Catholicism for Pentecostalism, many were only nominal Catholics to begin with.

Interestingly, at the same time that Pentecostals have been peeling off members from Catholic parishes, the Catholic Church has sought to assimilate Pentecostal spirituality into itself. In fact, Catholicism's own version of Pentecostalism, the Catholic Charismatic Renewal, dates back to the late 1960s. The

Catholic Church is responding to Protestant Pentecostalism by telling its members that they can be both Catholic and charismatic—that they can have the "best" of both worlds. (The difference between a Pentecostal and charismatic is that a charismatic is simply a Pentecostal who is also a part of a mainline denomination.)

Today there are an estimated 120 million charismatic Catholics worldwide with most of them in the Southern Hemisphere. One religious survey estimates that about 14 percent of all US Catholics, about 10 million, consider themselves to be charismatic, among them being a large number of Hispanics.[175] Worldwide, 11 percent of Catholics count themselves as charismatic/Pentecostal. In some Catholic Churches in the Southern Hemisphere, charismatics make up the majority of members. If Pentecostalism is Catholicism without priests, as Harvey Cox suggests, then it might be just as true that southern Catholicism is more and more becoming Pentecostalism with priests. As the Catholic Church in the United States becomes increasingly Hispanic, we might expect it also to take on more of a Pentecostal/charismatic complexion.

So while there is definitely competition between Catholicism and Protestant Pentecostalism, Catholicism, at least in the Global South, is taking on an increasingly Pentecostal face.

Ecumenism and interreligious dialogue

Ecumenism refers to relationships with Christians in other churches. *Interreligious dialogue* is the term that Catholics have used to refer to their relationships with people of non-Christian religions.

Ecumenism

Prior to Vatican II, Rome remained officially aloof to the modern ecumenical movement. With the Second Vatican Council in the 1960s, the Catholic Church entered the modern ecumenical era. At Vatican II, the Catholic Church declared that it was ready to become a major partner with other participating churches in the ecumenical movement. For more than 40 years now, Catholics have dialogued with leaders of the Eastern Orthodox churches and with most of the mainline Protestant churches.

In the early post-Vatican II era, a feeling of euphoria characterized ecumenical relationships and activities. The pope and the patriarch of Constantinople lifted the thousand-year-old curses of excommunication against each other and their respective churches. Many Protestant mainline church leaders engaged in dialogue with Roman Catholics, and both sides have spoken of doctrinal "convergences" between their respective churches. Officially, Rome's stance is that all Protestants remain "separated brethren," but during the discussions polemical tones of the past were replaced with expressions of mutual recognition as "Christian brothers and sisters."

Since then, the early euphoria among Catholic and Protestant dialogue participants has vanished. After 40 years of dialogue, Protestant participants are still faced with Rome's adamant insistence that recognition of the primacy and authority of the pope is necessary if a church body wants to be a true church with a real ministry. And Catholics are faced with the move to ordain women and accept openly practicing homosexuals as practiced by many mainline Protestants. The result is that Catholic-Protestant ecumenical progress toward unity has pretty much stalled. Clergy from both sides still make appearances at joint prayer services in which they pray for "unity," but no officially recognized full Eucharistic sharing between Catholics and a Protestant church body will happen anytime soon.

Rome's ecumenical efforts seem to have turned more to healing the division between itself and the Eastern Orthodox churches. Participants from both churches recognize that the process to heal the thousand-year-old division will be long and difficult. Rome's claim for papal primacy and authority over the whole Christian church is without a doubt the biggest sticking point. Both sides recognize their unity during the first Christian millennium as the starting point for resolving current differences. It appears that both the Catholics and Orthodox, while committed to the effort, realistically do not expect any big breakthroughs in the near future. The schism, both sides point out, did not occur overnight, and healing the schism won't happen overnight either.

Interreligious dialogue

Since Vatican II, Catholics have conducted various discussions with representatives of the other world religions. Rome has given particular attention to improving relations between Catholics and Jews. Catholic-Jewish relations certainly seem to have improved since Vatican II, but there also seems to be some growing frustration among some Catholics. To some, it seems that no matter how many times Catholic leaders denounce anti-Semitism, apologize for the Holocaust, and offer other gestures of goodwill to Jews, Jewish leaders come back with the response, "That's good, but it's still not enough."

John Allen speculates that we may see the Catholic Church's primary interreligious attention shift from Judaism to Islam, if it hasn't shifted already. Two reasons may be involved in this shift.

One obvious reason, Allen proposes, is the rising ascendancy of Islam. There are roughly one billion Catholics in the world and one billion Muslims. With the rise of Islamic fundamentalism in recent years, relations between Catholics and Muslims in countries where both are present—countries in the Middle East, Africa, Indonesia, the Philippines, etc.—have been strained. As more Catholic top leadership comes from the Global South, we may see that their interreligious attention is focused on what for them is a far more pressing concern.

The second reason for the shift is that Catholics in the Global South have never carried the kind of collective guilt over the Nazi Holocaust that European Catholics have.

Earlier interreligious discussions between Catholics and some Muslim leaders seem to have focused more on finding common religious beliefs, for example, both Catholics and Muslims refer to themselves as "people of the book," who believe in one God. More recently, the Vatican has been emphasizing that Christians and Muslims need to find ways to mutually coexist on this planet without agreeing on religious beliefs. The Vatican is trying to press Muslims to recognize religious freedom, including the right to convert, as a basic human right of all people. Catholics are also trying to press Muslims to recognize religious reciprocity. If Catholics in Italy, for instance, allow Muslims to build mosques in their country, then Muslims should reciprocate by recognizing the rights of Catholics to build churches and openly practice their religion in countries where Muslims are the majority, such as in Saudi Arabia. So far, Muslim leaders have dismissed the idea with the response, "It doesn't work that way." Catholics continue to press the point that mutual recognition of basic universal human rights is essential for any kind of peaceful coexistence. The hope is that more moderate Muslims can somehow influence the rest of the Islamic world in this regard.

In its interreligious relationships, similar to its ecumenical relations with the Eastern Orthodox, Rome seems to be taking a long-term approach. The current tensions took centuries to develop, and they will take a long time to resolve. The Catholic Church, with its enduring institution of the papacy, seems to be especially suited, humanly speaking, to using such a long-term approach to interreligious relations.

Conclusion

The first chapter of this book described the Catholic Church, using these eight characteristics:

- a huge church
- a diverse church
- a changing church
- an unchanging church
- a troubled church
- a sacramental church
- a hierarchical church
- a creedal (Christian) church

If we think of these characteristics in terms of trends, it is probably safe to assume that they are all trends that will continue into the future.

What does this mean for us Lutherans in our personal relationships with Catholics? Because Catholics form a huge—and growing—church, we Lutherans can expect that our paths will frequently cross. Catholics will continue to be our neighbors, friends, coworkers, and relatives.

Because Catholics are diverse in their personal beliefs, we should not assume that all or even most Catholics staunchly believe and profess everything that is officially taught in their church. Some do; others do not. Some may question, doubt, or even deny some of the most basic teachings of the Christian faith. On the other hand, we might be pleasantly surprised that some Catholics confess their faith in ways quite close to our Lutheran beliefs. They may say that Jesus Christ and his atoning death on the cross are the sinner's only hope for eternal life with God in heaven. If we hear Catholics profess such a Christ-centered faith, it makes our hearts glad, and we should tell them so.

Nor should such a Christ-centered profession of faith completely surprise us. The Catholic Church is a creedal church, and Catholics profess the common Christian creeds. The Scriptures are read in their churches. The ancient Bible-based songs of the liturgy are sung in their services every week. Where God's Word is read and sung, God promises to work his miracle of faith in Christ in people's hearts. When he does, it is in spite of, not because of, the false and unscriptural teachings of work-righteousness that pervade Roman Catholicism.

The Catholic Church remains a troubled church on many fronts. But it is our Lutheran conviction, as I believe is demonstrated in this book, that the greatest trouble plaguing the Catholic Church is its work-righteousness perversion of the gospel of God's unconditional gift of righteousness and the forgiveness of all sins, which were earned in full by Christ and received through faith in him. Rome continues to teach that while it is made possible for all by Christ, salvation is conditioned by our human works and virtues. This false teaching pervades Catholic theology to this day, and the effects of this false teaching are obvious. When asked the question in religious surveys of how they hope to get to heaven, most Catholics respond that they are trying hard to be good people.

If the Catholics we know express such a human, works-based hope, we can show no greater act of Christian love than to explain from Scripture in a kind and respectful way that God's law demands not just good intentions and efforts but complete obedience. It demands that we keep all God's commandments perfectly in every thought we think, every word we speak, and every act we do (Matthew 5:48). Scripture convinces us that we have all fallen short of the holiness God demands of us (Romans 3:20,23). For our sinful failings, we deserve eternal punishment in hell. But God, who is rich in mercy, sent his Son, Jesus Christ, not just to be a good example or to give us more laws but to be our Savior. He lived a perfect life as our substitute. He died on the cross to pay for all our sins. God announces in the gospel that he credits his Son's perfect righteousness to us and forgives all sins freely and unconditionally for Christ's sake. All who believe in Christ as their Savior possess his saving righteousness and forgiveness (John 3:16; Romans 3:23-26). Christ, and Christ alone, is the one on whom we base our hope of salvation. The gospel truth about what Christ has done for us and that Christ is the only basis of our Christian hope of salvation is what Roman Catholics need most to hear—again and again—as do all people. To that end may the Lord bless your proclamation of Christ and his gospel.

ENDNOTES

[1] In organizing the material for this book, I decided to follow much the same organization used by Professor John Brug in his Bible study entitled *Catholicism Today* (Milwaukee: Northwestern Publishing House, 2007). This also enables the book and the Bible study to be used together in a Bible study setting.

[2] The first five of these characteristics are taken from John Brug's *Catholicism Today* Bible study.

[3] Statistics for Catholics are from *Our Sunday Visitor's Catholic Almanac 2012* (Huntington, IN: Our Sunday Visitor, Inc., 2012). Statistics for Lutherans are from the Lutheran World Federation, http://www.lutheranworld.org/LWF_Documents/LWF-Statistics-2009.pdf (accessed 11/15/11).

[4] David Carlin, *The Decline and Fall of the Catholic Church in America* (Manchester, NH: Sophia Institute Press, 2003), pp. 389,390.

[5] Carlin, *The Decline and Fall,* pp. 390,391.

[6] Thomas J. Reese, *Inside the Vatican: The Politics and Organization of the Catholic Church* (Cambridge: Harvard University Press, 1996), p. 75.

[7] Documents of Vatican II, www.ewtn.com/library/councils/v2all.htm (accessed 5/31/13).

[8] Avery Dulles, *The Reshaping of Catholicism* (San Francisco: Harper & Row Publishers, 1998), pp. 19-33.

[9] *Code of Canon Law: Latin-English* (Washington DC: Canon Law Society of America, 1983), p. 119.

[10] The pope used to also claim the title "Patriarch of the West," that is, not claiming authority over the territory of the Eastern Orthodox Church, which is governed by the Patriarch of Constantinople (Istanbul), but that title was formally dropped by Pope Benedict XVI in 2006.

[11] "Dogmatic Decrees of the Vatican Council, Session IV, Chapter IV" in *The Creeds of Christendom,* Philip Schaff, editor, Vol. 2 (New York: Harper, 1877; reprinted by Baker Books, 1996), p. 270.

[12] "Vatican I, Session IV, Chapter III," Schaff, *The Creeds of Christendom,* Vol. 2, pp. 262,263.

[13] "Vatican I, Session IV, Chapter III," Schaff, *The Creeds of Christendom,* Vol. 2, pp. 260-263.

[14] Vatican II, Dogmatic Constitution on the Church, n. 22. All quotations of the documents of Vatican II are from *Vatican Council II: The Conciliar and Post Conciliar Documents,* Austin P. Flannery, general editor (Northport, NY: Costello Publishing Company, 1975).

[15] Vatican II, Dogmatic Constitution on the Church, n. 25.

[16] Vatican II, Decree on Ecumenism, n. 3.

[17] Smalcald Articles II, IV, 10-14, in *Concordia: The Lutheran Confessions,* edited by Paul Timothy McCain (St. Louis: Concordia Publishing House, 2005), pp. 269,270.

[18] Treatise on the Power and Primacy of the Pope, 39-41, McCain, *Concordia,* pp. 300,301.

[19] *Catechism of the Catholic Church,* Second Edition (Washington DC: United States Catholic Conference, Inc.; Vatican City: Libreria Editrice Vatican, 1994, 1997), nn. 552,880-892.

[20] Smalcald Articles II, II, 15, McCain, *Concordia,* pp. 265,266.

[21] Formula of Concord, Epitome, Summary Rule and Norm, 1,2, McCain, *Concordia,* p. 473.

[22] Formula of Concord, Solid Declaration, Summary Rule and Norm, 3, McCain, *Concordia,* p. 508.

[23] Session IV, 1. *Canons and Decrees of the Council of Trent,* edited by H. J. Schroeder (St. Louis: B. Herder Book Co., 1941), p. 17.

[24] Vatican II, Dogmatic Constitution on Divine Revelation, nn. 9,10.

[25] Martin Chemnitz, *Examination of the Council of Trent,* Vol. 1 (St. Louis: Concordia Publishing House, 1971), pp. 217-307.

[26] Chemnitz, *Examination,* Vol. 1, p. 227.

[27] Chemnitz, *Examination,* Vol. 1, p. 256.

[28] Chemnitz, *Examination,* Vol. 1, p. 274.

[29] For examples, see Karl Keating, *Catholicism and Fundamentalism* (San Francisco: Ignatius Press, 1988), and Robert Sungenis, *Not by Scripture Alone: A Catholic Critique of the Protestant Doctrine of Sola Scriptura* (Santa Barbara, CA: Queenship Publishing Company, 1997).

[30] Lyle W. Lange, *God So Loved the World: A Study of Christian Doctrine* (Milwaukee: Northwestern Publishing House, 2005), p. 68.

[31] Vatican II, Dogmatic Constitution on Divine Revelation, n. 11.

[32] For examples, see George A. Kelly, *The New Biblical Theorists: Raymond E. Brown and Beyond* (Ann Arbor, MI: Servant Books, 1983), pp. 153-160. See also Brian W. Harrison, "The Truth and Salvific Purpose of Sacred Scripture According to *Dei Verbum,* Article 11," *Living Tradition,* Organ of the Roman Theological Forum, No. 59, July 1995. http://www.rtforum.org/lt/lt59.html (accessed 1/5/09).

[33] *The New Jerome Biblical Commentary,* edited by Raymond S. Brown, Joseph A. Fitzmeyer, and Roland E. Murphy (Englewood Cliffs, NJ: Prentice-Hall, Inc., 1968, 1990).

[34] John Paul II, *Original Unity of Man and Woman: Catechesis on the Book of Genesis* (Boston: St. Paul Books and Media, 1981).

[35] Pontifical Biblical Commission, *The Interpretation of the Bible in the Church* (Libreria Editrice Vaticana, 1993. Reprinted by St. Paul Books and Media, 1993), p. 35.

[36] Pontifical Biblical Commission, *The Interpretation of the Bible,* pp. 72-75.

[37] John F. Brug, "Rome Endorses Higher Criticism," *Wisconsin Lutheran Quarterly,* Vol. 92, No.1 (Winter 1995), pp. 61,62.

[38] Alan Schreck, *The Catholic Challenge* (Ann Arbor, MI: Servant Publications, 1991), p. 23.

[39] Keating, *Catholicism and Fundamentalism,* p. 275.

[40] Dulles, *The Reshaping of Catholicism,* pp. 83,84.

[41] Vatican II, Dogmatic Constitution on Divine Revelation, n. 8.

[42] Vatican II, Dogmatic Constitution on Divine Revelation, n. 10.

[43] Lange, *God So Loved the World,* p. 52.

[44] William Webster, *The Old Testament Canon and the Apocrypha* (Battle Ground, WA: Christian Resources, Inc., 2002), p. 86.

[45] McCain, *Concordia,* p. 33.

[46] Council of Trent, Session 6, Schroeder, pp. 33,43,44.

[47] Council of Trent, Session 6, Canon 16. Schroeder, p. 44.

[48] For a more detailed exposition of James 2:14-16, see Mark Jeske, *James, 1,2 Peter, 1,2,3 John, Jude,* in The People's Bible series (Milwaukee: Northwestern Publishing House, 2002), pp. 27-30. See also the Apology V (III):123-132 [244-253], McCain, *Concordia,* pp. 118-120.

[49] For a traditional Catholic interpretation of this account, see Robert A. Sungenis, *Not by Faith Alone* (Santa Barbara, CA: Queenship Publishing Company, 1997), pp. 178-185.

[50] See Sungenis, *Not by Faith Alone,* pp. 355-363.

[51] Formula of Concord, Solid Declaration, Article 1, 60, McCain, *Concordia,* p. 519.

[52] Daniel F. McSheffery, "Indulgences in the Contemporary Church," *Homiletical & Pastoral Review,* Vol. XCVI, Nos. 11-12 (August–September 1996), p. 60.

[53] *Catechism of the Catholic Church,* nn. 1471-1479.

[54] McSheffery, "Indulgences in the Contemporary Church," p. 62.

[55] Pope John Paul II, "*Incarnationis Mysterium:* Bull of Indiction of the Great Jubilee of the Year 2000" (Vatican City: Libreria Editrice Vaticana; Washington, DC: United States Catholic Conference, 1999), pp. 34,35.

[56] John L. Allen, "A German Pope Heads for the Land of Luther," *National Catholic Reporter,* September 2, 2011, http://ncronline.org/print/26446 (accessed 9/2/11). Gottfried Martens, "JDDJ After Ten Years," *Logia,* Holy Trinity, 2009 (Vol. XVIII, No. 3), pp. 11-26.

[57] For more in-depth studies of JDDJ and the Lutheran-Catholic dialogues on justification, see Robert Preus, *Justification and Rome* (St. Louis: Concordia Publishing House, 1997); Gaylin R. Schmeling, "The Joint Declaration on the Doctrine of Justification," *Lutheran Synod Quarterly,* Vol. 39, No. 4, pp. 356-359; and *The Joint Declaration on the Doctrine of Justification in Confessional Lutheran Perspective* (St. Louis: The Lutheran Church—Missouri Synod, 1999).

[58] Vatican II, Dogmatic Constitution on the Church, n. 16.

[59] For an in-depth study of this topic, see Curtis A. Jahn, "*Extra Ecclesiam Nulla Salus* (Outside the Church No Salvation)," *Wisconsin Lutheran Quarterly,* Vol. 104, No. 2 (Spring 2007), pp. 105-122.

[60] Peter Kreeft, "Hauled Aboard the Ark," http://www.peterkreeft.com/topics/hauled-aboard.htm (accessed 9/6/11).

[61] At the time of the Reformation, the way the Lutheran confessors used the word *sacrament* was still somewhat in flux. Luther's coworker Philip Melanchthon says in the Apology of the Augsburg Confession: "If we call Sacraments 'rites that have the command of God, and to which the promise of grace has been added,' it is easy to decide what are true Sacraments . . . Baptism, the Lord's Supper, and Absolution (which is the Sacrament of Repentance) are truly Sacraments" (Apology XIII, par. 1,4, McCain, *Concordia*), p. 184. Melanchthon's definition does not limit sacraments to rites that use an earthly element. But to announce the forgiveness of sins does have Christ's command and promise (Matthew 18:15-20; John 20:21-23). Luther, on the other hand, employed the more limited definition when he spoke in the Large Catechism of "our two Sacraments instituted by Christ" (Large Catechism, Part 4, par. 1, McCain, *Concordia*), p. 423.

[62] Council of Trent, Session 7, Canon 1. Schroeder, p. 51.

[63] Large Catechism, Part IV, par. 18, McCain, *Concordia,* p. 425.

[64] Richard McBrien, *Catholicism* (San Francisco: HarperSanFranciso, 1994), p. 796.

[65] Augsburg Confession, Article VIII, par. 2, McCain, *Concordia,* p. 34.

[66] Small Catechism, Part IV, McCain, *Concordia,* p. 339.

[67] Small Catechism, Part VI, McCain, *Concordia,* p. 343.

[68] Council of Trent, Session 7, Canon 3. Schroeder, p. 52.

[69] From Wisconsin Lutheran Seminary Senior Dogmatics Notes, p. 172.

[70] Council of Trent, Session 7. Schroeder, p. 52.

[71] Vatican II, Constitution on the Sacred Liturgy, n. 14.

[72] McBrien, *Catholicism,* pp. 798,799.

[73] Vatican II, Dogmatic Constitution on the Church, n. 48.

[74] Mark Searle, "Infant Baptism Reconsidered," in *Alternative Futures for Worship: Baptism and Confirmation,* Vol. 2 (Collegeville, MN: The Liturgical Press, 1987), p. 15.

[75] Thomas Bokenkotter, *Dynamic Catholicism: A Historical Catechism* (New York: Doubleday, 1992), p. 186.

[76] Council of Trent, Session 7, Canons on the Sacraments in General, Canon 9. Schroeder, p. 52.

[77] John A. Hardon, *The Question and Answer Catholic Catechism* (Garden City, NY: Doubleday, 1981), pp. 233,234.

[78] Council of Trent, Session 7, Canons on Baptism, Canon 10. Schroeder, p. 54.

[79] Small Catechism, Baptism, Second, McCain, *Concordia,* p. 339.

[80] *Catechism of the Catholic Church,* n. 1304.

[81] Council of Trent, Session 7, Canons on Confirmation. Schroeder, pp. 54,55.

[82] Vatican II, Dogmatic Constitution on the Church, n. 11.

[83] *Code of Canon Law,* n. 897, p. 337.

[84] Small Catechism, Part VI, McCain, *Concordia,* p. 343.

[85] Smalcald Articles III, VI, 1,5, McCain, *Concordia,* p. 279.

[86] Council of Trent, Session 13, Canon 2. Schroeder, p. 79.

[87] *Catechism of the Catholic Church,* n. 1376.

[88] Council of Trent, Session 22, Chapter 2. Schroeder, p. 146.

[89] Council of Trent, Session 22, Chapter 9. Schroeder, p. 149.

[90] Vatican II, Dogmatic Constitution on the Church, n. 3, and Decree on the Ministry and Life of Priests, nn. 2,5.

[91] Vatican II, Dogmatic Constitution on the Church, n. 11. See also *Catechism of the Catholic Church,* n. 1368.

[92] James T. O'Connor, *The Hidden Manna: A Theology of the Eucharist* (San Francisco: Ignatius Press, 1988), pp. 309,310.

[93] See the Smalcald Articles, Part II, Article II, The Mass, McCain, *Concordia,* pp. 264-266.

[94] Council of Trent, Session 13, Canon 11. Schroeder, p. 80.

[95] Smalcald Articles II, II, 1, McCain, *Concordia,* p. 264.

[96] Cf. Council of Trent, Session 21. Canons 1-3. Schroeder, pp. 134,135.

[97] Cf. Vatican II, The Constitution on the Sacred Liturgy, n. 55.

[98] Formula of Concord, Solid Declaration, Article VII, p. 126, McCain, *Concordia,* p. 835.

[99] Judith Marie Kubicki, "Recognizing the Presence of Christ in the Liturgical Assembly," *Theological Studies,* 65:4 (December 2004), p. 818.

[100] "Sacraments Today: Belief and Practice Among U.S. Catholics, Executive Summary," p. 4. http://cara.georgetown.edu.sacraments.html (accessed 11/16/10).

[101] Luther's Small Catechism, Part V, McCain, *Concordia,* p. 341.

[102] *Catechism of the Catholic Church,* nn. 1456-1458.

[103] Smalcald Articles, III, III:14, McCain, *Concordia,* p. 273.

[104] *Catechism of the Catholic Church,* nn. 1461,1462,1495.

[105] Council of Trent, Session 14, Chapter 6. Schroeder, p. 95.

[106] Council of Trent, Session 14, Canon 9. Schroeder, p. 103.

[107] *The Vatican II Sunday Missal* (Boston: Daughters of St. Paul, 1974), p. 589.

[108] "Sacraments Today," p. 5. http://cara.georgetown.edu.sacraments.html (accessed 11/16/10).

[109] Joseph Martos, *Doors to the Sacred: A Historical Introduction to the Sacraments in the Catholic Church,* 2nd edition (Liguori, MO: Liguori/Triumph, 2001), p. 83.

[110] For a more detailed discussion of the James passage, see Jeske, *James, 1,2 Peter, 1,2,3 John, Jude,* pp. 49-52.

[111] McBrien, *Catholicism,* p. 844.

[112] Vatican II, The Constitution on the Sacred Liturgy, n. 73.

[113] McBrien, *Catholicism,* p. 847.

[114] *Catechism of the Catholic Church,* n. 1520.

[115] *Catechism of the Catholic Church,* nn. 1521,1522.

[116] "Sacraments Today," p. 5. http://cara.georgetown.edu.sacraments.html (accessed 11/16/10).

[117] Council of Trent, Session 24, Canon 1. Schroeder, p. 181.

[118] Council of Trent, Session 24, Canon 10. Schroeder, p. 182.

[119] See McBrien, *Catholicism,* pp. 856-858.

[120] Pope Paul VI, *Humanae Vitae* (Boston: St. Paul Books and Media, 1968), n. 4.

[121] Pope Paul VI, *Humanae Vitae,* n. 11.

[122] Pope Paul VI, *Humanae Vitae,* n. 14.

[123] Janet Smith, "Contraception: Why Not?" www.catholiceducation.org/articles/sexuality/se0002.html (accessed 2/10/11).

[124] The Web site of Christian Life Resources offers a number of articles from a biblical Lutheran perspective on family planning, birth control, and contraception: www.christianliferesources.com.

[125] Edward Peters, "Annulments in America," *Homiletic & Pastoral Review,* November 1996, pp. 58,59.

[126] Jeff Ziegler, "Annulment Nation," *The Catholic World Report,* March 2011, p. 17.

[127] John L. Allen, "The Vatican's Marriage Quandary," *The Wall Street Journal,* February 18, 2011 (accessed online 2/19/11).

[128] Vatican II, Dogmatic Constitution on the Church, n. 10. Decree on the Apostolate of Lay People, the entire document.

[129] Philip Schaff, *History of the Christian Church,* Vol. V (Grand Rapids: Wm. B. Eerdmans Publishing Company, 1907/1974), pp. 36-45; and Carl A. Volz, *The Medieval Church* (Nashville: Abingdon Press, 1997), p. 165.

[130] Pope John Paul II, "*Ordinatio Sacerdotalis:* Reserving Priestly Ordination to Men Alone," Apostolic Letter, May 22, 1994 (Washington, DC: United States Catholic Conference, 1994).

[131] John F. Brug, *The Ministry of the Word* (Milwaukee: Northwestern Publishing House, 2009), pp. 271,272.

[132] Hardon, *The Question and Answer Catholic Catechism,* nn. 1534,1538, pp. 304,305.

[133] Hardon, *The Question and Answer Catholic Catechism,* n. 1552, p. 307.

[134] Formula of Concord, Epitome, Article VIII, par. 12, McCain, *Concordia,* p. 492.

[135] Most, if not all, orthodox Lutheran theologians from Luther up to Karl Walther and Franz Pieper either accepted the *utero clauso* without questioning it or call it an open question, but they definitely do not categorically reject it as false teaching.

[136] Pius IX, *Apostolic Constitution Defining the Dogma of the Immaculate Conception* (Boston: St. Paul Books and Media, no date), p. 21. Also in Henry Denzinger, *The Sources of Catholic Dogma,* translated by Roy J. Deferrari (St. Louis: B. Herder Book Co., 1957), n. 1641, p. 413.

[137] Ludwig Ott, *Fundamentals of Catholic Dogma* (Rockford, IL: Tan Book Publishers, 1974), p. 200.

[138] Elliot Miller and Kenneth R. Samples, *The Cult of the Virgin Mary* (Grand Rapids: Baker Book House, 1992), p. 37.

[139] William Webster, *The Church of Rome at the Bar of History* (Edinburgh: The Banner of Truth Trust, 1995), pp. 82-84.

[140] Pius XII, *Apostolic Constitution Defining the Dogma of the Assumption* (Boston: St. Paul Books and Media, no date), nn. 44,45, p. 20. Also in Denzinger, *The Sources of Catholic Dogma,* n. 2333, p. 648.

[141] Keating, *Catholicism and Fundamentalism,* p. 275.

[142] Pius XII, *Apostolic Constitution Defining the Dogma of the Assumption,* p. 17. Also in Denzinger, *The Sources of Catholic Dogma,* n. 2331, p. 647.

[143] Saint Alphonsus Ligouri, *The Glories of Mary* (New York: Alba House, 1990).

[144] George Weigel, *Witness to Hope: The Biography of Paul John Paul II* (New York: HarperCollins Publishers, 1999), p. 57.

[145] Saint Louis de Montfort, *True Devotion to the Blessed Virgin* (Bay Shore, NY: Montfort Publications, 1980).

[146] Vatican II, Dogmatic Constitution on the Church, nn. 58-67.

[147] For a study of the pagan roots of Catholic Mariology, see Hermann Sasse, "Mary and the Pope: Remarks on the Dogma of the Assumption of Mary," *Logia,* Vol. XIX, No. 3 (Holy Trinity 2010), pp. 5-13. See also Lucien Dhalenne, "Antichristian Mariology," *Wisconsin Lutheran Quarterly,* Vol. 55, No. 3 (July 1958), pp. 167-192.

[148] John L. Allen Jr. "Fast-Track Saint," *Newsweek,* April 17, 2011. http://www.newsweek.com/2011/04/17/fast-track-saint.html (accessed 4/26/11).

[149] Bob O'Gorman and Mary Falkner, *The Complete Idiot's Guide to Understanding Catholicism* (Indianapolis: Alpha Books, 2000), pp. 10,11.

[150] Augsburg Confession, Article XXI, par. 1-4, McCain, *Concordia,* p. 44.

[151] Smalcald Articles, Part II, Article II, par. 25-28, McCain, *Concordia,* pp. 266,267.

[152] William A. Donohue, "John Jay 2011 Study on Sexual Abuse: A Critical Analysis," posted on the Web site of the Catholic League for Religious and Civil Rights, www.catholicleague.org (accessed 6/27/11). Marianne Medin, "Critics say new study misses real reasons for priest abuse crisis," Catholic News Agency, www.catholicnewsagency.com/news (accessed 5/25/11). Paul Shaughnessy, "The Gay Priest Problem," *The Catholic World Report,* November 2000, pp. 52-58. Richard Sipe, "Secret sex in the celibate system," *National Catholic Reporter,* http://ncronline.org (accessed 4/30/11). Louie Verrecchio, "John Jay Study: A $2 million exercise in political correctness," Catholic News Agency, May 26, 2011, www.catholicnewsagency.com (accessed 5/26/11). George Weigel, "Priests, Abuse, and the Meltdown of a Culture," *National Review Online,* May 19, 2011. Posted on the Web site of the Ethics and Public Policy Center, www.eppc.org (accessed 5/23/11).

[153] "Practicing Catholics unfazed by abuse scandals," www.catholicculture.org (accessed 5/5/10).

[154] Michael S. Rose, *Goodbye, Good Men* (Washington DC: Regency Publishing Co., 2002).

[155] Jeff Ziegler, "The State of Catholic Schools in the US," *The Catholic World Report,* June 2011, p. 26.

[156] Ziegler, *The Catholic World Report,* p. 28.

[157] Ziegler, *The Catholic World Report,* p. 27.

[158] Kenneth C. Jones, *Index of Leading Catholic Indicators: The Church Since Vatican II* (St. Louis: Oriens Publishing Company, 2003), pp. 14-16.

[159] Catholic Culture: Latest Headlines, "Over 1,800 US parishes have closed since 1990," http://www.catholicculture.org/news/headlines/index.cfm?storyid=11063 (accessed 7/19/2011).

[160] Catholic Culture: Latest Headlines, "Over 1,800 US parishes have closed since 1990."

[161] Pope John Paul II, *Ordinatio Sacerdotalis.*

[162] Jones, *Index of Leading Catholic Indicators,* p. 15.

[163] Brian McGuire, "Why There Are So Many Priests in Omaha," http:/www.catholic.net/us_catholic_news/print.phtml?article_id=91 (accessed 4/4/2001). Paul Likoudis, "The Vocation Manipulation—How Seminaries Weed Out Catholics," *The Wanderer.* Preprinted in *The Christian News,* November 13, 2000, p. 17. Michael S. Rose, "A Self-Imposed Shortage," http://www.catholic.net/collars_habits/print.phtml?article_id=58 (accessed 2/28/2001).

[164] Vatican II, Constitution on the Sacred Liturgy, n. 14.

[165] R. Michael Dunnigan, "Justice and Reconciliation: An Analysis of the Holy See's Instruction on the Latin Mass," *The Catholic World Report,* August/September 2011, pp. 35-38.

[166] John L. Allen, *The Future Church* (New York: Doubleday, 2009).

[167] Allen, *The Future Church,* pp. 32-41.

[168] Archbishop Timothy Dolan, "External Markers of Our Faith," http://blog.archny.org/?p=1567 (accessed 8/19/11).

[169] John L. Allen, "Big Picture at World Youth Day: 'It's the Evangelicals, Stupid!'" *National Catholic Reporter,* August 19, 2011, http://ncronline.org/print/26252 (accessed 8/19/11).

[170] Anna Williams, "For these millennials, faith trumps relativism," *USA Today,* August 14, 2011.

[171] Allen, *The Future Church,* pp. 378-413.

[172] Allen, *The Future Church,* p. 381.

[173] Quoted in Allen, *The Future Church,* p. 382.

[174] Allen, *The Future Church,* p. 387.

[175] Allen, *The Future Church,* p. 384.

SUBJECT INDEX

D

E

F

G

H

I

J

V

W

SCRIPTURE INDEX